THE HELPING RELATIONSHIP SOURCEBOOK

44422

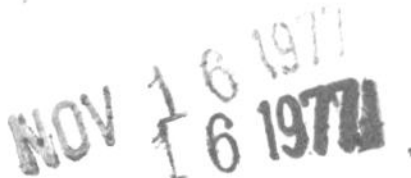

THE HELPING RELATIONSHIP SOURCEBOOK

Second Edition

edited by

Donald Avila
University of Florida

Arthur W. Combs
University of Florida

William W. Purkey
University of North Carolina
at Greensboro

WITHDRAWN

Allyn and Bacon, Inc.
Boston, London, Sydney, Toronto

Copyright © 1977, 1971 by Allyn and Bacon, Inc.,
470 Atlantic Avenue, Boston, Massachusetts 02210.

All rights reserved. Printed in the United States of America. No part of the material protected by this copyright notice may be reproduced or utilized in any form or by any means, electronic or mechanical, including photocopying, recording, or by any information storage and retrieval system, without written permission from the copyright owner.

Library of Congress Cataloging in Publication Data

Avila, Donald L comp.
The helping relationship sourcebook.

Includes bibliographies.
1. Helping behavior. 2. Counseling.
3. Humanistic psychology. I. Combs, Arthur Wright.
II. Purkey, William Watson. III. Title.
BF637.H4A9 1977 158′.2 77–7303
ISBN 0–205–05843–4

BF
637
.H4
A9
1977
c.2

This book is dedicated to
Shirley, Susan, and Imogene—
three of the greatest humanists we know.

Contents

Preface

Since the first edition of this book was published, some things have changed and some have not. The Vietnam war has ended; we have experienced the worst political scandal in our history; and we have had one of the worst recessions since the Great Depression. For the first time, we have been forced to come face-to-face with the fact that our natural resources can be totally exhausted and that we must do something about it.

It is too soon to tell where these events will take us, but it is certain that they will generate tremendous changes in our way of life and accelerate the process of "Future Shock." What have not changed, except to be exaggerated, are the general conditions existing at the time of the first volume and the sentiments which prompted the authors to produce the first publication. Consequently, we are restating those sentiments.

The search for personal fulfillment and satisfying relationships with others has been an endless quest for human beings. It's achievement in our time has become at once more necessary, possible, and precarious than ever. On the one hand, science has provided us with the means to fill our physical needs in a fashion never dreamed of previously and, in doing so, has released us to turn our energies to higher considerations. On the other hand, we find ourselves in jeopardy as the great human and social problems we have created threaten to overwhelm us. Troubled people everywhere are searching deeply within themselves for personal meaning and exploring relationships with others for solutions as never before. To aid in this search, the established professions of medicine, law, education, and religion are being asked to expand their traditional services and responsibilities. In their quest for purpose, peace, and fulfillment, humans have created new helping professions expressly designed to assist persons, singularly or in groups, to find more effective and satisfying ways of living with themselves and others.

Based upon the life sciences of biology, psychology, sociology, and anthropology, a whole new constellation of professions has come into being, each designed to aid in the greater fulfillment of human hopes and longing. Among those more recently developed helping professions are psychiatry, psychology, social work, and their myriad branches and practical applications. Some names of these helpers, like *counselor, psychotherapist, psychiatrist, probation officer, child psychologist, social worker,* and *psychiatric nurse* are household words. A host of other specialists, like crisis teachers, human development specialists, encounter group leaders, rehabilitation counselors, community educators, and labor-management arbitrators are less well-known to the lay person. There will be many more whose nature we cannot discern as yet because the need for helping persons becomes ever greater as our population expands and society becomes more complex. It is to the potential members of these professions and to those people already engaged in helping relationships that this book is directed.

In the earliest forms of the helping professions, it was generally believed that what helped the client, student, or patient was what the helper did or said. As a consequence, helpers conceived of their tasks as "diagnosing and treating," "teaching the facts," "giving advice," or exerting some overt or covert form of direction. This might be applied gently, as in persuasion or blandishment; loudly, as in exhortation and demand; or even physically, as in the use of force and punishment. With such a view, the training of helpers was primarily directed toward teaching proper techniques or methods.

With further study and experience, it has become apparent that the specific acts or behavior employed by the helper are far less important to the helping process than the nature of the relationships established between helper and helpee. The processes of helping are much more than mechanical questions of input and output. They are complex human encounters—personal interrelationships which determine the meaning of whatever content or technique the helper attempts to employ.

The success of the helping professions is dependent upon change in personal meaning. However, the dynamics of communication involve much more than what is said or done in a given setting. They are affected by many additional factors among which might be, Who said it? When? Under what conditions? With what tone of voice, attitude, stance, and personality characteristics? Techniques and information are important to the helping process, to be sure, but the relationships in which they are used are crucial. For this reason, training programs in the helping professions devote much time to the study of relationships, and the nature and dynamics of the helping encounter have become primary topics of psychological research.

Sufficient evidence has now been collected from this research to support the belief that the relationships required for most of the helping professions are highly similar. This is not surprising since all of these professions are in actuality forms of learning and therefore depend upon a common psychology. The basic goal of the helping professions is to invite others to learn new and more effective ways of perceiving one's self and one's relationships with the world. Whatever we discover about the proper conditions for bringing about this end must, therefore, have wide applicability to all of the helping professions.

The editors have learned something about helpers since the first edition of this book. That is, that they may have been using the term too narrowly the first time around. Because of the kind of people who found the first edition useful and the variety of places it has been used, the authors have come to believe that what constitutes a professional helper depends more on how people see their occupation than what their occupational title may be.

In the earlier edition, we directly referred to the more obvious persons engaged in helping relationships such as teachers, physicians, counselors and persons of the clergy. Much to our surprise, however, as time passed we discovered that the book was being used in the training of such groups as police officers, administrators, military personnel, and business men. We would like to acknowledge that phenomenon, and conclude that what constitutes a professional helper is in the mind of the helper and not the title of the profession with which he or she may be identified.

The editors would also like to point out that they are well aware of the thousands of people who support helping professions with their volunteer work. In fact, were it not for these people, many educational and community programs could not survive. Our public schools have always depended on volunteer help and are coming to depend on them more each year. Hospitals could not do nearly as adequate a job without volunteers. Community agencies such as crisis and drug centers, rape prevention programs, youth and aged recreation programs could not exist without the aid of people willing to give freely of their time and effort. This book has been prepared for them as much as any other group.

The editors stated two primary reasons for producing the first edition of the *Sourcebook*. We have maintained those two reasons and added a third. First, we have attempted to collect those papers of broad relevance to all helpers, which seem to shed most light upon the nature and dynamics of the helping relationship.

A second reason for creating this collection is the belief that serious students in the helping professions should be exposed to original sources in their field. So many survey texts are now available that it is possible for a student, even at the graduate level, to obtain a degree in one of the professions without ever having had this experience. This is a pity. No matter how well an interpretation of a person's work has been done by someone else, there is something special to be gained from hearing it "from the horse's mouth." It is not always easy to search out original documents, yet there is need to make them more readily available. The editors believe that the papers included here are among the most important and pertinent articles currently at hand for the helping professions. By publishing them in this form, we hope to make them more readily available to our own students and to others in the helping professions.

The third reason for the current edition is to serve as a source of encouragement. With the death of such men as Abraham Maslow, Sidney Jourard, and Earl Kelley, and the strong conservative trend in our nation as reflected in such statements as, "Lets return to basics," there has been a growing fear that humanism, too, is dying. That fear should be alieviated somewhat by the authors of the articles found in this text. Here can be heard the voices of humanists whom we have been listening to for a long time, and it is evident that people like Arthur Combs and Carl Rogers are still in the midst of promoting the humanistic cause. At the same time, it is also obvious that *new voices* are joining the movement as represented by Fred Richards, David Aspy, David Campbell, and others. These, and the many voices not included in this volume, should help reassure those who are experiencing some despair.

The present volume, although it can be used by itself, has been designed as a companion to *Helping Relationships: Basic Concepts for the Helping Professions.*[1] Many of the papers used in the development of the principles and practices presented in that book are included in this one. It is intended that the students be provided with a useful complement for introducing them to some of the original work upon which the above volume is based, and by giving an opportunity to delve much deeper into some of the ideas presented there.

This edition of *The Helping Relationship Sourcebook* is divided into five parts. Part 1 deals with some essential aspects of a helping relationship, the characteristics of helpers, and some of what is involved in the training of helpers. Part 2 focuses on the two major approaches to helping—humanistic and behavioristic—how they are different, how they may be integrated, and reasons for selecting one as the helper's basic frame of reference. Part 3 discusses some of the values important in help-

1. Arthur W. Combs, Donald L. Avila, and William W. Purkey, *Helping Relationships: Basic Concepts for the Helping Professions* (Boston: Allyn and Bacon, Inc., 1971). A new edition of this book is scheduled to be published by Allyn and Bacon, Inc. in 1978.

ing and a number of goals the helper might wish to achieve. Part 4 examines the helping process and the persons doing the helping. Part 5 deals with the persons being helped and their potential for growth.

Some of the articles in this volume are new and some have been retained from the first edition. As was true with all the articles in the first edition, the new ones have been selected because they were considered to be among the best available, consistent with the purpose of the editors, and primarily representative of modern humanistic orientations in psychological thought. This last criteria, admittedly a bias, is due in part to the personal commitments of the editors who lean toward that persuasion. It is also a consequence of the fact that much of humanistic psychology is designed expressly for understanding the problems of the human condition and so speaks more often and more directly to questions of concern to the helping professions.

The articles which appear again in this volume do so for the reasons stated above as well as for an additional reason. Several hundred students rated each article appearing in the first edition on a five point scale. They rated them in relation to two criteria: (1) how well the student believed the respective authors communicated their positions, and (2) how relevant they (the students) believed the content of the articles were to their needs. Only those articles receiving a rating of three or better were retained. If the individuals who rated these articles are at all representative of students throughout the country, and we have no reason to believe they are not, this edition should have more meaning for the readers for whom it is intended than did the first. The editors would like to thank Robert Spangler of East Tennessee State University, for his invaluable assistance in adding this new dimension to the present text.

In selecting these papers, the editors sought to achieve impact and relevance rather than touch on all aspects of the helping relationships. Instead, this collection is a sample, although we hope a representative one, of what, in the editors' opinions, are some of the best and most pertinent articles available. To those authors whose works are represented here, the editors express their deepest appreciation—first, for producing their fine articles, and, second, for permitting us to reproduce them.

D. A.
A. W. C.
W. W. P.

THE HELPING RELATIONSHIP SOURCEBOOK

1
THE PROFESSIONAL HELPER

The first three articles in this volume define the helping relationship, identify what a good helper is, and suggest what it might take to develop professional helpers. The reader, however, may find the way in which this is done a bit unusual.

Historically, training programs for helpers have been based on two phases. First, the novices are presented one or more theoretical positions. Second, they are taught the specific methods and techniques of their trade. Traditionally, it has been considered important to know whether one was a psychoanalytic psychiatrist, student-centered teacher, existential psychologist, or whatever. Educators have searched for the perfect teaching style, ministers for the ideal method of delivery, counselors and therapists for the most effective technique, and physicians for the best bed-side manner.

In recent years, however, a growing number of individuals are beginning to believe that theoretical backgrounds, methods, styles, and techniques are not essential to the success of helping relationships or in determining a good helper. They believe there is a universal process that constitutes a successful helping relationship, irrespective of one's theoretical position, and that people must possess some basic human characteristics before they can be successful helpers. Otherwise, all the methods and techniques available will not make them one.

In the first article, Carl Rogers explicitly states this belief about the helping relationship, "I have long had the strong conviction—some might say it was an obsession—that the therapeutic relationship is only a special instance of interpersonal relationships in general, and that the same lawfulness governs all such relationships." He then proceeds to discuss what he believes are the characteristics necessary for the establishment of a successful helping relationship.

For some years, Arthur Combs has supervised a series of studies at the University of Florida designed to discover the personal characteristics of good helpers. In the second paper of this volume, he reports the findings from some of this research. The results of these studies are provocative, but the overall conclusion is even more so. It suggests that techniques, methods, and styles have very little to do with the success or failure of helpers. If the results of these studies are correct, it appears that a helper's basic beliefs and values, rather than their grand schemes, methods, techniques, or years of training, are the real determiners of whether or not they will be effective or ineffective as a helper. In the article, Combs identifies what some of these beliefs and values are.

Fred Richards continues with the theme that the personal characteristics of helpers are their most important assets. His article is an excellent review of much of the research relating to this position. Although the discussion focuses on counselors as helpers, what is said is characteristic of and generalizable to all helpers. Richards also suggests some elements that could be incorporated into the training program of helpers to enhance the development of positive values and beliefs.

The Characteristics of a Helping Relationship

CARL R. ROGERS

I have long had the strong conviction—some might say it was an obsession—that the therapeutic relationship is only a special instance of interpersonal relationships in general, and that the same lawfulness governs all such relationships. This was the theme I chose to work out for myself when I was asked to give an address to the convention of the American Personnel and Guidance Association at St. Louis, in 1958.

Evident in this paper is the dichotomy between the objective and the subjective which has been such an important part of my experience during recent years. I find it very difficult to give a paper which is either wholly objective or wholly subjective. I like to bring the two worlds into close juxtaposition, even if I cannot fully reconcile them.

My interest in psychotherapy has brought about in me an interest in every kind of helping relationship. By this term I mean a relationship in which at least one of the parties has the intent of promoting the growth, development, maturity, improved functioning, improved coping with life of the other. The other, in this sense, may be one individual or a group. To put it in another way, a helping relationship might be defined as one in which one of the participants intends that there should come about, in one or both parties, more appreciation of, more expression of, more functional use of the latent inner resources of the individual.

Now it is obvious that such a definition covers a wide range of relationships which usually are intended to facilitate growth. It would certainly include the relationship between mother and child, father and child. It would include the relationship between the physician and his patient. The relationship between teacher and pupil would often come

From *Personnel and Guidance Journal,* 1958, 37, 6–16. Copyright 1958 American Personnel and Guidance Association. Reprinted with permission of author and publisher.

under this definition, though some teachers would not have the promotion of growth as their intent. It includes almost all counselor-client relationships, whether we are speaking of educational counseling, vocational counseling, or personal counseling. In this last-mentioned area it would include the wide range of relationships between the psychotherapist and the hospitalized psychotic, the therapist and the troubled or neurotic individual, and the relationship between the therapist and the increasing number of so-called "normal" individuals who enter therapy to improve their own functioning or accelerate their personal growth.

These are largely one-to-one relationships. But we should also think of the large number of individual-group interactions which are intended as helping relationships. Some administrators intend that their relationship to their staff groups shall be of the sort which promotes growth, though other administrators would not have this purpose. The interaction between the group therapy leader and his group belongs here. So does the relationship of the community consultant to a community group. Increasingly the interaction between the industrial consultant and a management group is intended as a helping relationship. Perhaps this listing will point up the fact that a great many of the relationships in which we and others are involved fall within this category of interactions in which there is the purpose of promoting development and more mature and adequate functioning.

THE QUESTION

But what are the characteristics of those relationships which *do* help, which do facilitate growth? And at the other end of the scale is it possible to discern those characteristics which make a relationship unhelpful, even though it was the sincere intent to promote growth and development? It is to these questions, particularly the first, that I would like to take you with me over some of the paths I have explored, and to tell you where I am, as of now, in my thinking on these issues.

THE ANSWERS GIVEN BY RESEARCH

It is natural to ask first of all whether there is any empirical research which would give us an objective answer to these questions. There has not been a large amount of research in this area as yet, but what there is, is stimulating and suggestive. I cannot report all of it but I would like to make a somewhat extensive sampling of the studies which have been done and state very briefly some of the findings. In so doing, oversimplification is necessary, and I am quite aware that I am not doing full justice to the researches I am mentioning, but it may give you the feeling that factual advances are being made and pique your curiosity enough to examine the studies themselves, if you have not already done so.

Studies of Attitudes

Most of the studies throw light on the attitudes on the part of the helping person which make a relationship growth-promoting or growth-inhibiting. Let us look at some of these.

A careful study of parent-child relationships made some years ago by Baldwin (1945) and others at the Fels Institute contains interesting evidence. Of the various clusters of parental attitudes toward children, the "acceptant-democratic" seemed most growth-facilitating. Children of these parents with their warm and equalitarian attitudes showed an accelerated intellectual development (an increasing I.Q.), more originality, more emotional security and control, less excitability than children from other types of homes. Though somewhat slow initially in social development, they were, by the time they reached school age, popular, friendly, non-aggressive leaders.

Where parents' attitudes are classed as "actively rejectant" the children show a slightly decelerated intellectual development, relatively poor use of the abilities they do possess, and some lack of originality. They are emotionally unstable, rebellious, aggressive, and quarrelsome. The children of parents with other attitude syndromes tend in various respects to fall in between these extremes.

I am sure that these findings do not surprise us as related to child development. I would like to suggest that they probably apply to other relationships as well, and that the counselor or physician or administrator who is warmly emotional and expressive, respectful of the individuality of himself and of the other, and who exhibits a non-possessive caring, probably facilitates self-realization much as does a parent with these attitudes.

Let me turn to another careful study in a very different area. Whitehorn and Betz (1956) investigated the degree of success achieved by young resident physicians in working with schizophrenic patients on a psychiatric ward. They chose for special study the seven who had been outstandingly helpful, and seven whose patients had shown the least degree of improvement. Each group had treated about fifty patients. The investigators examined all the available evidence to discover in what ways the A group (the successful group) differed from the B group. Several significant differences were found. The physicians in the A group tended to see the schizophrenic in terms of the personal meaning which various behaviors had to the patient, rather than seeing him as a case history or a descriptive diagnosis. They also tended to work toward goals which were oriented to the personality of the patient, rather than such goals as reducing the symptoms or curing the disease. It was found that the helpful physicians, in their day by day interaction primarily made use of active personal participation—a person-to-person relationship. They made less use of procedures which could be classed as "passive permissive." They were even less likely to use such procedures as interpretation, instruction or advice, or emphasis upon the practical care of the patient. Finally, they were much more likely than the B group to develop a relationship in which the patient felt trust and confidence in the physician.

Although the authors cautiously emphasize that these findings relate only to the treatment of schizophrenics, I am inclined to disagree. I suspect that similar facts would be found in a research study of almost any class of helping relationship.

Another interesting study focuses upon the way in which the person being helped perceives the relationship. Heine (1950) studied individuals who had gone for psychotherapeutic help to psychoanalytic, client-centered, and Adlerian therapists. Regardless of the type of therapy, these clients report similar changes in themselves. But it is their perception of the relationship which is of particular interest to us here. When asked what accounted for the changes which had occurred, they expressed some differing explanations, depending on the orientation of the therapist. But their agreement on the major elements they had found helpful was even more significant. They indicated that these attitudinal elements in the relationship accounted for the changes which had taken place in themselves: the trust they had felt in the therapist; being understood by the therapist; the feeling of independence they had had in making choices and decisions. The therapist procedure which they had found most helpful was that the therapist clarified and openly stated feelings which the client had been approaching hazily and hesitantly.

There was also a high degree of agreement among these clients, regardless of the orientation of their therapists, as to what elements had been unhelpful in the relationship. Such therapist attitudes as lack of interest, remoteness or distance, and an over-degree of sympathy, were perceived as unhelpful. As to procedures, they had found it unhelpful when therapists had given direct specific advice regarding decisions or had emphasized past history rather than present problems. Guiding suggestions mildly given were perceived in an intermediate range—neither clearly helpful nor unhelpful.

Fiedler, in a much quoted study (1953), found that expert therapists of differing orientations formed similar relationships with their clients. Less well known are the elements which characterized these relationships, differentiating them from the relationships formed by less expert therapists. These elements are: an ability to understand the client's meanings and feelings; a sensitivity to the client's attitudes; a warm interest without any emotional over-involvement.

A study by Quinn (1950) throws light on what is involved in understanding the client's meanings and feelings. His study is surprising in that it shows that "understanding" of the client's meanings is essentially an attitude of *desiring* to understand. Quinn presented his judges only with recorded therapist statements taken from interviews. The raters had no knowledge of what the therapist was responding to or how the client reacted to his response. Yet it was found that the degree of understanding could be judged about as well from this material as from listening to the response in context. This seems rather conclusive evidence that it is an attitude of wanting to understand which is communicated.

As to the emotional quality of the relationship, Seeman (1954) found that success in psychotherapy is closely associated with a strong and growing mutual liking and respect between client and therapist.

An interesting study by Dittes (1957) indicates how delicate this relationship is. Using a physiological measure, the psychogalvanic reflex, to measure the anxious or threatened or alerted reactions of the client, Dittes correlated the deviations on this measure with judges' ratings of the degree of warm acceptance and permissiveness on the part of the therapist. It was found that whenever the therapist's attitudes changed even slightly in the direction of a lesser degree of acceptance, the number of abrupt GSR deviations significantly increased. Evidently when the relationship is experienced as less acceptant the organism organizes against threat, even at the physiological level.

Without trying fully to integrate the findings from these various studies, it can at least be noted that a few things stand out. One is the fact that it is the attitudes and feelings of the therapist, rather than his theoretical orientation, which are important. His procedures and techniques are less important than his attitudes. It is also worth noting that it is the way in which his attitudes and procedures are perceived which makes a difference to the client, and that it is this perception which is crucial.

"Manufactured" Relationships

Let me turn to research of a very different sort, some of which you may find rather abhorrent, but which nevertheless has a bearing upon the nature of a facilitating relationship. These studies have to do with what we might think of as manufactured relationships.

Verplanck (1955), Greenspoon (1955) and others have shown that operant conditioning of verbal behavior is possible in a relationship. Very briefly, if the experimenter says "Mhm," or "Good," or nods his head after certain types of words or statements, those classes of words tend to increase because of being reinforced. It has been shown that by using such procedures one can bring about increases in such diverse verbal categories as plural nouns, hostile words, statements of opinion. The person is completely unaware that he is being influenced in any way by these reinforcers. The implication is that by such selective reinforcement we could bring it about that the other person in the relationship would be using whatever kinds of words and making whatever kinds of statements we had decided to reinforce.

Following still further the principles of operant conditioning as developed by Skinner and his group, Lindsley (1956) has shown that a chronic schizophrenic can be placed in a "helping relationship" with a machine. The machine, somewhat like a vending machine, can be set to reward a variety of types of behaviors. Initially it simply rewards—with candy, a cigarette, or the display of a picture—the lever-pressing behavior of the patient. But it is possible to set it so that many pulls on the lever may supply a hungry kitten—visible in a separate enclosure—with a drop of milk. In this case the satisfaction is an altruistic one. Plans are being developed to reward similar social or altruistic behavior directed toward another patient, placed in the next room. The only limit to the kind of behavior which might be rewarded lies in the degree of mechanical ingenuity of the experimenter.

Lindsley reports that in some patients there has been marked clinical improvement. Personally I cannot help but be impressed by the description of one patient who had gone from a deteriorated chronic state to being given free grounds privileges, this change being quite clearly associated with his interaction with the machine. Then the experimenter decided to study experimental extinction, which, put in more personal terms, means that no matter how many thousands of times the lever was pressed, no reward of any kind was forthcoming. The patient gradually regressed, grew untidy, uncommunicative, and his grounds privilege had to be revoked. This (to me) pathetic incident would seem to indicate that even in a relationship to a machine, trustworthiness is important if the relationship is to be helpful.

Still another interesting study of a manufactured relationship is being carried on by Harlow and his associates (1953), this time with monkeys. Infant monkeys, removed from their mothers almost immediately after birth, are, in one phase of the experiment, presented with two objects. One might be termed the "hard mother," a sloping cylinder of wire netting with a nipple from which the baby may feed. The other is a "soft mother," a similar cylinder made of foam rubber and terry cloth. Even when an infant gets all his food from the "hard mother" he clearly and increasingly prefers the "soft mother." Motion pictures show that he definitely "relates" to this object, playing with it, enjoying it, finding security in clinging to it when strange objects are near, and using that security as a home base for venturing into the frightening world. Of the many interesting and challenging implications of this study, one seems reasonably clear. It is that no amount of direct food reward can take the place of certain perceived qualities which the infant appears to need and desire.

Two Recent Studies

Let me close this wide-ranging—and perhaps perplexing—sampling of research studies with an account of two very recent investigations. The first is an experiment conducted by Ends and Page (1957). Working with hardened chronic hospitalized alcoholics who had been committed to a state hospital for sixty days, they tried three different methods of group psychotherapy. The method which they believed would be most effective was therapy based on a two-factor theory of learning; a client-centered approach was expected to be second; a psychoanalytically oriented approach was expected to be least efficient. Their results showed that the therapy based upon a learning theory approach was not only not helpful, but was somewhat deleterious. The outcomes were worse than those in the control group which had no therapy. The analytically oriented therapy produced some positive gain, and the client-centered group therapy was associated with the greatest amount of positive change. Follow-up data, extending over one and one-half years, confirmed the in-hospital findings, with the lasting improvement being greatest in the client-centered approach, next in the analytic, next in the control group, and least in those handled by a learning theory approach.

As I have puzzled over this study, unusual in that the approach to which the authors were committed proved *least* effective, I find a clue, I believe, in the description of the therapy based on learning theory. Essentially it consisted (a) of pointing out and labeling the behaviors which had proved unsatisfying, (b) of exploring objectively with the client the reasons behind these behaviors, and (c) of establishing through re-education more effective problem-solving habits. But in all of this interaction the aim, as they formulated it, was to be impersonal. The therapist "permits as little of his own personality to intrude as is humanly possible." The "therapist stresses personal anonymity in his activities, i.e., he must studiously avoid impressing the patient with his own (therapist's) individual personality characteristics." To me this seems the most likely clue to the failure of this approach, as I try to interpret the facts in the light of the other research studies. To withhold one's self as a person and to deal with the other person as an object does not have a high probability of being helpful.

The final study I wish to report is one just being completed by Halkides (1958). She started from a theoretical formulation of mine regarding the necessary and sufficient conditions for therapeutic change (1957). She hypothesized that there would be a significant relationship between the extent of constructive personality change in the client and four counselor variables: (a) the degree of empathic understanding of the client manifested by the counselor; (b) the degree of positive affective attitude (unconditional positive regard) manifested by the counselor toward the client; (c) the extent to which the counselor is genuine, his words matching his own internal feeling; and (d) the extent to which the counselor's response matches the client's expression in the intensity of affective expression.

To investigate these hypotheses she first selected, by multiple objective criteria, a group of ten cases which could be classed as "most successful" and a group of ten "least successful" cases. She then took an early and late recorded interview from each of these cases. On a random basis she picked nine client-counselor interaction units—a client statement and a counselor response—from each of these interviews. She thus had nine early interactions and nine later interactions from each case. This gave her several hundred units which were now placed in random order. The units from an early interview of an unsuccessful case might be followed by the units from a late interview of a successful case, etc.

Three judges, who did not know the cases or their degree of success, or the source of any given unit, now listened to this material four different times. They rated each unit on a seven point scale, first as to the degree of empathy, second as to the counselor's positive attitude toward the client, third as to the counselor's congruence or genuineness, and fourth as to the degree to which the counselor's response matched the emotional intensity of the client's expression.

I think all of us who knew of the study regarded it as a very bold venture. Could judges listening to single units of interaction possibly make any reliable rating of such subtle qualities as I have mentioned? And even if suitable reliability could be obtained, could eighteen counselor-client interchanges from each case—a minute sampling of the hundreds or thousands of such interchanges which occurred in each case—possibly bear any relationship to the therapeutic outcome? The chance seemed slim.

The findings are surprising. It proved possible to achieve high reliability between the judges, most of the inter-judge correlations being in the 0.80's or 0.90's, except on the last variable. It was found that a high degree of empathic understanding was significantly associated, at a .001 level, with the more successful cases. A high degree of unconditional positive regard was likewise associated with the more successful cases, at the .001 level. Even the rating of the counselor's genuineness or congruence—the extent to which his words matched his feelings—was associated with the successful outcome of the case, and again at the .001

level of significance. Only in the investigation of the matching intensity of affective expression were the results equivocal.

It is of interest too that high ratings of these variables were not associated more significantly with units from later interviews than with units from early interviews. This means that the counselor's attitudes were quite constant throughout the interviews. If he was highly empathic, he tended to be so from first to last. If he was lacking in genuineness, this tended to be true of both early and late interviews.

As with any study, this investigation has its limitations. It is concerned with a certain type of helping relationship, psychotherapy. It investigated only four variables thought to be significant. Perhaps there are many others. Nevertheless it represents a significant advance in the study of helping relationships. Let me try to state the findings in the simplest possible fashion. It seems to indicate that the quality of the counselor's interaction with a client can be satisfactorily judged on the basis of a very small sampling of his behavior. It also means that if the counselor is congruent or transparent, so that his words are in line with his feelings rather than the two being discrepant; if the counselor likes the client, unconditionally; and if the counselor understands the essential feelings of the client as they seem to the client—then there is a strong probability that this will be an effective helping relationship.

SOME COMMENTS

These then are some of the studies which throw at least a measure of light on the nature of the helping relationship. They have investigated different facets of the problem. They have approached it from very different theoretical contexts. They have used different methods. They are not directly comparable. Yet they seem to me to point to several statements which may be made with some assurance. It seems clear that relationships which are helpful have different characteristics from relationships which are unhelpful. These differential characteristics have to do primarily with the attitudes of the helping person on the one hand and with the perception of the relationship by the "helpee" on the other. It is equally clear that the studies thus far made do not give us any final answers as to what is a helping relationship, nor how it is to be formed.

How Can I Create a Helping Relationship?

I believe each of us working in the field of human relationships has a similar problem in knowing how to use such research knowledge. We cannot slavishly follow such findings in a mechanical way or we destroy the personal qualities which these very studies show to be valuable. It seems to me that we have to use these studies, testing them against our own experience and forming new and further personal hypotheses to use and test in our own further personal relationships.

So rather than try to tell you how you should use the findings I have presented I should like to tell you the kind of questions which these studies and my own clinical experience raise for me, and some of the tentative and changing hypotheses which guide my behavior as I enter into what I hope may be helping relationships, whether with students, staff, family, or clients. Let me list a number of these questions and considerations.

1. Can I *be* in some way which will be perceived by the other persons as trustworthy, as dependable or consistent in some deep sense? Both research and experience indicate that this is very important, and over the years I have found what I believe are deeper and better ways of answering this question. I used to feel that if I fulfilled all the outer conditions of trustworthiness—keeping appointments, respecting the confidential nature of the interviews, etc.—and if I acted consistently the same during the interviews, then this condition would be fulfilled. But experience drove home the fact that to act consistently acceptant, for example, if in fact I was feeling annoyed or skeptical or some other non-acceptant feeling, was certain in the long run to be perceived as inconsistent or untrustworthy. I have come to recognize that being trustworthy does not demand that I be rigidly consistent but that I be dependably real. The term "congruent" is one I have used to describe the way I would like to be. By this I mean that whatever feeling or attitude I am experiencing would be matched by my awareness of that attitude. When this is true, then I am a unified or integrated person in that moment, and hence I can *be* whatever I deeply *am*. This is a reality which I find others experience as dependable.

2. A very closely related question is this: Can I be expressive enough as a person that what I am will be communicated unambiguously? I believe that most of my failures to achieve a helping relationship can be traced to unsatisfactory answers to these two questions. When I am experiencing an attitude of annoyance toward another person but am unaware of it, then my communication contains contradictory messages. My words are giving one message, but I am also in subtle ways communicating the annoyance I feel and this confuses the other person and makes him distrustful, though he too may be unaware of what is causing the difficulty. When as a parent or a therapist or a teacher or an administrator I fail to listen to what is going on in me, fail because of my own defensiveness to sense my own feelings, then this kind of failure seems to result. It has made it seem to me that the most basic learning for anyone who hopes to establish any kind of helping relationship is that it is safe to be transparently real. If in a given relationship I am reasonably

congruent, if no feelings relevant to the relationship are hidden either to me or the other person, then I can be almost sure that the relationship will be a helpful one.

One way of putting this which may seem strange to you is that if I can form a helping relationship to myself—if I can be sensitively aware of and acceptant toward my own feelings—then the likelihood is great that I can form a helping relationship toward another.

Now, acceptantly to be what I am, in this sense, and to permit this to show through to the other person, is the most difficult task I know and one I never fully achieve. But to realize that this *is* my task has been most rewarding because it has helped me to find what has gone wrong with interpersonal relationships which have become snarled and to put them on a constructive track again. It has meant that if I am to facilitate the personal growth of others in relation to me, then I must grow, and while this is often painful it is also enriching.

3. A third question is: Can I let myself experience positive attitudes toward this other person—attitudes of warmth, caring, liking, interest, respect? It is not easy. I find in myself, and feel that I often see in others, a certain amount of fear of these feelings. We are afraid that if we let ourselves freely experience these positive feelings toward another we may be trapped by them. They may lead to demands on us or we may be disappointed in our trust, and these outcomes we fear. So as a reaction we tend to build up distance between ourselves and others—aloofness, a "professional" attitude, an impersonal relationship.

I feel quite strongly that one of the important reasons for the professionalization of every field is that it helps to keep this distance. In the clinical areas we develop elaborate diagnostic formulations, seeing the person as an object. In teaching and in administration we develop all kinds of evaluative procedures, so that again the person is perceived as an object. In these ways, I believe, we can keep ourselves from experiencing the caring which would exist if we recognized the relationship as one between two persons. It is a real achievement when we can learn, even in certain relationships or at certain times in those relationships, that it is safe to care, that it is safe to relate to the other as a person for whom we have positive feelings.

4. Another question the importance of which I have learned in my own experience is: Can I be strong enough as a person to be separate from the other? Can I be a sturdy respecter of my own feelings, my own needs, as well as his? Can I own and, if need be, express my own feelings as something belonging to me and separate from his feelings? Am I strong enough in my own separateness that I will not be downcast by his depression, frightened by his fear, nor engulfed by his dependency? Is my inner self hardy enough to realize that I am not destroyed by his anger, taken over by his need for dependence, nor enslaved by his love, but

that I exist separate from him with feelings and rights of my own? When I can freely feel this strength of being a separate person, then I find that I can let myself go much more deeply in understanding and accepting him because I am not fearful of losing myself.

5. The next question is closely related. Am I secure enough within myself to permit him his separateness? Can I permit him to be what he is—honest or deceitful, infantile or adult, despairing or over-confident? Can I give him the freedom to be? Or do I feel that he should follow my advice, or remain somewhat dependent on me, or mold himself after me? In this connection I think of the interesting small study by Farson (1955) which found that the less well adjusted and less competent counselor tends to induce conformity to himself, to have clients who model themselves after him. On the other hand, the better adjusted and more competent counselor can interact with a client through many interviews without interfering with the freedom of the client to develop a personality quite separate from that of his therapist. I should prefer to be in this latter class, whether as parent or supervisor or counselor.

6. Another question I ask myself is: Can I let myself enter fully into the world of his feelings and personal meanings and see these as he does? Can I step into his private world so completely that I lose all desire to evaluate or judge it? Can I enter it so sensitively that I can move about in it freely, without trampling on meanings which are precious to him? Can I sense it so accurately that I can catch not only the meanings of his experience which are obvious to him, but those meanings which are only implicit, which he sees only dimly or as confusion? Can I extend this understanding without limit? I think of the client who said, "Whenever I find someone who understands a *part* of me at the time, then it never fails that a point is reached where I know they're not understanding me again . . . What I've looked for so hard is for someone to understand."

For myself I find it easier to feel this kind of understanding, and to communicate it, to individual clients than to students in a class or staff members in a group in which I am involved. There is a strong temptation to set students "straight," or to point out to a staff member the errors in his thinking. Yet when I can permit myself to understand in these situations, it is mutually rewarding. And with clients in therapy, I am often impressed with the fact that even a minimal amount of empathic understanding—a bumbling and faulty attempt to catch the confused complexity of the client's meaning—is helpful, though there is no doubt that it is most helpful when I can see and formulate clearly the meanings in his experiencing which for him have been unclear and tangled.

7. Still another issue is whether I can be acceptant of each facet of this other person which he presents to me. Can I receive him as he is? Can I communicate this attitude? Or can I only receive him condition-

ally, acceptant of some aspects of his feelings and silently or openly disapproving of other aspects? It has been my experience that when my attitude is conditional, then he cannot change or grow in those respects in which I cannot fully receive him. And when—afterward and sometimes too late—I try to discover why I have been unable to accept him in every respect, I usually discover that it is because I have been frightened or threatened in myself by some aspect of his feeling. If I am to be more helpful, then I must myself grow and accept myself in these respects.

8. A very practical issue is raised by the question: Can I act with sufficient sensitivity in the relationship that my behavior will not be perceived as a threat? The work we are beginning to do in studying the physiological concomitants of psychotherapy confirms the research by Dittes in indicating how easily individuals are threatened at a physiological level. The psychogalvanic reflex—the measure of skin conductance—takes a sharp dip when the therapist responds with some word which is just a little stronger than the client's feeling. And to a phrase such as, "My you *do* look upset," the needle swings almost off the paper. My desire to avoid even such minor threats is not due to a hypersensitivity about my client. It is simply due to the conviction based on experience that if I can free him as completely as possible from external threat, then he can begin to experience and to deal with the internal feelings and conflicts which he finds threatening within himself.

9. A specific aspect of the preceding question but an important one is: Can I free him from the threat of external evaluation? In almost every phase of our lives—at home, at school, at work—we find ourselves under the rewards and punishments of external judgments. "That's good"; "that's naughty." "That's worth an A"; "that's a failure." "That's good counseling"; "that's poor counseling." Such judgments are a part of our lives from infancy to old age. I believe they have a certain social usefulness to institutions and organizations such as schools and professions. Like everyone else I find myself all too often making such evaluations. But, in my experience, they do not make for personal growth and hence I do not believe that they are a part of a helping relationship. Curiously enough a positive evaluation is as threatening in the long run as a negative one, since to inform someone that he is good implies that you also have the right to tell him he is bad. So I have come to feel that the more I can keep a relationship free of judgment and evaluation, the more this will permit the other person to reach the point where he recognizes that the locus of evaluation, the center of responsibility, lies within himself. The meaning and value of his experience is in the last analysis something which is up to him, and no amount of external judgment can alter this. So I should like to work toward a relationship in which I am not, even in my own feelings, evaluating him. This I believe can set him free to be a self-responsible person.

10. One last question: Can I meet this other individual as a person who is in process of *becoming*, or will I be bound by his past and by my past? If, in my encounter with him, I am dealing with him as an immature child, an ignorant student, a neurotic personality, or a psychopath, each of these concepts of mine limits what he can be in the relationship. Martin Buber, the existentialist philosopher of the University of Jerusalem, has a phrase, "confirming the other," which has had meaning for me. He says "Confirming means . . . accepting the whole potentiality of the other. . . . I can recognize in him, know in him, the person he has been . . . *created* to become. . . . I confirm him in myself, and then in him, in relation to this potentiality that . . . can now be developed, can evolve." [1] If I accept the other person as something fixed, already diagnosed and classified, already shaped by his past, then I am doing my part to confirm this limited hypothesis. If I accept him as a process of becoming, then I am doing what I can to confirm or make real his potentialities.

It is at this point that I see Verplanck, Lindsley, and Skinner, working in operant conditioning, coming together with Buber, the philosopher or mystic. At least they came together in principle, in an odd way. If I see a relationship as only an opportunity to reinforce certain types of words or opinions in the other, then I tend to confirm him as an object—a basically mechanical, manipulable object. And if I see this as his potentiality, he tends to act in ways which support this hypothesis. If, on the other hand, I see a relationship as an opportunity to "reinforce" *all* that he is, the person that he is with all his extent potentialities, then he tends to act in ways which support *his* hypothesis. I have then—to use Buber's term—confirmed him as a living person, capable of creative inner development. Personally I prefer this second type of hypothesis.

Conclusion

In the early portion of this paper I reviewed some of the contributions which research is making to our knowledge *about* relationships. Endeavoring to keep that knowledge in mind I then took up the kind of questions which arise from an inner and subjective point of view as I enter, as a person, into relationships. If I could, in myself, answer all the questions I have raised in the affirmative, then I believe that any relationships in which I was involved would be helping relationships, would involve growth. But I cannot give a positive answer to most of these questions. I can only work in the direction of the positive answer.

This has raised in my mind the strong suspicion that the optimal help-

1. M. Buber and C. Rogers, transcription of dialogue held April 18, 1957, Ann Arbor, Mich. Unpublished manuscript.

ing relationship is the kind of relationship created by a person who is psychologically mature. Or to put it in another way, the degree to which I can create relationships which facilitate the growth of others as separate persons is a measure of the growth I have achieved in myself. In some respects this is a disturbing thought, but it is also a promising or challenging one. It would indicate that if I am interested in creating helping relationships I have a fascinating lifetime job ahead of me, stretching and developing my potentialities in the direction of growth.

References

Baldwin, A. L.; Kalhorn, J.; and Breese, F. H. "Patterns of Parent Behavior." *Psychological Monographs,* 58 (1945): 1–75.

Betz, B. J., and Whitehorn, J. C. "The Relationship of the Therapist to the Outcome of Therapy in Schizophrenia." In *Psychiatric Research Reports #5. Research Techniques in Schizophrenia.* Washington, D.C.: American Psychiatric Assn., 1956, pp. 89–117. See also, "A Study of Psychotherapeutic Relationships Between Physicians and Schizophrenic Patients," *American Journal of Psychiatry* 3 (1954): 321–331.

Dittes, J. E. "Galvanic Skin Response as a Measure of Patient's Reaction to Therapist's Permissiveness." *Journal of Abnormal and Social Psychology,* 55 (1957): 295–303.

Ends, E. J., and Page, C. W. "A Study of Three Types of Group Psychotherapy with Hospitalized Male Inebriates." *Quarterly Journal of the Study of Alcohol,* 18 (1957): 263–277.

Farson, R. E. "Introjection in the Psychotherapeutic Relationship." Doctoral diss., University of Chicago, 1955.

Fiedler, F. E. "Quantitative Studies on the Role of Therapists' Feelings Toward Their Patients." In O. H. Mowrer, ed., *Psychotherapy: Theory and Research.* New York: Ronald Press, 1953, chapter 12.

Greenspoon, J. "The Reinforcing Effect of Two Spoken Sounds on the Frequency of Two Responses." *American Journal of Psychology,* 68 (1955): 409–416.

Halkides, G. "An Experimental Study for Four Conditions Necessary for Therapeutic Change." Doctoral diss., University of Chicago, 1958.

Harlow, H. F. "The Nature of Love." *American Psychologist,* 13 (1958): 673–685.

Heine, R. W. "A Comparison of Patients' Reports on Psychotherapeutic Experience with Psychoanalytic, Nondirective, and Adlerian therapists." Doctoral diss., University of Chicago, 1950.

Lindsley, O. R. "Operant Conditioning Methods Applied to Research in Chronic Schizophrenia." *Psychiatric Research Reports #5.* Research Techniques in Schizophrenia. Washington, D.C.: American Psychiatric Assn., 1956, pp. 118–153.

Page, C. W., and Ends, E. J. "A Review and Synthesis of the Literature Suggesting a Psychotherapeutic Technique Based on Two-Factor Learning Theory." Unpublished manuscript, loaned to the writer.

Quinn, R. D. "Psychotherapists' Expressions as an Index to the Quality of Early Therapeutic Relationships." Doctoral diss., University of Chicago, 1950.

Rogers, C. R. "The Necessary and Sufficient Conditions of Psycho-Therapeutic Change." *Journal of Consulting Psychology,* 21 (1957): 95–103.

Seeman, J. "Counselor Judgments of Therapeutic Process and Outcome." In C. R. Rogers and R. F. Dymond, eds., *Psychotherapy and Personality Change*. Chicago: University of Chicago Press, 1954, chapter 4.

Verplanck, W. S. "The Control of the Content of Conversation: Reinforcement of Statements of Opinion. *Journal of Abnormal and Social Psychology,* 51 (1955): 668–676.

An Overview and Next Steps

A. W. COMBS

What can we conclude from this series of studies and what directions do they suggest for further research? While these studies leave many questions unanswered and can hardly be regarded as definitive, they nevertheless provide additional support for basic concepts in perceptual theory, shed new light on the nature of the helping professions, and point the way to promising hypotheses for further research.

SUPPORT FOR PERCEPTUAL THEORY

The basic premise of perceptual psychology is that behavior is a function of the perceptual field of the behaver at the instant of action. Most research in human behavior has traditionally been carried on from an external point of view. That is to say, understanding of behavior has been sought from the frame of reference of the outside observer. The thesis of perceptual psychology, on the other hand, is that behavior can also be understood (and sometimes more effectively) when examined from the standpoint, not of the outsider, but of the behaver himself. The results of these studies tend to corroborate that position. They do more. Attempts to distinguish the behavior of professional workers in terms of objective criteria like knowledge possessed, or methods used, or behavior exhibited have generally been disappointing in the past. Several of the studies reported here, however, have demonstrated that significant relationships do, indeed, exist between perception and behavior. Even

From A. W. Combs, *Florida Studies in the Helping Professions;* University of Florida Monographs: Social Sciences No. 37, University of Florida Press: Gainesville, 1969, pp. 69–78. Reprinted by permission of the author and the publisher.

more, they suggest that a perceptual approach to the study of professional workers may provide us with more useful understanding of these persons than has heretofore been possible. Thus, these studies not only support the perceptual hypothesis, but suggest that this approach may be more fruitful in advancing our efforts to understand the helping professions. They seem to place in our hands a new and promising tool for further research.

A major difficulty in perceptual psychology is the problem of measurement. Measurement in more orthodox approaches to psychology can be a pretty straightforward matter of recording observations or counting responses. The study of perception is more difficult since perceptions lie inside people and are not open to direct observation. Because perception can only be approached (at least, at present) by some form of inference, additional problems of reliability of measurement are posed for the researcher using this frame of reference. For some psychologists these problems have seemed so difficult that they have raised serious questions of whether such procedures can be dignified by the term "research" at all. The question requires an answer. The position of the perceptual psychologist is that techniques of inference can, indeed, provide reliable data if the researcher approaches the problem of measurement with the same discipline, care, and rigor demanded of science in any other field of exploration.

In these studies inferences about the perceptual organization of professional workers have been obtained from a wide variety of original sources including observations, interviews, "critical incidents," responses to problem situations, and stories told by the subject. Inferences were obtained by using the observer himself as an instrument of measurement. Observers also demonstrated in these studies that such inferences could be made with highly acceptable degrees of reliability and that such data could be effectively used for the exploration of an important aspect of human behavior.

THE NATURE OF THE HELPING PROFESSIONS

The Common Origins of the Helping Professions

The original impetus for these studies grew out of a suspicion that, while the various forms of the helping professions differ with respect to their purposes, clientele, and techniques, nevertheless, they are basically alike in the psychology through which they operate. It seemed to us that the crux of the problem of "helping" lay not in some mysterious special technique. Rather the various helping professions seem really to be expressions of a kind of basic "good" human interrelationship. That is to say, these professions appear to represent the concentration and crystallization of the best we know about human interrelationships for the sake of the person or persons to be helped. The helping professions seem to us not different from life experience but selected from human experience. Within the limited sample represented by these studies, this thesis is given some support.

Ideally, the case for this observation would certainly be stronger had our studies investigated identical criteria with identical techniques in each of the professions we examined. Unfortunately, that is hindsight which suggests the need for further research, to be sure, but does us little good now. From the data we do have, however, there is sufficient evidence to suggest that the perceptual organization of persons who are effective helpers, at least for counselors, elementary teachers, Episcopal priests, and student nurses, have a number of common kinds of perceptions. Our original hunches seem to be supported and we are encouraged to continue exploring in these directions.

The Importance of Perceptual Organization as a Distinguishing Characteristic

Our early theoretical consideration of these matters led us to the belief that the widespread failure of research efforts to distinguish between effective and ineffective workers in the helping professions was largely due to concentration on symptoms rather than causes. Observed behavior is the end of a process, an expression of it. As such, many diverse behaviors may occur as expressions of a single aspect of individual beliefs or perceptions. Conversely, different perceptual experiences can result in highly similar kinds of behavior. To distinguish clearly between effective and ineffective workers in the helping professions it seemed to us required penetration to the causes of behavior, a hypothesis supported by the observation of other workers that persons are often helped by highly diverse behaviors if the intent of the helper is positive. The accuracy of this reasoning is certainly given support by the findings of these studies. Our studies with elementary teachers, counselors, and Episcopal priests, especially, seem to lend credence to the importance of the perceptual variable in distinguishing between effective and ineffective helpers. The results for our college teachers, when effectiveness is judged by students, at least, also seem to corroborate our hypotheses. The findings of our study with student nurses, however, while not denying our original hypothesis, certainly did not corroborate it.

THE GENERAL FRAME OF REFERENCE OF PROFESSIONAL HELPERS

Three of our studies showing significant differences between effective and ineffective professional workers investigated the frame of reference in which the helper approached his task (Table 1). All these investigated the people-things dichotomy, two examined the internal-external approach dimension, and one further examined the perceptual-facts and the immediate-historical dichotomies as well. In view of the fact that the helping professions are designed to help people, it is not surprising to find that workers who tend to be people-oriented are likely to be more effective. The remaining items explored in this category seem to represent a characteristic internal or perceptual approach which effective helpers take toward their students, clients, or parishioners. Such a characteristic frame of reference in the helper would presumably cause him to behave in ways that others would describe as sensitive or empathic, both qualities often described as desirable in counselors, teachers, pastors, and nurses.

THE HELPER'S PERCEPTIONS OF PEOPLE

It is apparent that effective helpers in all four of the professions indicated in Table 2 are characterized by a generally positive view of their subjects and a belief in the capacity of the human organism to save itself. It makes a great deal of difference whether helpers perceive their clients as able or unable. If a counselor, teacher, or priest does not regard his clients as able he can hardly permit them, let them, or trust them to act on their own; to do so would be a violation of responsibility. Apparently, effective helpers tend to see the persons they work with in essentially positive ways as dependable, friendly, and worthy people.

Table 1 Frame of Reference Categories Showing Significant Differences in Three Studies

Category	Counselors	Teachers	Priests
People—things	S[a]	S	S
Internal—external	S	S	NM
Perceptual—facts	NM[b]	S	NM
Immediate—historical	NM	S	NM

a. S = Significant difference.
b. NM = Not measured.

Table 2 Perceptions of Other Categories Showing Significant Differences in Four Studies

Category	Counselors	Teachers	Priests	Professors[a]
Able–unable	S[b]	S	S	S
Dependable–undependable	S	S	NM	S
Friendly–unfriendly	S	S	NM	NM
Worthy–unworthy	S	S	NM	S
Internally motivated–not	NM[c]	S	NM	S
Helpful–hindering	NM	S	NM	NM

a. Effectiveness determined from student ratings only.
b. S = Significant difference.
c. NM = Not measured.

This hardly seems like a startling revelation. Indeed, it sounds like little more than good common sense. It is necessary to remind ourselves, however, that these are not factors which helpers *say* about themselves, but characteristic ways of perceiving inferred from their behavior. Effective behavers do not simply verbally ascribe to these qualities, they *behave* in terms of them.

THE HELPER'S PERCEPTIONS OF SELF

Two characteristics stand out in an examination of Table 3. In the first place effective helpers appear to see themselves as one with mankind, as sharing a common fate. Poor helpers, on the other hand, have a tendency to see themselves as apart from others, as different from them. If the success of helping professions depends upon relationships established

Table 3 Perceptions of Self Categories Showing Significant Differences in Four Studies

Category	Counselors	Teachers	Priests	Professors[a]
Identified–unidentified	S[b]	S	S	NS[d]
Enough–not enough	S	S	NM	NS
Dependable–undependable	NM[c]	S	NM	NM
Worthy–unworthy	NM	S	NM	NS
Wanted–unwanted	NM	S	NM	S

a. Effectiveness determined from student ratings only.
b. S = Significant difference.
c. NM = Not measured.
d. NS = Not significant.

between helpers and helpees, as modern theory would seem to suggest, it is easy to see why this characteristic would distinguish between good helpers and poor ones. It is difficult to establish effective relationships with a helper unwilling to get involved.

A second major characteristic of a good helper seems to be the existence of an essentially positive view of self. Such views of self seem to be characteristic also of self-actualizing personalities as reported in the literature. A positive view of self provides the kind of internal security which makes it possible for persons who possess such views of self to behave with much more assurance, dignity, and straightforwardness. With a firm base of operations to work from such persons can be much more daring and creative in respect to their approach to the world and more able to give of themselves to others as well.

THE HELPER'S PERCEPTIONS OF HIS TASK

Effective helpers apparently tend to see their tasks more as freeing than controlling (Table 4). Such a finding certainly gives much support to the growth philosophy underlying most current counseling approaches and to the student-centered concept of teaching advocated by many modern educators. The concern of effective helpers with larger rather than smaller issues also seems to be consistent with the freeing purpose.

The self-revealing characteristic found in the effective helpers seems congruent with the identified-unidentified characteristic of self found in Table 4. Many writers have indicated that self-disclosure is closely related to healthy personality and the capacity to enter into intimate human relationships.

Table 4 Perceptions of Purpose Categories Showing Significant Difference in Three Studies

Category	Counselors	Teachers	Priests
Self revealing–self concealing	S[a]	S	NM
Freeing–controlling	S	S	S
Altruistic–narcissistic	S	NM	NM
Larger–smaller	S	S	NM
Involved–uninvolved	NM[b]	S	S
Process–goals	NM	S	NM

a. S = Significant difference.
b. NM = Not measured.

METHODS IN THE HELPING PROFESSIONS

In the original formulation of hypotheses for our studies of the helping professions our seminar listed seven continua which we thought might discriminate between effective and ineffective helpers in connection with the methods they used to carry out their tasks. None of these hypotheses has yet been subjected to test. In our earlier experiments this was because the problem was of less interest to us than hypotheses about the helper's frame of reference, perceptions of self and others, or perception of purposes. Later, we postponed further research on this question because changes in our thinking about the question of methods led us in somewhat different directions.

It will be recalled from our earlier discussion that a review of the literature had shown only very disappointing results with respect to distinguishing between effective and ineffective helpers on the basis of the methods which they used. In our early thinking about this matter it seemed to us we might find more clear-cut differences between effective and ineffective helpers if we looked, not at the methods they used per se, but rather, at the ways in which they were perceiving methods. Accordingly, our early seminar listed eleven continua for examination. As a consequence of our later studies, however, we have come to see the problem as follows. If the self as instrument concept of effective operation in the helping professions is valid, then the search for "right" methods is doomed before it begins. Since helpers as persons are unique, the hope of finding a "common uniqueness," by definition, is a hopeless search. It occurred to us then that perhaps the question of methods in the helping professions is not a matter of adopting the "right" method, but a question of the helper discovering the right method for *him*. That is to say, the crucial question is not "what" method, but the "fit" of the method, its appropriateness to the self of the helper, to his purposes, his subjects, the situation, and so forth. We now believe the important distinction between the good and poor helper with respect to methods is not a matter of his perceptions of methods, per se, but the *authenticity* of whatever methods he uses. There is already some evidence for this in our findings that good helpers are self-revealing, involved, and identified.

We suspect a major problem of poor helpers is the fact that their methods are unauthentic, that is, they tend to be put on, contrived. As such they can only be utilized so long as the helper keeps his mind on them. That, of course, is likely to be disastrous on two counts. In the first place it separates him from his client or student, and the message conveyed is likely to be that he is not "with it," is not really interested, or is a phony. Second, it is almost never possible to maintain attention to the "right" method for very long. As a consequence the poor helper relapses frequently to what he believes or his previous experience has taught him, and so the method he is trying to use fails because of the tenuous, interrupted character of his use of it.

We are about persuaded the question of the helper's perceptions concerning methods are of minor significance. Helpers will find the methods to carry on their tasks effectively if perceptions of self, others, purposes, and the general frame of reference are congruent with that of effective helpers. The validity of this position, of course, remains to be investigated. It is our hope that others will join us in exploring whether or not authenticity is truly the key question with respect to methods.

HOW MANY PERCEPTUAL FACTORS?

In our studies of the perceptual organization of effective helpers we have so far demonstrated that at least twenty-one perceptual characteristics distinguish between good and poor helpers. In our original seminar we listed forty-three hypotheses for exploration. There seems to be no doubt that still others could be added to this list. There is an important question to be answered, however, concerning the number of truly significant variables involved in this matter. All of us engaged in these researches have the very strong feeling that there may, in fact, be comparatively few perceptual criteria related to effective and ineffective operations in the helping professions. In choosing hypotheses from our original list for investigation it became quite clear to us that some of these were duplications. They also seemed to vary considerably in terms of fundamental importance. Even among some of the perceptual characteristics we investigated in the studies reported here, it is apparent from simple observation that items overlap. In addition, in the factor analysis of children's perceptions carried out by Combs and Soper (1963), forty-seven of the forty-nine categories under investigation were reduced to one global factor which these authors called "a feeling of general adequacy." In order to determine the number of truly discreet perceptual characteristics involved in the discrimination of effective and ineffective helpers, we believe a factor analysis study of this matter is called for. Unfortunately, such a study would require a most expensive design and to this point we have not been able to find either the time or finances required to properly carry out such a project. Perhaps, some day, we, or someone else, may.

Ever since the various forms of the helping professions came into being the problem of discriminating between effective and ineffective workers has been a knotty one. We believe these investigations have opened some new avenues for understanding of the matter with broad implications for practical application. To this point we have been primarily interested in exploring these questions for their possible implications in the training of effective persons in the helping professions. This has already borne fruit in suggesting new approaches to the professional education of teachers based upon a perceptual approach to the problem (Combs 1965). Benton (1964), Gooding (1964), and Dickman (1967) have touched slightly on the implications of their studies for the training of priests, teachers, and nurses. These are matters deserving much more speculation, experiment, and application.

To this point our researchers have been primarily concerned with exploring the perceptual organization of helpers in order to shed light on theoretical questions and to suggest areas of innovation for training more effective helpers in teaching, counseling, nursing, and pastoral care. The measurement techniques we have employed in these studies are at this stage still far less refined that we could wish. In time they will improve and new ones develop as well. If further studies continue the favorable trends we have seen so far, it is likely these measurement techniques may also contribute important new approaches to the selection and evaluation of effective helpers.

It is apparent that the studies reported here are little more than pilot studies. Like any research worthy of the name they raise far more questions than they have settled. For those of us involved in these investigations they have been exciting and stimulating explorations in what seem to us to be fruitful new directions.

We believe these studies represent but a small and tentative beginning of research into a most promising new approach to understanding the helping professions. What started as a series of hunches in 1957 has now become a conviction that we are on or close to the right track. If these concepts are not the truth, then we are encouraged by our studies to believe they are very like it. It is our earnest hope that this presentation may encourage others to join us on this path to further discovery.

References

Benton, J. A. "Perceptual Characteristics of Episcopal Pastors." Doctoral diss., University of Florida, 1964.

Combs, A. W. *The Professional Education of Teachers.* Boston: Allyn and Bacon, 1965.

———, and Soper, D. W. *The Relationship of Child Perceptions to Achievement and Behavior in the Early School Years.* Cooperative Research Project No. 814, University of Florida, Gainesville, Florida, 1963.

Dickman, J. F. "The Perceptual Organization of Person-Oriented versus Task-Oriented Student Nurses." Doctoral diss., University of Florida, 1967.

Gooding, C. T. "An Observational Analysis of the Perceptual Organization of Effective Teachers." Doctoral diss., University of Florida, 1964.

Counselor Training: Educating For the Beautiful and Noble Person

FRED RICHARDS

During the past three decades psychologists have focused increasingly upon the healthy personality to clarify, define, and objectify the optimal end of the growth process in human nature. A vital part of this revolutionary reconstruction of the image of man has been a re-evaluation of the counseling relationship and a new model of the counselor or helper as one becoming fully human, fully growing and fully functioning in every aspect of his life. Systematic exploration into the interpersonal dynamics of the therapeutic process and the facilitative dimensions of counselor functioning suggests that the more effective counselors are also the more fully human, the most actualizing. Such research findings challenge us to devise counselor training programs which have as their main thrust the facilitation of the maximum growth of the trainee. They urge us to employ training programs educating for what Landsman (1968) calls the "beautiful and noble person."

Thirty years ago, Carl Rogers presented a paper entitled, "New Concepts in Psychotherapy," which attempted to formulate a newer approach to counseling and therapy. Rogers' approach emphasized, as we know, the profound significance of the counselor/counselee relationship and the human qualities of the counselor. Years later, Rogers (1967, p. 181) wrote:

> Some years ago I formulated the view that it was not the special professional knowledge of the therapist, nor his intellectual conception of therapy. . . nor his techniques, which determined his effectiveness. I hypothesized that what was most important was the extent to which he possesses certain personal attitudes in the relationship. I endeavored to

From the *Colorado Journal of Educational Research,* 1972, 12 (1), 11–16. Reprinted by permission of the author and publisher.

> define three of these which I regarded as basic—the realness, genuineness or congruence of the therapist; the degree of emphatic understanding of his client which he experienced and communicated; and the degree of unconditional positive regard or non-possessive liking which he felt toward his client.

Rogers' theoretical formulations focused on those personal qualities characteristic of that person other humanistic psychologists were beginning to define as the "ultimate" in human growth and development. These psychologists were seeking to postulate an ideal image of the most human realization of man's potential. During thirty years of exploration and research into what man may become or could be, Rogers and others have variously described this human potential as: self-actualization, integration or individuation, adequacy, authenticity, fully-functioning, the transparent self, the beautiful and noble person. While their descriptions have varying emphasis, the authors agree that the human being they decribe is one "realizing the potentialities of the person . . . becoming fully human, everything that the person can become" (Maslow, 1968, p. 153). These various descriptions of full humanness appear to converge at one point: the truly healthy personality, in part, can be operationally defined as a person functioning on high levels of empathy, genuineness and positive regard. As Maslow (1970) points out, it has become "clearer and clearer that the best 'helpers' are the most fully human persons . . . the best way to become a better 'helper' is to become a better person."

Descriptions of the healthy personality by humanistic psychologists emphasize the convergence of these personal qualities in the superior person.* Describing the qualities the effective counselor communicates in therapeutic relationship, Rogers (1967) writes that the counselor can sense and identify with the client's private world of inner meanings and feelings and communicate his understanding at levels where the client is vaguely aware. The effective counselor is openly, freely, spontaneously himself; he is genuinely there, authentic, *sans* a front or facade. He also accepts, respects and cares about his client in a nonpossessive way. He is warm and caring. He does not judge or evaluate the client, but lets the client *be*.

Landsman (1961, 1967, 1968) describes the beautiful and noble person or the best self "as an individual's functioning on the highest levels of his uniquely human characteristics" (1967, p. 32). Intelligent, productive, self-actualizing, he is the "helper" possessing the qualities of warmth, kindness, gentleness, courage, and compassion. He has sharp, accurate perceptions of reality. He accepts, likes, enjoys, expresses and understands himself. Joyfully, passionately, fully, he goes out to meet, experi-

* See Welch and Rodwick, "*Communicating the Sciences: The Scientist as a Healthy Personality.*"

ence and respond to his world. Deeply caring and committed to the growth and well-being of others, he is the compassionate, facilitative helper, (Landsman, 1968).

In short, the effective counselor is the compassionate person at the positive end of the passionate-productive-compassionate continuum describing the growth process of Landsman's beautiful and noble person, (Landsman, 1968). It appears that counselor training programs committed to producing effective counselors should have as their goal the maximum growth and full-humanness of the trainees.

Research on the facilitative dimensions of empathy, genuineness and positive regard have produced results with important implications for the structuring of counselor training programs. Research by Carkhuff (1967), Carkhuff and Berenson (1967), Carkhuff and Truax (1966), Pierce, Carkhuff and Berenson (1967), and Truax and Carkhuff (1964) found that low levels of counselor functioning have deteriorative influences on client personality change and that high levels of therapist offered conditions evoke the greatest constructive change in the client. That is, counselors both promote and inhibit or retard the growth of their clients! Alexik and Carkhuff (1967) found that low level functioning counselors are manipulated by the client's depth of self-exploration. In one study, Kratochvil, Aspy and Carkhuff (1967) concluded that the counselor's direction of growth or change in levels of functioning has a profound effect upon constructive changes in the client. Foulds (1969) found that counselors communicating high levels of facilitative conditions are more self-actualizing than low functioning counselors.

Carkhuff and Berenson (1967), Carkhuff, Kratochvil, and Friel (1968) and Pierce, Carkhuff and Berenson (1967) found that training programs function at the level of the trainers who conduct them; the levels of trainer or supervisor functioning may facilitate or retard the trainee's level of functioning and constructive personality change. Bergin and Solomon (1963) concluded that graduates of training programs functioned at unusually low levels. Carkhuff, Kratochvil and Friel (1968) also found that graduates of training programs function at lower levels than they did when first entering the program, and that the more and less adequate trainees left the program while the middle or average range of trainees remained.

The above mentioned research findings must be viewed with some caution, however. Combs (1970, p. 7) correctly warns that counselor "training programs must concern themselves with perception and less with acts and methods." Researchers emphasizing the latter too often attempt to measure the interpersonal functioning of the counselor/subjects while employing an approach greatly lacking in the dimensions of interpersonal functioning they seek to measure. Often little or no consideration is given to the perceptual organization or personal meanings of the behavior who is the subject of the research. The counselor/subject's level of functioning is evaluated in terms of whether or not his verbal behavior conforms to the expectations of the rating scales designed by researchers who consider themselves "the experts." On the other hand, it is incorrect to assume "that the way to become expert is to do what the expert does." (Combs, 1964, p. 371). It is also true an effective counselor is not necessarily a person who employs any particular method. An effective counselor is one whose methods fit him (Combs, 1970, p. 6). Often the basic response repertoire of the counselor/subject—his particular "method"—is considered ineffective or low functioning because the researcher fails to consider important what causes the subject's behavior, i.e. his perception and not the researcher's perception of the client and the situation.

Even though the above research into the interpersonal dynamics of the counseling relationship has its evident shortcomings, it alarmingly and convincingly suggests that present training programs may be educating for mediocrity rather than human magnificence, may be producing "nonhelpers" rather than helpers. Mediocrity, even though it has a professional polish, is not enough. Training programs not honestly committed to educating for the best, the ultimate realizations of human growth and development, become part of the very interpersonal environment that drives a client to the counselor in the first place.

Having commented on the chronic lack of healthy, human nourishment available in our society, Carkhuff and Berenson write (1967, p. 1):

> The hope, it would appear, lies in the development through both training and constructive personal change, of the whole person/counselor, the person who does not view counseling and therapy as distinct from life, but rather, counseling as a way of life. The only reasonable starting point from which to increase the quality and quantity of nourishment in all human relationships is the whole counselor, a person acutely aware of his own experience.

The whole person/counselor is both competent and compassionate. He is a grower, one committed to his own personal constructive change and the growth of others. He has vast resources, is fully alive, full of energy and zest for life. He employs a thorough knowledge of research and research tools to discriminate and communicate high levels of facilitative conditions (Carkhuff and Berenson, 1967). Briefly, he is self-actualizing; he is passionately, productively, and compassionately alive.

What kind of training program would best educate for such a man? Carkhuff and Berenson and others suggest an integrated didactic and experiential approach to counselor training with a focus upon the trainee's personal growth and self-actualization (Carkhuff and Berenson, 1967; Carkhuff, Kratochvil and Friel, 1968; Carkhuff and Truax, 1965a,

1965b). The training program would provide a "living, flourishing, productive pocket of health" where trainees would interrelate with trainers who would be models of the effective whole person/counselor, models of the person who "is involved in a life long search for actualization for others as well as for himself, and is readily amenable to the sharing of his search with others (Carkhuff and Berenson, 1967, pp. 205 and 46).

A program characterized by the above and providing vast opportunities or evoking behaviors ascribed to Landsman's beautiful and noble person has exciting possibilities. Landsman's systematic exploration of positive experiences suggested to him the fascinating possibility "that the maximization of positive human experience is perhaps the key to the maximization of self-actualization" (Landsman, 1961, p. 51). He postulates an experiential continuum which describes the growth process of the self-actualizer moving beyond normality toward superior functioning as the beautiful and noble person (Landsman, 1968). Landsman clearly insists that the first phase, the passionate-self-positive context, is absolute; a positive attitude toward self is a necessary basis for movement toward higher levels of functioning on the continuum. The second or productive phase is characterized by increased productivity, efficiency, single-minded commitment of one's resources, talents and energies to personally meaningful tasks or goals. Here the mode of productivity is that most expressive of one's essential personality. The third phase, the compassionate person, is the highest level. Here one is the socially effective person, the exciter, the growth facilitator, the loving-caring person. Here one is, if you will, the whole person/counselor.

The following only suggests possible directions for a training program which would operationalize or confirm Landsman's continuum. No effort to outline a complete program is intended. What the authors attempt to do here is to give a brief overview of what might well be the emphasis in each phase of a program. The selection of staff members and students is considered only briefly, although some research has attempted to deal with this problem (Whiteley, Sprinthall, Mosher, Donaghy, 1967).

It is assumed that the counselor trainers or supervising personnel would be some of the best persons available, those functioning on higher levels and actively and continually committed to their own growth. Selection of counselor-trainees should include a candid discussion of the risk factor implicit in the growth-process emphasis of the program. Important is that perspective counselor-trainees choose to participate in such a process only after exploring and sharing with one or more members of the staff their own perceptions of what such a program means to them. Counselor-trainees accepted into the program would become involved in an intense mini-program, a one to three week session reflecting both the climate and challenge of the full program. The mini-program would function as an experiential selection phase, a selection process grounded in the very qualities of interpersonal functioning the program hopes to facilitate and one that provides an opportunity for students to leave the program, if they choose to do so, after an intense and personal interaction with other students and the staff.

The Passionate Self Phase: A conscious committed effort to create a climate of non-evaluation, non-threat and unconditional positive regard. A real attempt on the part of all personnel to communicate high levels of the facilitative conditions to the trainees. A commitment to the creation of community celebrating the separateness and uniqueness of each individual. A commitment to being, working, playing and sharing together to facilitate the maximum well-being of all concerned.

The emphasis should be upon dialogue in community with others, the discovery of significant others among the staff and students, sensitivity training, encountering, confronting, being with oneself and others, joy, closeness, sharing, mutual acceptance and respect, spontaneity. Students would help others to discover their potential creativity by sharing unique talents and skills, would design their own "program" of ongoing growth as the whole person/counselor, would strive to increase their openness to others, themselves and the world. They would meet with other students and staff members to discuss ideas, share insights, or self-disclose and listen to the self-disclosures of others. Students would be encouraged to set aside time each week to meditate alone, sit quietly, walk, hike and simply enjoy learning the art of responding more fully to their inner selves and their environment.

Students would keep detailed cumulative records or journals of their experiences with self, others and the world, would share these records or journals with significant others, and would use them to better perceive and understand more deeply their own growth process. They would participate in preparatory seminars to explore the personal meanings and implications of the passionate-productive-compassionate continuum and related areas in psychology, literature and other fields. Important here is that each trainee's experience frees him increasingly to explore and share his changing perceptions of himself and others. Such a climate would be an invitation to explore his feelings of personal adequacy and move toward accepting any and all aspects of his perceptual world. A goal of such seminars would be to give the students a personally meaningful overview of the process in which they were personally involved, enable them to perceive their unique and separate, though perhaps shared, experience of the process, and give them a sense of being an accepted member of a community committed to the growth and well-being of *all* its members.

The Productive Self Phase: This phase would build upon, grow or emerge out of the former phase. In the first phase trainees would be helped, through extensive interaction with staff members and other students, to realize that their process of self-exploration and self-discovery may move forward on their terms and that it is at times a very slow and laborious one. Consequently the decision to move forward would be a shared one. The trainees would only move into the second phase when adequate enough to do so and when such movement was personally meaningful. Thus the length of each phase would vary according to how the trainee perceived his own growth experience after sharing his perceptions of the experience with significant others.

In the productive-self phase the emphasis would be respectable but creative research in areas dealing, directly or indirectly, with personal blocks to further growth, personal problems, conflicts, meanings, urges toward growth experienced by the student in the initial phase of the program. Productivity with significant others would be emphasized, also the increased realization of goals or the satisfaction of needs newly perceived in the first phase and now a personally meaningful basis for research, new projects and new directions in one's program.

Students might work extensively with research scales to increase their ability both to discriminate and communicate a core of facilitative conditions to others. Rather than a mechanistic use of the scales in which the trainee attempts to become a carbon copy of "the effective counselor" by "learning" or mimicking taped responses rated high on the scales, the trainee would function in terms of *his* initial and changing perception of how *he* sees the various levels of functioning as defined by the observational instruments. Most important is that the trainee become his instrument, that he increasingly becomes "a person who has learned to use himself as an effective instrument" (Combs, 1964, p. 373). Working extensively with the scales the trainee would seek to acquire a deep awareness of how *he* functions most authentically as a helper.

Trainees would also work with video and/or audio tape-recorded examples of therapists functioning at different levels of facilitation. They would also participate in sessions in which each student would respond to the taped sessions of supervising staff members and students who, at the compassionate-self-phase, would be actively involved in the counseling experience. Again, it is important that such "evaluation" take place in an atmosphere of trust, acceptance and respect, that the facilitative qualities considered characteristic of the whole/person counselor be equally that of the program in general.

The second phase student-trainees would role play as both "counselor" and "counselee." Immediate feedback from video and/or audio tapings of these sessions would be evaluated by those who volunteer to be taped and by fellow students. Students perceiving themselves as functioning at low levels on the core of facilitative dimensions would role play as "counselees" with those students functioning at higher facilitative levels serving as "counselors." As student "counselees" increase their sense of adequacy they would move into the role of "counselor." Both "counselors" and "counselees" would record, by using journals, cassettes, charts, etc., their change in levels of interpersonal functioning. They would continue to keep journals—an extension of the first-phase journals—which would relate their levels of functioning to their understanding and perception of their personal growth.

In this phase, as in all phases of the program, the educative process would be always an active participation in one's own growth and the growth of others. As aspiring helpers in a counselor training program they would be helpers in their relationships with one another. In the context of the experience of community nurtured in the first phase, evaluation of trainee functioning in the second-phase taped sessions are intended to be facilitative rather than threatening. Mistakes would not be failures but the cutting edge dimensions of one's personal growth process to be accepted, disclosed and assimilated into one's perception of himself and his role as a helper. To view the instruments as a means of "degrading" rather than facilitating the trainee to grow and learn in a climate of non-threat would be inimical to the training program suggested here. In fact, if the selection of students for the counseling program, viewed here as a vital and significant phase of the program, could distinguish between "growers" and "non-growers," "failure" in the context of such a climate might be a near impossibility. Perhaps no significant data is available on this matter because an educative process pregnant with vast opportunities for positive facilitative experiences toward the increased actualization of the student has never been tried!

The Compassionate Self Phase: This phase would again be an extension and continuation of the first two phases. But the emphasis here would be the active involvement of the trainee in the counseling relationship. He would function as the compassionate helper. Phase-two students' evaluation of the trainee's video and/or audio taped sessions, done in a climate of community and mutual helping, would give the trainee immediate feedback. The trainee would focus his passion and productivity on the increase of his capacity to function as an effective helper in every facet of the program. He could assist in research and carry out his own; he might extend his role as helper by co-leading seminars with staff members and by advising or assisting students participating in earlier phases of the program.

Using his own cumulative records or journals, tape-recorded sessions of his second-phase "counseling" and third-phase counseling experience, the student would do an extensive self-evaluation of his own growth process and his perceptions of his increased professional competence as a helper—an evaluation of himself as a whole person/counselor. This analysis or self-evaluation would be extended and supported by personally meaningful research in counseling psychology and related areas and/or a project of excellence whose focus and form would be determined by the needs of the student. The project of excellence would be an extension or expression of the unique concerns and directions of each of the counselor-trainees and a contribution to the counseling field. It would be an integration of the various aspects of the total impact of the trainee's experience and involvement in the program. Important here is that the student obtains a deep cognitive/affective or personally meaningfully understanding of *his mode of counseling,* that his own unique mode is related, by him, to the total counseling field, that he become increasingly aware of himself as the whole person/counselor, that he gain insight into the unique direction of his own development and growth, that he knows what he's about, where he's been, where he is, and where he can and may be going.

Participation in a training program that strives to achieve and practice the same high levels of interpersonal functioning it desires of its trainees would, it is hypothesized, free the trainees to discover and begin to develop their own maximum potential for becoming effective facilitators of growth. Hopefully, the trainee's experience in the counselor training program will prepare him to function not only as an increasingly effective counselor, but as an increasingly effective human being as well, as the beautiful and noble person.

References

Alexik, Mae, and Carkhuff, Robert R. "The Effects of the Manipulation of Client Depth of Self-Exploration Upon High and Low Functioning Counselors." *Journal of Clinical Psychology,* 23 (1967): 210–212.

Bergin, A. E., and Solomon, S. "Personality and Performance Correlates of Graduate Training." *American Psychologist,* 18 (1963): 393.

Carkhuff, Robert R. "Toward a Comprehensive Model of Facilitative Interpersonal Processes." *Journal of Counseling Psychology,* 14 (1967): 67–72.

———, and Truax, Charles B. "Training in Counseling and Psychotherapy: An Evaluation of an Integrated Didactic and Experiential Approach." *Journal of Consulting Psychology,* 29 (1965): 333–336. (a)

——— "Lay Mental Health Counseling: The Effects of Lay Group Counseling." *Journal of Consulting Psychology,* 29 (1965): 426–431. (b)

——— "Toward Explaining Success and Failure in Interpersonal Learning Experiences." *Personnel and Guidance Journal,* 44 (1966): 723–728.

———, and Berenson, G. *Beyond Counseling and Therapy.* New York: Holt, Rinehart and Winston, Inc., 1967.

———; Kratochvil, Daniel; and Friel, Theodore. "Effects of Professional Training: Communication and Discrimination of Facilitative Conditions." *Journal of Counseling Psychology,* 15 (1968): 68–74.

Combs, Arthur W. "The Perceptual Approach to the Helping Professions." *Journal of the Association for the Study of Perception,* 5 (11), (Fall 1970): 1–7.

——— "The Personal Approach to Good Teaching." *Educational Leadership,* (March 1964): 369–377, 399.

Foulds, Melvin L. "Self-Actualization and the Communication of Facilitative Conditions During Counseling." *Journal of Counseling Psychology,* 16 (2), (1969): 132–136.

Kratochvil, Daniel, Aspy, David, and Carkhuff, Robert R. "The Differential Effects of Absolute Level and Direction of Growth in Counselor Functioning Upon Client Level of Functioning." *Journal of Clinical Psychology,* 23 (1967): 216–217.

Landsman, Ted. "Human Experience and Human Relationship." In *Personality Theory and Counseling Practices.* First Annual Personality Conference, University of Florida, Gainesville, Florida, January 5, 6, and 7, 1961, pp. 42–52.

Landsman, Ted. "To Be or Not to Be . . . One's Best Self." In *To Be or Not To Be . . . Existential-Psychological Perspectives on the Self.* Sidney M. Jourard ed. University of Florida Social Sciences Monograph No. 34. Gainesville, Florida: University of Florida, 1967, pp. 37–49.

Landsman, Ted. "Positive Experience and the Beautiful Person." Presidential Address, the Southeastern Psychological Association, April 5, 1968.

Maslow, Abraham H. *Toward a Psychology of Being.* 2nd ed. Princeton, N.J.: D. Van Nostrand Co., Inc., 1968.

Maslow, Abraham H. "Introduction" to new edition of *Religion, Values, and Peak Experiences.* New York: Viking Press, Fall, 1970. (mimeographed copy from author)

Pierce, R.; Carkhuff, R. R.; and Berenson, B. G. "The Differential Effects of High and Low Functioning Counselors Upon Counselors in Training." *Journal of Clinical Psychology,* 23 (1967): 212–215.

Rogers, Carl and Stevens, Barry. *Person to Person: The Problem of Being Human.* Walnut Creek, California: Real People Press, 1967.

Truax, Charles B. and Carkhuff, Robert R. "The Old and the New Theory and Research in Counseling and Psychotherapy." *Personnel and Guidance Journal,* 42 (9), (1964): 860–866.

Whiteley, John M., Sprinthall, Norman A., Mosher, Ralph L. and Donaghy, Rolla T. "Selection and Evaluation of Counselor Effectiveness." *Journal of Counseling Psychology,* 14 (3), (1967): 226–234.

2
THE PSYCHOLOGICAL BASES FOR HELPING

At the present time, two major viewpoints dominate the helping professions—humanism and behaviorism. One or the other position constitutes the psychological bases for almost every program for the training of helpers currently in operation. It is with these approaches that we are concerned with in Part II *of this volume.*

In the first article, William Hitt presents the two positions as controversial, which they often are. Discussions of humanism (or, a specific humanistic approach such as phenomenology) and behaviorism often end in a heated argument and total rejection of one side by the other. Hitt presents an analysis of the major differences between what he has termed "Two Models of Man," and reaches some important conclusions about the role of these models in our society.

For some time, Donald Avila and William Purkey have advocated an integration of humanism and behaviorism. They believe that the most fruitful course to follow in the helping professions is one that attempts to discover what positive contributions each position can make toward realizing the goals of helping. In their paper, they illustrate how they believe self-concept theory and behaviorism can fit together to make a more appropriate model for humankind than can the two treated separately.

For many years, Arthur Combs has maintained that a humanistic or phenomenological frame of reference is the most appropriate one for the helping professions. In the third paper of this section, he states why he believes this to be true, presents the criteria necessary for an adequate phenomenological psychology, and discusses some specific aspects of his own brand of humanistic psychology.

Two Models of Man

WILLIAM D. HITT

A symposium sponsored by the Division of Philosophical Psychology of the American Psychological Association clearly pointed up the cleavage in contemporary theoretical and philosophical psychology. The symposium was held at Rice University to mark the inception of the Division of Philosophical Psychology as a new division of the APA. Participants included Sigmund Koch, R. B. MacLeod, B. F. Skinner, Carl R. Rogers, Norman Malcolm, and Michael Scriven. The presentations and associated discussions were organized in the book: *Behaviorism and Phenomenology: Contrasting Bases for Modern Psychology* (Edited by T. W. Wann, 1964).

THE ARGUMENT

As indicated in the title of the book, the main argument of the symposium dealt with phenomenology versus behaviorism. This argument also could be described as one between existential psychology and behavioristic psychology. The presentations dealt with two distinct models of man and the scientific methodology associated with each model. The discussions following each presentation may be described as aggressive, hostile, and rather emotional; they would suggest that there is little likelihood of a reconciliation between the two schools of thought represented at the symposium.

To illustrate the nature of the argument, some of the statements made by the participants are presented below.

From *American Psychologist,* 1969, 24, 651–658. Copyright 1969 by the American Psychological Association. Reprinted by permission of the author and publisher.

In Support of Behaviorism

Skinner (1964)
An adequate science of behavior must consider events taking place within the skin of the organism, not as physiological mediators of behavior, but as part of behavior itself. It can deal with these events without assuming that they have any special nature or must be known in any special way. . . . Public and private events have the same kinds of physical dimensions [p. 84].

Malcolm (1964)
Behaviorism is right in insisting that there must be some sort of conceptual tie between the language of mental phenomena and outward circumstances and behavior. If there were not, we could not understand other people, nor could we understand ourselves [p. 152].

Attacks on Behaviorism

Koch (1964)
Behaviorism has been given a hearing for fifty years. I think this generous. I shall urge that it is essentially a role-playing position which has outlived whatever usefulness its role might once have had [p. 6].

Rogers (1964)
It is quite unfortunate that we have permitted the world of psychological science to be narrowed to behavior observed, sounds emitted, marks scratched on paper, and the like [p. 118].

In Support of Phenomenology

MacLeod (1964)
I am . . . insisting that what, in the old, prescientific days, we used to call "consciousness" still can and should be studied. Whether or not this kind of study may be called a science depends on our definition of the term. To be a scientist, in my opinion, is to have boundless curiosity tempered by discipline [p. 71].

Rogers (1964)
The inner world of the individual appears to have more significant influence upon his behavior than does the external environmental stimulus [p. 125].

Attacks on Phenomenology

Malcolm (1964)
I believe that Wittgenstein has proved this line of thinking (introspectionism) to be disastrous. It leads to the conclusion that we do not and

cannot understand each other's psychological language, which is a form of solipsism[1] [p. 148].

Skinner (1964)

Mentalistic or psychic explanations of human behavior almost certainly originated in primitive animism [p. 79]. . . . I am a radical behaviorist simply in the sense that I find no place in the formulation for anything which is mental [p. 106].

This appears to be the heart of the argument:

The behaviorist views man as a passive organism governed by external stimuli. Man can be manipulated through proper control of these stimuli. Moreover, the laws that govern man are essentially the same as the laws that govern all natural phenomena of the world; hence, it is assumed that the scientific method used by the physical scientist is equally appropriate to the study of man.

The phenomenologist views man as the *source* of acts; he is free to choose in each situation. The essence of man is *inside* of man; he is controlled by his own consciousness. The most appropriate methodology for the study of man is phenomenology, which begins with the world of experience.

These two models of man have been proposed and discussed for many years by philosophers and psychologists alike. Versions of these models may be seen in the contrasting views of Locke and Leibnitz (see Allport, 1955), Marx and Kierkegaard, Wittgenstein and Sartre, and, currently, Skinner and Rogers. Were he living today, William James probably would characterize Locke, Marx, Wittgenstein, and Skinner as "tough-minded," while Leibnitz, Kierkegaard, Sartre, and Rogers would be viewed as "tender-minded." Traditionally, the argument has been one model versus the other. It essentially has been a black-and-white argument.

The purpose of this article is to analyze the argument between the behaviorist and the phenomenologist. This analysis is carried out by presenting and discussing two different models of man.

CONTRASTING VIEWS OF MAN

The two models of man are presented in terms of these contrasting views:

1. Man can be described meaningfully in terms of his behavior; or man can be described meaningfully in terms of his consciousness.
2. Man is predictable; or man is unpredictable.

1. Solipsism is defined as the theory that only the self exists, or can be proven to exist.

3. Man is an information transmitter; or man is an information generator.
4. Man lives in an objective world; or man lives in a subjective world.
5. Man is a rational being; or man is an arational being.
6. One man is like other men; or each man is unique.
7. Man can be described meaningfully in absolute terms; or man can be described meaningfully in relative terms.
8. Human characteristics can be investigated independently of one another; or man must be studied as a whole.
9. Man is a reality; or man is a potentiality.
10. Man is knowable in scientific terms; or man is more than we can ever know about him.

Each of these attributes is discussed below.

SUPPORT FOR BOTH MODELS

The evidence offered below in support of each of the two models of man is both empirical and analytical. Perhaps some of the evidence is intuitive, but it at least seems logical to the author of this article.

Man Can Be Described Meaningfully in Terms of His Behavior; or Man Can Be Described Meaningfully in Terms of His Consciousness

According to John B. Watson, the founder of American behaviorism, the behavior of man and animals was the only proper study for psychology. Watson strongly advocated that

> Psychology is to be the science, not of consciousness, but of behavior. . . . It is to cover both human and animal behavior, the simpler animal behavior being indeed more fundamental than the more complex behavior of man. . . . It is to rely wholly on objective data, introspection being discarded [Woodworth & Sheehan, 1964, p. 113].

Behaviorism has had an interesting, and indeed productive, development since the time of Watson's original manifesto. Tolman, Hull, and a number of other psychologists have been important figures in this development. Today, Skinner is the leading behaviorist in the field of psychology. Skinner (1957) deals with both overt and covert behavior; for example, he states that "thought is simply *behavior*—verbal or nonverbal, covert or overt [p. 449]."

As a counterargument to placing all emphasis on behavior, Karl

Jaspers, an existential psychologist and philosopher, points up the importance of consciousness or self-awareness. According to Jaspers (1963), consciousness has four formal characteristics: (*a*) the feeling of activity—an awareness of being active; (*b*) an awareness of unity; (*c*) awareness of identity; and (*d*) awareness of the self as distinct from an outer world and all that is not the self (p. 121). Jaspers (1957) stresses that "Man not only exists but knows that he exists [p. 4]."

It is apparent from this argument that psychologists over the years have been dealing with two different aspects of man—on the one hand, his actions, and on the other, his self-awareness. It seems reasonable that man could be described in terms of either his behavior *or* his consciousness or both. Indeed, behavior is more accessible to scientific treatment, but the systematic study of consciousness might well give the psychologist additional understanding of man.

Man Is Predictable; or Man Is Unpredictable

Understanding, prediction, and control are considered to be the three objectives of science. Prediction and control are sometimes viewed as evidence of the scientist's understanding of the phenomenon under study. The objective of prediction rests on the assumption of determinism, the doctrine that all events have sufficient causes. Psychological science has traditionally accepted the objective of predicting human behavior and the associated doctrine of determinism.

Indeed, there have been some notable successes in predicting human behavior. Recent predictions of the number of fatalities resulting from automobile accidents on a given weekend, for example, have been within 5–10% of the actual fatalities. College administrators can predict fairly accurately the number of dropouts between the freshman and sophomore years. Further, a psychometrician can readily predict with a high degree of accuracy the distribution of scores resulting from an achievement test administered to a large sample of high school students. As another example, the mean reaction time to an auditory stimulus can be predicted rather accurately for a large group of subjects. All of these examples lend support to the doctrine of determinism.

There also have been some notable failures in attempts to predict human behavior. For example, the therapist has had little success in predicting the effectiveness of a given form of therapy applied to a given patient. Similarly, the guidance counselor has had relatively little success in predicting the occupation to be chosen by individual high school students. Such failures in predicting human behavior sometimes prompt one to question the basic assumption of determinism.

To illustrate the complexity associated with predicting the behavior of man—as contrasted with that of other complex systems—consider the following illustration. Suppose that a research psychologist has made a detailed study of a given human subject. He now tells the subject that he predicts that he will choose Alternative A rather than Alternative B under such and such conditions at some future point in time. Now, with this limited amount of information, what do you predict the subject will do?

The evidence suggests that there is support for both sides of this issue. It is difficult to argue with the deterministic doctrine that there are sufficient causes for human actions. Yet these causes may be unknown to either the observer or the subject himself. Thus, we must conclude that man is both predictable and unpredictable.

Man Is an Information Transmitter; or Man Is an Information Generator

The information theorists and cyberneticists have formulated a model of man as an information transmitter. W. Ross Ashby (1961), the cyberneticist, has proposed a basic postulate that says that man is just as intelligent as the amount of information fed into him.

> Intelligence, whether of man or machine, is absolutely bounded. And what we can build into our machine is similarly bounded. The amount of intelligence we can get into a machine is absolutely bounded by the quantity of information that is put into it. We can get out of a machine as much intelligence as we like, if and only if we insure that at least the corresponding quantity of information gets into it [p. 280].

Ashby believes that we could be much more scientific in our study of man if we would accept this basic postulate and give up the idea that man, in some mysterious manner, generates or creates new information over and above that which is fed into him.

The information-transmitting model of man is indeed very compelling. It promises considerable rigor and precision; it is compatible with both empiricism and stimulus-response theory; and it allows the behavioral scientist to build on past accomplishments in the fields of cybernetics, systems science, and mechanics.

But, alas, man does not want to be hemmed in by the information-transmitting model. Man asks questions that were never before asked; he identifies problems that were never before mentioned; he generates new ideas and theories; he formulates new courses of action; and he even formulates new models of man. Now to say that all of these human activities are merely a regrouping or recombining of existing elements is an oversimplification, a trivialization of human activity. Further, the assumption that all information has actually been in existence but hidden since the days of prehistoric man is not intuitively satisfying.

Considering the evidence in support of man both as an information transmitter and as an information generator, would it be reasonable to view man as both a *dependent* variable and an *independent* variable?

Man Lives in an Objective World; or Man Lives in a Subjective World

Man lives in an objective world. This is the world of facts and data. This is a reliable world; we agree that this or that event actually occurred. This is a tangible world; we agree that this or that object is actually present. This is the general world that is common to all.

But man also lives in a subjective world. This is the individual's private world. The individual's feelings, emotions, and perceptions are very personal; he attempts to describe them in words but feels that he can never do complete justice to them.

In making this comparison between the objective world and subjective world, it is important to distinguish between two types of knowledge. We can know *about* something, or we can personally *experience* something. These two forms of knowledge are not the same.

We conclude that man is both object and subject. He is visible and tangible to others, yet he is that which thinks, feels, and perceives. The world looks at man, and he looks out at the world.

Are both the objective world and the subjective world available to the methods of science? Empiricism in general and the experimental method in particular can be applied to the objective world; phenomenology can be applied to the subjective world. In his efforts to understand man, perhaps the psychologist should attempt to understand both worlds.

Man Is a Rational Being; or Man Is an Arational Being

Man is sometimes referred to as a rational animal. He is intelligent; he exercises reason; he uses logic; and he argues from a scientific standpoint. Indeed, man is considered by man to be the *only* rational animal.

An individual's action or behavior, of course, is sometimes considered irrational. This is the opposite of rational. The irrational person defies the laws of reason; he contradicts that which is considered rational by some particular community of people.

But man also is arational. This characteristic transcends the rational-irrational continuum; it essentially constitutes another dimension of man's life. As an example of man being arational in his life, he makes a total commitment for a way of life. This commitment may be for a given faith, a religion, a philosophy, a vocation, or something else. It may be that any analysis of this decision would reveal that it was neither rational nor irrational—it merely was.

Man's actions are guided by both empirical knowledge and value judgment. Empirical knowledge belongs to the rational world, whereas value judgment often belongs to the arational world. According to Jaspers (1967): "An empirical science cannot teach anybody what he ought to do, but only what he can do to reach his ends by statable means [p. 60]."

To achieve greater understanding of man, it would seem essential that the psychologist investigate man's arational world as well as his rational world.

One Man Is Like Other Men; or Each Man Is Unique

A major goal of science is to develop general laws to describe, explain, and predict phenomena of the world. These laws are frequently based upon the study of one sample of objects or events and are then expected to be valid for a different sample of objects or events. It then follows that a major goal of psychology is to formulate general laws of man. In fact, without the possibility of developing general laws of human behavior, can psychology even be considered a science?

There is a considerable amount of evidence to support the possibility of developing general laws of human behavior. For example, the results of the reaction-time experiments have held up very well over the decades. Moreover, the many conditioning experiments conducted over the past several decades—either classical or operant—certainly suggest that man is governed by general laws applicable to all. Further, the cultural anthropologist and social psychologist have clearly pointed up the similarity of people in a given culture, suggesting that they might be taken from the same mold.

On the other hand, there is considerable evidence to support the concept of individual uniqueness. For example, there are thousands of possible gene combinations and thousands of different environmental determinants, all of which bring about millions of different personalities. Further, it is apparent that no two people ever live in exactly the same environment. As someone once said about two brothers living in the same house, with the same parents, and with the same diet: "Only one of the boys has an older brother." Then, too, we might reflect on a statement made by William James (1925): "An unlearned carpenter of my acquaintance once said in my hearing: 'There is very little difference between one man and another; but what little there is, *is very important*' [pp. 242–243]."

Our conclusion from this brief analysis is that the evidence appears to support both models of man: (*a*) that he is governed by general laws that apply to all of mankind, and (*b*) that each individual is unique in a nontrivial way.

Man Can Be Described Meaningfully in Absolute Terms; or Man Can Be Described Meaningfully in Relative Terms

If we believe that man can be described in absolute terms, we view such descriptions as being free from restriction or limitation. They are independent of arbitrary standards. Contrariwise, if we believe that man can be described in relative terms, we see him as existing or having his specific nature only by relation to something else. His actions are not absolute or independent.

If the concept of absoluteness is supported, we must accept the idea of general laws for all of mankind, and we also must accept the related idea that man is governed by irrefutable natural laws. On the other hand, if the concept of relativism is supported, we probably can have no general laws of man; we must realize that everything is contingent upon something else; and we can be certain of nothing.

It would appear that there is evidence to support the concept of absoluteness in psychology. The basic psychophysical laws, for example, might be characterized as irrefutable natural laws. Similarly, the basic laws of conditioning seem to be free from restriction or limitation. This evidence might lead us to conclude that man can be described in absolute terms.

But before we can become smug with this false sense of security, the relativist poses some challenging questions. For example: What is considered intelligent behavior? What is normal behavior? What is an aggressive personality? What is an overachiever? At best, it would seem that we could answer such questions only in relative terms. The answers would be contingent on some set of arbitrary standards.

What can we conclude? Perhaps man can be described meaningfully in either absolute terms or relative terms, depending on what aspect of man is being described.

Human Characteristics Can Be Investigated Independently of One Another; or Must Be Studied as a Whole

The question here is: Can man be understood by analyzing each attribute independently of the rest, or must man be studied as a whole in order to be understood? Another way of phrasing the question is: Can we take an additive approach to the study of man, or is a holistic or Gestalt approach required?

There is some evidence to support an additive approach to the study of man. Consider the following areas of research: psychophysics, physiological psychology, motor skills, classical and operant conditioning, and sensation. All of these areas have produced useful results from experimentation involving the manipulation of a single independent variable and measuring the concomitant effects on a single dependent variable. Useful results have been produced by investigating a single characteristic independently of other characteristics.

Other areas of research, however, point up the value of a holistic point of view. Research in the area of perception, for example, has demonstrated the effect of individual motivation on perception. Similarly, studies of human learning have shown the great importance of motivation and intelligence on learning behavior. Further, as one more example, research in the area of psychotherapy has revealed that the relation between the personality of the therapist and that of the patient has a significant influence on the effectiveness of the therapy. All of these examples illustrate the importance of the interactions and interdependencies of the many variables operating in any given situation.

Support for a holistic view of man is seen in the works of Polanyi and Tielhard de Chardin, to mention only two. Polanyi (1963) gives this example: "Take a watch to pieces and examine, however carefully, its separate parts in turn, and you will never come across the principles by which a watch keeps time [p. 47]." Tielhard de Chardin (1961) says:

> In its construction, it is true, every organism is always and inevitably reducible into its component parts. But it by no means follows, that the sum of the parts is the same as the whole, or that, in the whole, some specifically new value may not emerge [p. 110].

What can be concluded from this discussion? First, it would seem that a detailed analysis of man is essential for a systematic understanding. Yet, synthesis also is required in order to understand the many interactions and interdependencies. We can conclude that the most effective strategy for the behavioral scientist might be that used by the systems analyst—a working back and forth between analysis and synthesis.

Man Is a Reality; or Man Is a Potentiality

Is man a reality? If so, he exists as fact; he is actual; he has objective existence. Or is man a potentiality? If so, he represents possibility rather than actuality; he is capable of being or becoming. The question here is: Can we study man as an actually existing entity—as we would study any other complex system—or must we view man as a completely dynamic entity, one that is constantly emerging or becoming?

There is support for the view of man as an actuality. The numerous results from the many years of research in the area of experimental psychology, for example, suggest that man is definable and measurable, and is capable of being investigated as an actually existing complex system. Further, the many current studies in the area of cybernetics, which point up similarities between man and machine, lend credence to the concept of man as an existing system.

There also is evidence to support the view of man as a potentiality. For example, case studies have revealed that long-term criminals have experienced religious conversions and then completely changed their way of life. Further, complete personality transformations have resulted from psychoanalysis and electroshock therapy. Indeed, man is changeable, and any given individual can become something quite different from what he was in the past.

Maslow (1961) has stressed the importance of human potentiality:

> I think it fair to say that no theory of psychology will ever be complete that does not centrally incorporate the concept that man has his future within him, dynamically active at this present moment [p. 59].

What can we conclude? Only that man is both a reality and a potentiality. He represents objective existence, yet he can move toward any one of many different future states that are essentially unpredictable.

Man Is Knowable in Scientific Terms; or Man Is More Than We Can Ever Know About Him

This final issue is basic to the entire study of man, and is closely tied to all the previous issues discussed. Is man knowable in scientific terms, or is man more than we can ever know about him?

There are many centuries of evidence to support the idea that man is scientifically knowable. Aristotle, for example, applied the same logic to his study of man as he did to other phenomena in the world. Further, volumes of data resulting from psychological experiments since the time of Wundt's founding of the first experimental psychology laboratory in 1879 indicate that man is scientifically knowable. Then, too, the many laboratory experiments and field studies recently conducted by the different disciplines included in the behavioral and social sciences certainly suggest that man is scientifically knowable.

Yet, there also is support for the idea that man is more than we can ever know about him. Man has continued to transcend himself over the past million or so years, as demonstrated by the theory of evolution.

Further, on logical grounds, it can be demonstrated that man becomes something different every time he gains new knowledge about himself, which would suggest that man is truly an "open system."

It is apparent that we know very little about man. William James (1956) says: "Our science is a drop, our ignorance a sea [p. 54]." Erich Fromm (1956) believes that "Even if we knew a thousand times more of ourselves, we would never reach bottom [p. 31]."

What can we conclude? We must conclude that man is scientifically knowable—at least to a point. Yet there is no evidence to support the idea that man is—or ever will be—*completely* knowable.

Conclusions

This paper has presented two models of man:

The behavioristic model. Man can be described meaningfully in terms of his behavior; he is predictable; he is an information transmitter; he lives in an objective world; he is rational; he has traits in common with other men; he may be described in absolute terms; his characteristics can be studied independently of one another; he is a reality; and he is knowable in scientific terms.

The phenomenological model. Man can be described meaningfully in terms of his consciousness; he is unpredictable; he is an information generator; he lives in a subjective world; he is arational; he is unique alongside millions of other unique personalities; he can be described in relative terms; he must be studied in a holistic manner; he is a potentiality; and he is more than we can ever know about him.

This analysis of behaviorism and phenomenology leads to these conclusions:

1. The acceptance of either the behavioristic model or a phenomenological model has important implications in the everyday world. The choice of one versus the other could greatly influence human activities (either behavior or awareness) in such areas as education, psychiatry, theology, behavioral science, law, politics, marketing, advertising, and even parenthood. Thus, this ongoing debate is not just an academic exercise.
2. There appears to be truth in both views of man. The evidence that has been presented lends credence to both the behavioristic model and the phenomenological model. Indeed, it would be premature for psychology to accept either model as the final model.
3. A given behavioral scientist may find that both models are useful, depending upon the problem under study. The phenomenological

model, for example, might be quite appropriate for the investigation of the creative process in scientists. On the other hand, the behavioristic model might be very useful in the study of environmental factors that motivate a given population of subjects to behave in a certain manner.

4. Finally, we must conclude that the behaviorist and the phenomenologist should listen to each other. Both, as scientists, should be willing to listen to opposing points of view. Each should endeavor to understand what the other is trying to say. It would appear that a dialogue is in order.

References

Allport, G. W. *Becoming: Basic Considerations for a Psychology of Personality.* New Haven: Yale University Press, 1955.

Ashby, W. R. "What Is An Intelligent Machine?" *Proceedings of the Western Joint Computer Conference,* 19 (1961) : 275–280.

de Chardin, P. T. *The Phenomenon of Man.* New York: Harper & Row, 1961 (Harper Torchback Edition) .

Fromm, E. *The Art of Loving.* New York: Harper & Row, 1956.

James, W. *The Will to Believe and Other Essays on Popular Philosophy.* New York: Dover, 1956 (Orig. publ. 1896) .

James, W. "The Individual and Society." In *The Philosophy of William James.* New York: Modern Library, 1925 (Orig. publ. 1897) .

Jaspers, K. *Man in the Modern Age.* New York: Doubleday, 1957 (Orig. publ. in Germany, 1931) .

———. *General Psychopathology.* Manchester, England: Manchester University Press, 1963. (Publ. in U.S.A. by University of Chicago Press.)

———. *Philosophy Is for Everyman.* New York: Harcourt, Brace & World, 1967.

Koch, S. "Psychology and Emerging Conceptions of Knowledge as Unitary." In T. W. Wann, ed., *Behaviorism and Phenomenology: Contrasting Bases for Modern Psychology.* Chicago: University of Chicago Press, 1964.

MacLeod, R. B. "Phenomenology: A Challenge to Experimental Psychology." In T. W. Wann, ed., *Behaviorism and Phenomenology: Contrasting Bases for Modern Psychology.* Chicago: University of Chicago Press, 1964.

Malcolm, N. "Behaviorism As a Philosophy of Psychology." In T. W. Wann, ed., *Behaviorism and Phenomenology: Contrasting Bases for Modern Psychology.* Chicago: University of Chicago Press, 1964.

Maslow, A. H. "Existential Psychology—What's In It For Us?" In R. May, ed., *Existential Psychology.* New York: Random House, 1961.

Polanyi, M. *The Study of Man.* Chicago: University of Chicago Press, 1963 (First Phoenix Edition) .

Rogers, C. R. Toward a Science of the Person. In T. W. Wann, ed., *Behaviorism and Phenomenology: Contrasting Bases for Modern Psychology.* Chicago: University of Chicago Press, 1964.

Skinner, B. F. *Verbal Behavior.* New York: Appleton-Century-Crofts, 1957.

Skinner, B. F. "Behaviorism at Fifty." In T. W. Wann, ed., *Behaviorism and Phe-*

nomenology: Contrasting Bases for Modern Psychology. Chicago: University of Chicago Press, 1964.

Wann, T. W., ed. *Behaviorism and Phenomenology: Contrasting Bases for Modern Psychology.* Chicago: University of Chicago Press, 1964.

Woodworth, R. S., and Sheehan, M. R. *Contemporary Schools of Psychology.* New York: Ronald Press, 1964.

Self-Theory and Behaviorism: A Rapprochement

DONALD AVILA AND
WILLIAM PURKEY

From the point of view of these authors a sad state of affairs presently exists in psychology and education. Central to this problem is the notion that to accept either behaviorism or self-theory as one's major psychological orientation automatically excludes acceptance of the other. That this assumption is all too prevalent is evidenced by Hitt's description of a recent symposium on behaviorism *vs.* phenomenology, which included some of the most prominent psychologists in the nation:

> The presentations dealt with two distinct models of man and the scientific methodology associated with each Model. The discussions following each presentation may be described as aggressive, hostile, and rather emotional; they would suggest that there is little likelihood of a reconcilliation between the two schools of thought represented at the symposium . . . [1969, p. 651].

We contend that this either-or-state of affairs is destructive, self-deluding and, if we read the temper of the younger psychologists and educators correctly, a position held only by those who look to the past rather than to the future.

Both self-theory and behaviorism offer important contributions to psychology and education. To make them mutually exclusive automatically blinds us to the significant contributions that each can make to our understanding of man. To be half blind is bad enough, but when an antagonistic situation develops that is characterized by aggression, hostility and anger, our vision is distorted even more.

We submit that to view self-theory and behaviorism as mutually exclusive and antagonistic is not only fruitless, but also misleading. Modern

From *Psychology in the Schools,* 1972, 9 (2), 124–126. Reprinted by permission of the authors and publisher.

behaviorists recognize central processes as essential to an understanding of behavior, while self-theorists are fully aware of the documented power of reinforcement to modify human behavior. It is becoming increasingly evident that both approaches are parts of a single continuum in the incredibly complex processes of understanding people and influencing their behavior. The purpose of this paper is to explain how we have been able to include both behaviorism and self-theory in our thinking about the dynamics of human activity.

First, we see self-theory as a valuable working hypothesis about the nature of man—in fact, self-theory could serve as a framework for a basic philosophy of life. Thanks to the writing and research of self-theorists, we have valuable insights about the nature of individuals, their perceptions, their needs, and their goals. Further, emerging evidence (Murphy & Spohn, 1968; Purkey, 1970) supports the commonsense notion that behavior is determined by the individual's subjective perceptions of the situation rather than by the situation itself. Thus, we have the indispensable construct of the phenomenological world.

Central to the phenomenological world is one's self-awareness. All of the beliefs, opinions, and attitudes that an individual holds about himself have come to be called self-concept. This concept of self and its related facets of self-esteem, self-enhancement, self-consistency, and self-actualization provide rich hypotheses for researchers and valuable guides for those in the helping professions (Combs, Avila, & Purkey, 1971).

People who work in helping relationships have pointed out the importance of a warm, accepting environment in which a person is treated with respect, dignity, warmth, and care. Furthermore, they have shown that the individual who is being helped needs to accept mutual responsibility for the helping relationship. Finally, the research of self-theorists has demonstrated that the way a professional helper feels about himself and his client or student has as much to do with the outcome of the interaction as the specific technique used, if not more. (Combs, Soper, Gooding, Benton, Dickman, & Usher, 1969).

In sum, self-theory provides heuristic guidelines by which to fulfill our professional responsibilities, be they counseling, therapy, teaching, or research. On the other hand, self-theory does seem to have difficulty when it comes to the question of "how." How does one change a self-concept, a perception, or a particular bit of behavior? How can one set up conditions and provide experiences for one's clients and students that will prove to be self-enhancing? This is the point at which we believe behaviorism enters the scene.

Behaviorism, after all, is not a theory, although a person certainly can develop a theoretical position from the approach. Behaviorism is a process and a method (essentially the scientific method) from which psychologists and educators have developed many useful principles and techniques. These principles and techniques can be used to accomplish the purpose of self-theory: *to convince each individual that he is valuable, responsible, and capable of influencing his own destiny.*

The behaviorist has little trouble with the "how" aspects of a given problem. For example, what better way is there to help a person to have positive experiences than to set up situations full of positive contingencies of reinforcement, *i.e.,* situations in which the individual has an excellent chance of success. If a person who has been a failure begins to experience success, he also will begin to change his feelings about himself and others and his perception of the world. This is exactly what the self-theorists want to accomplish. The point has been clarified by Andrews and Karlin (1971), who demonstrated that behavioristic processes can be used to build autonomy in the individual, facilitate his freedom, and strengthen his self-image. Rice (1970) also has demonstrated that the goals of self-theory can be realized by use of behavior modification.

Thus it seems to these authors that enhancement and reinforcement, changing self-concepts and behavior modification are related closely and may sometimes be the same thing. Furthermore, the authors believe that the future of psychology lies in a unification of these two positions, not in the wasted energy of continued conflict.

References

Andrews, L. M., and Karlin, M. *Requiem for Democracy?* New York: Holt, Rinehart, & Winston, 1971.

Combs, A. W.; Avila, D. L.; and Purkey, W. W. *Helping Relationships: Basic Concepts for the Helping Professions.* Boston, Mass.: Allyn & Bacon, 1971.

Combs, A. W.; Soper, D. W.; Gooding, C. T.; Benton, J. A., Jr.; Dickman, J. F.; and Usher, R. H. *Florida Studies in the Helping Professions.* University of Florida Social Science Monograph No. 37. Gainesville: University of Florida Press, 1969.

Hitt, W. D. "Two Models of Man." *American Psychologist,* 24, (1969) : 651–658.

Murphy, G., and Spohn, H. E. *Encounter with Reality.* Boston: Houghton Mifflin, 1968.

Purkey, W. W. *Self Concept and School Achievement.* Englewood Cliffs, N.J.: Prentice-Hall, 1970.

Rice, D. R. "Educo-Therapy: A New Approach to Delinquent Behavior." *Journal of Learning Disabilities,* 3 (1970) : 16–23.

Why the Humanistic Movement Needs a Perceptual Psychology

ARTHUR W. COMBS

Years ago, while working as a lobbyist for the New York State psychologists, I came to have a great respect for what politicians call, "the ground swells of human opinion." Successful politicians are always attuned to these implicit needs of people. They know that to oppose them is folly. The real masters among the politicians are those with the peculiar genius for combining deep sensitivity to the implicit yearnings of people with effective techniques for giving expression and direction to them. For me, the humanist movement is one of these great ground swells, perhaps the most important in our time. It represents a basic shift in human thought, a deep welling up of a new commitment to human dignity and integrity. One sees it worldwide in the decline of colonialism, the rise of the have-not nations, freedom for women, UNESCO, the United Nations. Here at home it seems to me to be implicit in the rise of labor, the elimination of child labor, the concern for education, Social Security, Civil Rights, Medicare, and, most recently, the War on Poverty.

All of us are tremendously impressed with the breakthroughs of the physical sciences, those instances when a new idea or new technique makes possible rapid strides forward in control of the physical world. But breakthroughs occur in the social sciences as well, and I am convinced the humanist movement is one of these. I am further certain that when this movement reaches its full potential, its implications for human welfare will make those of the physical sciences pale by comparison.

I believe the humanist movement in psychology is but a single expression in that discipline of the same deep stirrings in human thought going

From the *Journal of the Association for the Study of Perception,* 1974, 9, 1–13. Reprinted by permission of the author and publisher.

on everywhere else. Each humanist is attempting to bring some aspect of the basic concept into clearer figure, to give it organization and direction, to discover with greater clarity and sharpness its meaning for the science of behavior. We have called ourselves by different names; Personalists, Transactionalists, Phenomenologists, Self psychologists, Existentialists, and Perceptualists, to name but a few. Like the blind man approaching the elephant, we have acquired a multitude of part answers. There is need now for a unifying system which will provide: (A) A frame of reference capable of encompassing and giving meaning to these diverse contributions, and (B) A theoretical structure capable of pointing the way to new directions for research and innovation. The theme of this paper is to suggest that perceptual psychology can provide a start toward that end.

CRITERIA FOR PERCEPTUAL PSYCHOLOGY

Let us begin by establishing some criteria in terms of which an encompassing theory for humanism must be judged. I suggest the following:

Criterion I. *An adequate frame of reference for humanism must be capable of dealing especially with the internal life of persons.* The very heart of humanism is its concern with those qualities of man's experience which make him most human—his values, beliefs, understandings, feelings, motives, goals and purposes. It is, in fact, the failure of traditional psychology to deal with these matters satisfactorily that has led many psychologists to embrace the humanistic persuasion.

Criterion II. *A humanistic psychology must be systematic.* It must begin with simple assumptions and, thereafter, provide understanding and prediction of behavior through internally consistent variations, constructs and development from these fundamental axioms.

Criterion III. *It must be congruent with existing systems of psychology.* Presumably if a thing is true it is true forever. A humanistic view of psychology must not, therefore, reject what is sound from other views. Rather, it must provide a framework in which they can be better comprehended and extended.

Criterion IV. *It must be testable.* It must possess a reasonable research methodology capable of disciplined application and must meet the customary scientific demands for rigor and reliability.

Criterion V. *It must be capable of including within its structure as many as possible of the concepts proposed by leadng humanist thinkers.* In this process some reinterpretation is acceptable but inclusion must occur without destructive violence to basic considerations.

The above criteria have to do with purely theoretical questions. An academic theory for humanism, however, is not enough. The humanist movement in psychology is to a very large extent a consequence of the failure of traditional approaches to provide sufficient answers for problems of professional practice. Most humanists are deeply involved in some kind of helping practice; teaching, therapy, social action, etc. Even those who do not make a living in these ways are deeply concerned for the implications of humanist concepts for human welfare and personal living. A humanist theory must also provide assistance for thinking about these kinds of problems. I, therefore, suggest three additional practical criteria which a humanist theory must meet if it is to provide a satisfactory framework for constructive action.

Criterion VI. *It must provide effective guides to action for the understanding and prediction of individual behavior.* Its principles should have maximum applicability to the solution of practical problems of human growth and welfare.

Criterion VII. *It must be capable of general use outside the laboratory.* It must contribute effectively to solutions to the great human problems of our time, especially in education, social interaction and treatment.

Criterion VIII. *It must be dynamic and immediate in application rather than descriptive and historic.* The primary problem of the practitioner is the production of change. To do this effectively requires a theory of behavior emphasizing immediate rather than historical causation.

HOW DOES PERCEPTUAL PSYCHOLOGY MEET THESE CRITERIA?

With reference to Criterion I, a humanistic psychology must be capable of dealing with the things that make man human, his feelings, purposes, beliefs, and understandings about himself and his world. Traditional approaches to psychology have, almost exclusively, dealt with man as object. They have sought the meaning of behavior from an external frame of reference, from the point of view of the outside observer. This places psychological science under a terrific handicap for it eliminates from consideration large sources of data which might otherwise contribute richly to understanding behavior. With observation restricted only to the objectively observable conditions, traditional psychology has been unable to deal satisfactorily with such internal matters as motives, aspirations, feelings, purposes, and self awareness.

There are two great frames of reference we may employ to observe behavior. We can look at it *externally,* through the eyes of an outside observer or, we may look at it *internally,* through the experience of the behaver himself. So long as one restricts himself to the external view, many matters of concern to the humanist can never be adequately dealt with. Humanism requires an internal frame of reference capable of dealing more directly and effectively with man's inner life. In my view this calls for a perceptual psychology. It seems to me a great waste to restrict the study of behavior to a single frame of reference. Surely, we need to use every device possible to push forward the frontiers of our knowledge. I believe psychologists must understand and use *both* the external and internal frames of reference. As a matter of fact this is what all psychologists do anyhow, whether they recognize it or not. Even the most objective psychologist will tell you his rats run their mazes "because they are hungry," while every psychologist concerned with people's meanings must make his inferences from external observation. The choice is not to throw one's lot with the internal or external camp but to use these ways of looking for those areas of study in which each is appropriate.

Humanism, especially, demands a phenomenological psychology, a psychology of personal meaning. And that is precisely what perceptual psychology offers, for perceptions are the personal meanings of events for the behaver, the raw data with which the humanist must operate. They are the individual's experience of events, and all the matters of special interest to the humanist, feelings, values, beliefs, purposes, even the self, can be expressed in perceptual terms. There may be some who wish to quarrel with my use of the term *perception* as synonymous with personal meaning. It will be difficult, however, to reject the thesis that humanism demands a psychology whose data is meaning by whatever term we wish to describe it.

I think the movement of humanism to a perceptual psychology is inevitable. If it is not the "Third Force" which Maslow spoke of in tracing humanist history, it is surely very like it. Objective, S-R Psychology was the first of the great movements in American psychology. This is an external view of human behavior seeking its answers in the direct observations of outside observers. The second great movement, brought about by Freud and his contemporaries, started the drift to humanism. It began to be concerned with the phenomenological problem, what was going on inside the behaver. Someone has suggested that "Freud was the first psychologist to listen to his patients!" The practice of psychoanalysis, of necessity, was concerned with the internal life of patients and consequently students of this point of view persisted in introducing the internal life of the subject into psychological discussions. These intrusions of phenomenology into traditional psychology were at first resisted. But gradually, many such concepts, however grudgingly, came to be accepted as a needed point of view, albeit for the *"non-scientific"* aspects of the profession. Looking back on it now it appears that psychoanalysis was really a bridge from an external view of behavior to the internal one now demanded by modern humanism. What is needed now is a sharper, clearer expression of the phenomenological position and that means, for me, a systematic, perceptual psychology.

I shall never forget the occasion of my own adoption of the internal frame of reference. It remains the most exciting intellectual experience of my life. When I completed my doctor's degree at Ohio State I was full to overflowing with the orthodox, objective, behavioristically oriented traditions then characteristic of that university. I was also unhappy, because much of what I had learned did not provide me with the answers I needed for the human problems in which I was enagaged in teaching, and the practice of clinical psychology. The psychology with which I was then equipped simply could not provide me with the answers I needed for my daily work. Then, on a train in 1947 one night, I took from my briefcase a reprint which had been given me by Donald Snygg entitled, "The Need for a Phenomenological System in Psychology," published in 1941. What an experience! As I read the article, answers to dozens of questions I had been wrestling with started to fall into place. In great excitement I sat there for several hours examining one after another the traditional problems of psychological thought translating each one from an external to an internal frame of reference. I was astounded to find how systematically they dove-tailed into a consistent gestalt. So many problems I had been struggling with fell neatly and systematically into place while a thousand new problems, released by my shift in frame of reference, began to arise in their place. In those few hours I experienced a tremendous "peak experience," a kind of intellectual conversion. As soon as I got off the train, I called Dr. Snygg and made an appointment for the following day. Out of that conference and the mutual stimulation of the next two years came the outline for the first edition of *Individual Behavior** setting forth our conception of a perceptual psychology. Since then I have continued to refine and expand the position but have so far not found it necessary to greatly alter its basic outline. It can and does provide a comprehensive, systematic structure for dealing with the problems of humanism for me.

If this "testimonial" to my personal experience with perceptual psy-

* Now in its third edition under a new title: Combs, A. W., Richard, A. C. & Richards, F., *Perceptual Psychology: A Humanistic Approach to the Study of Persons,* Harper & Row, New York, 1975.

chology offends, I am sorry, but I am human as well as humanist and I think it is good for young members of the profession to know that science is not always dry and dusty. It has its moments of high drama and personal fulfillment as well.

Regarding Criterion II, an effective humanistic psychology must begin with simple assumptions and thereafter develop its position through internally consistent constructs and variations of these fundamental axioms. Perceptual psychology meets this criterion.

It begins with two assumptions:

First: All behavior is lawful. This is a necessary assumption of any science. Without it, there could be no science.

Second: All behavior, without exception, is completely determined by and pertinent to, the perceptual field of the behaving organism. That is to say, how a person behaves at any moment will be a direct consequence of the peculiar field of awareness existing for him at that instant. This field of awareness is characteristic of life itself and exists, so far as we can observe, in every living thing from the lowly amoeba (which turns toward food and away from danger) up through the scale of animal life to man with his immensely expanded apparatus for awareness. Whatever the behavior, it is the direct consequence of this field of meaning, called the phenomenal or perceptual field.

The perceptual field is fluid in the sense that it is open to change as a consequence of experience and the operation of need. It also has stability as it becomes organized around its most central aspects, especially perceptions of "self" and perceptions of the external world called "anchorages" or "expectancies." Change in the field occurs by a process of differentiation into figure and ground and perceptions may exist at any level of differentiation from ground to clear figure.

Behavior at any moment is a product of the total field of perceptions, existing at that moment, some of which may be in very clear figure, and others, which may be so obscure the behaver could not report them to an outsider if he was asked to do so. This conception of the perceptual field including all levels of awareness has often been misunderstood by critics of perceptual psychology who have assumed the term, "perception," refers only to those aspects of experience which can be reported by the subject. This is an error. Perception refers to the phenomenal experience of the individual whether reportable by him or not. Perceptual psychologists, however, avoid the use of the terms "conscious" and "unconscious" because these seem to imply a kind of dichotomy or "place where." They prefer to speak of "levels of awareness" which allows for the existence of perceptions at any degree of differentiation from clear, reportable figure to vague and indistinct ground. Perception, as we have used it, is synonymous with meaning and meanings may exist at any level of awareness in the phenomenal field.

Beginning from the assumption of a perceptual field it is thereafter possible step by step to build a systematic explanation of behavior which is both internally consistent and capable of application to most of the phenomena about which psychologists are interested. The basic problems for investigation center on perception and the dynamics of its development and operation in the behaver's phenomenal field. To this point at least seven influences upon perception can be isolated for special study. They are:

1. *The physical organism.* This is the vehicle in which perceiving occurs; Kelley calls it, "the meat-house in which we live." The physical organism both affects the individual's perceptions and, in turn, is affected by the individual's perceptions.
2. *Time.* The perceptions possible to an individual are in part a function of the time of exposure.
3. *Opportunity.* Since perceptions are differentiated, in part, as a consequence of the individual's experience, the opportunities he has been exposed to will, of course, have a vital effect on the nature of the perceptions he possesses.

These three variables of perception (the organism, time and opportunity) have long been studied in traditional approaches to psychology. They include the hereditary, physiological and environmental forces affecting the individual's behavior throughout his life time. To these three, perceptual psychology would add at least four more which have been given much less attention in orthodox frames of references.

4. *Need.* The perceptual view of behavior postulates a single need, namely, the need for adequacy or the maintenance and enhancement of self. This basic need can be traced through the phylogenetic scale beginning with the lowest forms of animal life, where it appears as mere "irritability," to its expression in a human being's search for self actualization or self fulfillment. It may find expression through many kinds of goals, some of which have often been described by other psychologists as "needs." The organism's search for fulfillment of the basic need for maintenance and enhancement of self provides the motive power for every behavior and exerts a selective effect upon all his perceptions.
5. *The self concept.* From a phenomenological orientation, the self concept is understood as an organization or gestalt of perceptions about the self. It includes all those aspects of an individual's experience which seem to him to be "I" or "me." Once established, the self concept has tremendous effects upon perception and so upon behavior. It is apparent that we have hardly scratched the surface of understanding the full importance of the self concept, as it is certainly one of the most currently popular areas for research. Unfortunately, there is also a great

deal of confusion about the concept. It has frequently been treated as synonymous with the self report, a quite different term. The self concept is an organization of perceptions relating to the self. The self report, on the other hand, is what an individual is willing, able, or can be tricked into saying about himself. To treat these two terms as though they were identical is a great pity for it creates all manner of confusion in the literature.

6. *Goals and values.* These organizations of perception are learned as a consequence of experience and in turn, have extensive selective effects upon further perception.
7. *The organization of the field.* The existing organization of the perceptual field at any moment has an effect upon what further perceptions may occur within the field. We have only begun to understand the significance of the variable. One of its effects can be seen, for example, in the tunnel vision produced under the experience of threat or high anticipation.

In time we may discover still other variables affecting the nature and development of meaning. Meantime, it is already apparent that many of the problems of traditional psychology can be dealt with quite adequately in this frame of reference. Many others, which orthodox positions have been notably inadequate to handle, readily lend themselves to solution in a perceptual orientation. This is especially true in theory for problems of motivation, values, the self, and holistic aspects of learning or, in more practical areas for problems of adjustment, treatment, human capacities and fulfillment. There is, of course, much yet to be done, but the outlines are apparent and a good start has been made toward the development of a systematic, internally consistent perceptual psychology. It is tailormade for humanist problems, and capable of pointing the way to fruitful further exploration.

Our third criterion for the acceptability of a perceptual system requires that it complement rather than deny positions which have gone before and stood the test of empirical investigation. It is a very human trait to think in dichotomous terms, to assume the establishment of a new position demands the abandonment of those which have gone before. Such an attitude is most unfortunate and badly mangles the possibilities of scientific progression. Perceptual psychology does not deny its antecedents, it complements them. It is not designed to replace traditional psychology, but to deal with problems more orthodox approaches have not yet been able to handle adequately. Human behavior can be looked at externally or internally. The observations made in each instance will also be true in its own frame of reference. The question is not, which frame of reference is right? The proper question is, which frame of reference is most appropriate to supply the answers needed for the problems posed?

While it is possible for some psychologists concerned primarily with research or theoretical matters to be almost exclusively involved in one frame of reference or another, the applied psychologist who is worthy of his title, must, almost certainly, be capable of looking at his problems from *both* points of view. Two tools for dealing with problems are likely to provide more effective answers than one.

Criterion four demands a testable system. Is this so for perceptual psychology? The answer is yes. In the first place, a great deal of research originating in orthodox traditions lends itself to a perceptual orientation. Sometimes this is true directly, sometimes through reinterpretation of objectively obtained results. Even in 1949, Dr. Snygg and I were able to quote from 222 sources for corroboration of our position. By 1959, we could call upon 619 references. Perceptual psychology, however, need not rely solely upon researches carried out in orthodox traditions. It is rapidly developing a methodology of its own.

An internal frame of reference for the study of behavior has a much more difficult problem than that posed in the external tradition. Its subject matter does not lie outside the behaver but inside. Its methods therefore, cannot be so simple and direct as those in the external tradition. This fact has made many orthodox psychologists uneasy for it seems to call for subjective methods of gathering data or a return to introspection which psychology rejected some fifty years ago. As a matter of fact, introspection is no more acceptable for perceptual psychology than it is for more orthodox approaches. The impression that such methods are acceptable in perceptual research seems to arise from two sources. It comes, in part, from the traditional definition of perception as "a mediating process within the individual about which he is able to give some report" which would, indeed, call for introspective methods. We have already seen earlier in this paper, however, that the definition of perception employed in perceptual psychology relates to *all* aspects of meaning not just those the subject can or will divulge on demand. The misconception is compounded by the unhappy fact that a number of current researchers have naively accepted introspective reports as acceptable data for psychological research.

The primary method of perceptual psychology is not introspection but inference, a highly respectable scientific technique which can be subjected to rigorous control. It is a method long employed in the physical sciences for approaching their most difficult problems. Without the use of inference, science would be forever restricted to that which was immediate and palpable. It could never deal with what was unseen or what lay in the future. The use of inference creates special problems, to be sure, but can and should meet the same exacting requirements as any science.

The use of inference for gathering data in perceptual psychology requires the use of the observer himself as a research instrument. This is a matter that causes many traditional psychologists great uneasiness. It need not. While the human instrument is not so neatly subject to control as a mechanical or electric one, like any other instrument of research, it can be calibrated and adjusted so that its readings have high degrees of reliability. There is already much evidence in existing research on values, beliefs, and the self concept to demonstrate that inferential approaches can provide us valid and useful data. The technique has also a long and distinguished history in the interpretations of projective instruments. In time, no doubt, we will develop many more techniques.

At this early stage of the development of a perceptual orientation it is to be expected that we would not have the precise, highly polished techniques of the objective frame of reference with ninety years of experience behind it. Compared to those older devices, some of our current techniques for exploration in a perceptual orientation must necessarily seem rather crude. This need not worry us, however, or divert us from the pursuit of understanding. Someone has to begin and, as Dr. Snygg once suggested, "The Conestoga Wagon was a crude transportation device but it made possible the opening up of a continent."

Some years ago the Social Science Research Council formulated a series of criteria for the validation of a theoretical position. These tests were as follows:

1. Feelings of subjective certainty.
2. Conformity with known facts.
3. Mental manipulation.
4. Predictive power.
5. Social agreement.
6. Internal consistency.

Applying these criteria to perceptual psychology, the system stands up quite as well as any other.

Although perceptual psychology deals with the internal life of the individual, the perceptual psychologist, like any other, must begin his studies with careful objective observations. That is a legitimate demand. To require of the perceptual psychologist, however, that he utilize the same constructs and methods as those in traditional psychology is going too far. A new frame of reference, of necessity, must develop its own constructs and methods. If it did not it would not be a new frame of reference! The essence of science is not a common method but disciplined, responsible observation. This can legitimately be demanded of perceptual psychology. It can also be delivered.

Criterion five demands that a perceptual system be capable of including the concepts of leading humanists. In my own experience perceptual psychology more than meets this criterion. With little or no distortion to their fundamental tenets the concepts of Maslow, Rogers, Van Kaam, Allport, May, Bugental, Murray, Moustakas, Jourard, to name but a few, readily fit in a perceptual framework. Some, in fact, have consciously adopted a perceptual orientation for the expression of much of their work.

Turning now to the practical aspects of humanistic theory, our sixth criterion demands applicability to the problems of the individual case. Orthodox approaches to psychology with emphasis upon the stimulus and restricted to external observations have often failed to provide practitioners with the precise information they need for carrying out applied functions. It is not enough for the counselor, or teacher or social worker to be able to say "the chances are." He must often be able to predict the behavior of students, patients or clients with far greater accuracy. As we have pointed out earlier it is the search for a more precise understanding of individual behavior which has led many psychologists into the ranks of humanism. A theory especially applicable to the individual case is precisely what perceptual psychology offers. It regards behavior as merely symptom, the external expression of internal perceptual organization. Its primary subject matter is the perceptions of subjects and these, of course, are always unique and individual. It is precisely because we felt perceptual psychology was especially pertinent for handling the problems of the unique case that Dr. Snygg and I chose the title, *Individual Behavior,* for our book setting forth this point of view.

The seventh criterion calls for a dynamic, immediately useful psychology. To understand behavior in the traditional approaches to psychology it has always been necessary to know the character of the stimulus. Accordingly, the practitioner was usually faced with the necessity of uncovering the events in his client's life which had produced his behavior. He sought these explanations in his client's successes and failures, in childhood trauma or in the relationships of the individual with the significant people in his past. This is a historic view of causation, after the fact. It explains how current behavior came about but often provides no great help in changing it. A perceptual view of behavior, on the other hand, approaches the understanding of behavior from the present. It sees the causes of behavior in the person's *current* feelings, beliefs, purposes, or ways of seeing himself and his world. This provides a dynamic, immediate view of causation.

Such a view of causation is immensely important for people engaged in activities involving human interaction. If behavior is truly a function of perception, then it is possible to modify behavior by changing perceptions in the present even if we do not have knowledge of how the subject got this way! That idea has already found expression in most of our modern psychotherapies which, either implicitly or explicitly, assume that human behavior can be modified in the present even if we do not know all of the factors which caused it in the past. In my own practice of psychotherapy I find that the clients I have who spend long hours exploring their past, are almost exclusively graduate students in psychology! They have thoroughly learned that their behavior is a function of the past, so when they come for help, they may spend long hours in an exploration of the past. Sooner or later, however, they arrive at the conclusion, "Well, now I know why I feel like I do," but almost at once, this statement is followed by, "But damn it all, I still feel that way!"

Our last criterion calls for a psychology capable of general use in the solution of pressing human problems.

The essence of humanism is a concern for man. Even the humanists among us most preoccupied with philosophical and theoretical problems are also deeply concerned with the human condition and how it can be improved. For many of us, problems of application are crucial. Humanistic psychology must contribute to the fulfillment of human potential. Since it deals with immediate causes, perceptual psychology, almost automatically, provides direction for action whether in the classrooom, clinic, consultation room or in solving social problems of the ghetto.

Let us take as an example the question of self actualization. Self-actualized people seem to see themselves in positive ways. That is to say, they see themselves as people who are liked, wanted, acceptable, able, and so on. Non-self-actualized people tend to see themselves in negative ways. Now, knowing that self-actualized people see themselves as liked, wanted, acceptable and able we have immediate clues to action. To produce such people (which is, after all, the goal of counseling, social work, and education) it is necessary for us to ask these questions: How can a person feel liked unless somebody likes him? How can a person feel wanted unless somebody wants him? How can a person feel acceptable unless somebody accepts him? How can a person feel able unless somewhere he has some success? In the answers we find to these questions we have immediate clues for action.

Humanistic psychology ought not be a secret society cloaked in obscurity and carrying on its business in a foreign language. Most of us in the humanist movement are concerned that our studies should make a difference to the human condition. We, therefore, need to be able to communicate with our students, clients, patients, and the public generally in language and ideas which are readily and accurately comprehended. Psychological constructs couched in perceptual terms have an immediate applicability to the experience of the man in the street. They have a quality of "of courseness" for him. It is a heartwarming experience to watch the way students exposed to perceptual thought pick up its concepts with enthusiasm and seek for ways to apply them to their own experience and problems. I think a humanistic psychology should be like that.

I am satisfied that perceptual psychology can adequately meet the criteria for a humanistic psychology. It is only fair to say, however, that this opinion is by no means universally accepted. Indeed, some critics of perceptual psychology have serious doubts it can be regarded as a psychology at all! In this discussion I have already dealt with some of their most cogent criticisms. There are several more I should like to mention.

One of the most frequent complaints has been that perceptual psychology is much too simple. It is quite true that many of the principles of perceptual psychology are deceptively simple. Simplicity, however, is hardly a matter for the condemnation of a theory. Indeed, it is one of its greatest strengths. Parsimony is, after all, a major goal of theory building. What could be simpler, for example, than the physical formula $E=MC^2$? I regard this criticism as more of a compliment than a weakness. The simple and obvious can have vast implications.

Some critics have also complained that the constructs of perceptual psychology are too fluid and are used as both product and process. They feel uncomfortable dealing with constructs like the self concept which is both a product of perception and a modifier of perception. While this two-sided aspect of such a construct makes it inconvenient for some forms of analysis, it in no way destroys its validity as data for a science. The rock in the streambed is a product of the erosion caused by the stream but also affects the flow of water. Thus it is both product and process and a force to be dealt with in understanding the stream and its behavior. Simply because a construct can be objectively measured is no guarantee it is the most accurate possible description of events. One could make a good case for the notion that the concept of the stimulus itself, although capable of objective observation, is not the *real* stimulus at all. A handful of jelly beans the day before Easter is not the same stimulus to a child as the same quantity of jelly beans the day after! The search for absolute concepts is an illusion. If behavior is a function of perception then a quite satisfactory perceptual psychology can be constructed whether there is anything really present to be perceived or not!

Finally, a criticism voiced by some humanists has found perceptual psychology lacking because it is too deterministic. A humanistic psychology, they maintain, must leave room for choice and self determination. The age old free-will problem thus rises to haunt us once again. It need not, however, for perceptual psychology provides us with *both* a deterministic explanation of behavior and a creative human being. Its basic axiom that all behavior is the product of the behaver's perceptual field at the moment of action provides us with a completely determined basis for behavior and so satisfies the requirement of a science that its subject matter be lawful. It also disposes of the possibility of "choice." On the other hand, the perceptual field is affected by at least the seven variables we mentioned earlier in this discussion among which, especially, are the self concept and the need for maintenance and enhancement. The operation of these variables on the selection of perception assures that the behavior of any individual will be unique and personal. Behavior is still determined by the field but the nature of the field is modified by need for fulfillment and the self concept. This uniqueness of behavior observed by an outsider is labeled "choice," although it is really nothing of the kind. It could have been predicted had we known enough of the nature of the behaver's field.

So it is that perceptual psychology eliminates choice or free will with one hand, but gives us a creative individual whose every behavior is a unique and personal expression of his self with the other. So it is possible to satisfy both the rigorous requirements of a science and the needs of a humanist movement, a deterministic psychology and a creative dynamic human being.

In closing we may ask, why search for a psychology for the expression of humanism anyhow? Why not just be eclectic? Why not use whatever works? Certainly, not every worker in humanistic psychology needs to have the same frame of reference. An eclectic approach using "whatever works" may be quite acceptable so long as an individual is not responsible for other people. For persons engaged in professional work, however, eclecticism will never do. There is no special virtue in having no position. Persons with responsibility for others cannot behave in so haphazard a manner. What they do must be a *predictable* process. This calls for the clearest, most consistent theoretical position possible in the light of current knowledge, to serve as a frame of reference for selecting action. The value of theory is to provide just such guidelines.

There are two great frames of reference for looking at human behavior. We may approach the problem externally, from the point of view of an outside observer, or internally, from the point of view of the behaver himself. The humanist movement began very largely because so many of us found the external approach inadequate to deal with our every day problems. I believe psychology has been drifting toward an internal frame of reference for a generation or more, sometimes consciously, sometimes unconsciously. Different students have also been moving at varying rates of speed and each has made the transition in more or less degree. Maslow once expressed the feeling that in twenty years humanism would become *THE* psychology and I think he was right. It is time we made explicit now what we have been implicitly drifting toward. We need a clearcut stand in the new frame of reference and a systematic psychology to give it expression. I believe perceptual psychology can provide that position.

Many humanists have already adopted a perceptual approach as a vehicle for solving their problems. I do not believe a perceptual orientation is the last word nor the only possibility for an adequate expression of the humanist position. It is, however, the only position I have been able to find so far which adequately meets the criteria I have stated in this paper. It has also been stimulating and helpful to me in my professional work and fits most adequately my own thinking, experience and needs.

As Donald Snygg and I commented in our first presentation of this point of view in 1949, "As fallible human beings we can only hope that this is 'if not the truth, then very like the truth'."

3

BELIEFS, VALUES, AND GOALS IN THE HELPING PROCESS

Objectivity is often stressed in the helping relationship. There are even times when the greatest degree of objectivity will best accomplish the purposes a helper is striving for. However, a helper can never be completely objective and there are times when helpers can be so objective that they may defeat their own purposes.

Every helper has a set of values, beliefs, and goals. No matter where helpers are or what they are doing, these things greatly determine what decisions they make and what behavior they will engage in. In a real sense, this means that objectivity is a highly relative and never absolute state. We can make no decisions or perform any helping act without being tremendously affected by the subjective values and goals that we hold.

This is as it should be. No one should engage in a helping relationship without a well-developed set of beliefs about what helpers are like and what they need. To do otherwise would be to blindly fumble around, trying first one thing, then another, in the hope that something might be of help to the person with whom we're working. That would be a totally inexcusable state of affairs.

Being unable to avoid the development of attitudes, beliefs, values, and goals is not a problem—it is simply a given. What is important for a professional helper is that beliefs be carefully thought out, defined as neatly as possible, be experimentally and logically consistent, and that goals evolve naturally from these systematic beliefs. It is the purpose of this section of the Sourcebook *to present some of the best statements we have seen on the kinds of beliefs and values that members of helping professions should hold and the goals they should be attempting to achieve.*

In the first article, Earl Kelley, with a warm and caring style, outlines what he believes should be a basic attitude held by all helpers about those they help.

Donald Snygg begins his presentation by examining beliefs held about human beings by laymen and nonpsychologists. He then reviews some psychological explanations of human behavior which differ from his. Next he explains what he, and the editors of this book, believe to be a more appropriate frame of reference for behavior. Snygg's position has much relevance for our time because he is trying to explain a model best suited to a rapidly changing society—something we desperately need!

Beliefs, values, and goals are so interdependent that we can hardly speak of one without speaking of the others. Sometimes they are actually the same thing. This is evident in Charlotte Buhler's article. "Human Life Goals in the Humanistic Perspective" is an excellent discussion of the development of one's self, the basis of fulfillment, and the difference between actualized and nonactualized persons. These topics provide a foundation for the development of consistent beliefs, values, and goals.

The Meaning of Wholeness

EARL C. KELLEY

Recently there has been more and more attention given to the psychosomatic nature of the human organism. Even some of those who make their living by ministering to our health have taken it up, at least in some degree. It is now fairly common to have an M.D. make indirect allusions to this fact.

The human organism has two selves, living together in the same body structure. There is the physical self and the psychological self. This is not intended to be a denial of the unity of man, but we have to admit that there are two of them because they feed on different stuffs. The physical self feeds on such things as meat and vegetables; the psychological self feeds on the perceptive stuff of growth, such as what people say, music, sunsets, or, according to one's lot, squalor, degradation. The perceptive stuff of growth cannot be seen, as the physical stuff can. If we could see it, it is possible that we might come to have a whole new set of attitudes toward those less fortunate than we. I say it is just possible, realizing that our attitudes are built on a whole set of circumstances that have nothing to do with compassion or any other of the more human emotions.

At any rate, we have paid far more attention to the physical self than we have to the psychological self. It is hard to say which is the more important because both are essential. The psychological self cannot even exist without a body. I suppose one could cite examples of the physical self existing without much psychological self, but such people are hardly even human, although they are entitled to our compassion, our love, and our best efforts.

From *ETC: A Review of General Semantics,* 1969, 26 (1). Copyright 1969 by the International Society for General Semantics. Reprinted with permission.

The point here is that we have paid too little attention to the psychological self in the past, and while every person must have a body to inhabit, what a person feels is far more important than what he knows. What he knows is important, of course, because that is what he uses to behave with. And the eventual pay-off is in behavior—what a person does. The task of the educator is to pay much attention to the perceptive stuff of growth. This he can do without fear of the neglect of the physical self. The various athletic coaches will see to that.

One of the most important facts about the perceptive stuff of growth is that it is selective, so that the individual sees what he has had experience to see and what is in line with his purposes. The purposive nature of the human individual is described more fully in Chapter 6 of *Education and the Nature of Man*.[1] I will not go into it again in this paper. At any rate, experience alone is not enough to account for what happens. The fact that no two people see the same thing at the same spot in the same way is truly significant. The fact that no two people perceive alike is particularly true in the case of our dealings with other people. It seems to me that other people are the most complex things that we have to view. And this accounts for much of what has seemed to us to be strange indeed. In the first psychology course I ever took the instructor had an "incident" occur and then asked each of us to write what we thought we had seen. When it came about that none of us had seen the same thing we all laughed merrily and then the teacher proceeded as though it were not so—as though people *do* see the same thing in the same way.

The psychological self has boundaries. These are invisible, as all of the psychological self is. But without boundaries there would be no entity. This self has two overwhelming needs. One is to defend itself; the other is to "keep" other people—to maintain and strengthen its social relationships. How to defend one's self and to do it without alienating other people must surely be the biggest adjustment that the human organism faces. It is simple to defend one's self if that is the only consideration. But everybody has to have other people in order to be provided with the perceptive stuff of growth. Without other people we would become like plants; in fact, there is some evidence that even plants are quite dependent on each other. We are therefore built by the people with whom we come in contact, and we build them. This is an answer to the age-old question, "Am I my brother's keeper?" We had better be; he is the stuff of which we are built, and the quality of life we enjoy depends on him.

It helps me to think of this boundary as a screen. Of course there is no screen, but there seems to be a flow in and out, as there would be if there were a screen. Those things which are perceived to be enhancing are admitted, and those that are seen to be endangering are kept out.

1. Kelley and Rasey (New York: Harper, 1952).

It seems that the outward flow is sometimes kept more open than the inward flow. Fearful people build thick screens. We once had a friend, quite a frequent visitor in our home, who was almost all output and very little intake. She would come in and say, "How are you?" If I were to say I just murdered my wife and her body lay in the next room, this woman would say, "You must hear what has just happened to me!" She never really comprehended that my retirement was approaching and that we would move away, though it was often mentioned in her presence.

If intake and defense were all there was to life, we would not have needed to evolve beyond the oyster. It has a good thick covering and lies at the bottom of the sea, opening up as long as there is food to be had, and closing when it feels endangered. But there is more to life than the oyster knows; and we are not oysters.

Sometimes the flow of the perceptive stuff of growth is cut off altogether in both directions. The people who do this we call catatonic. They just exist. There are infants who just exist too—infants who never cry or smile or babble. We call these autistic, and every large city has a ward in its hospital for them. So far as I know, nobody knows what causes a baby to be autistic, although there has been recent research on them. The research leads to a certain amount of speculation, however; it seems likely that these infants have looked out upon a hostile world and have decided to have none of it. These infants seldom live beyond eighteen months.

Whether infant or adult, and whether complete or incomplete, such people shut off the stuff out of which they are built and become prisoners in their own fortresses.

We need to develop people with open selves, or as nearly open as can be achieved. Thus they will learn more readily. I have found in my teaching that if I could achieve this, learning would be greatly increased. And so, particularly in the later years, I worked more on this than on anything else. If I could bring about confidence and reduce or abolish fear, the learner would become more and more able to take in what there was to take from his environment. In the main, this is where all of today's large classes and impersonal relationships break down; this is one of the causes of the present rebellion. I once knew a professor of history who proclaimed that he did not *want* to know his students because he might become fond of them and this would cause a loss of interest in his subject matter. Such attitudes destroy what I hold to be the primary function of the teacher—that of relating to and building people. Of course we have to have something for them to learn, and they will not all learn the same things anyway.

Too often teachers teach in such a way as to make their learners value themselves less and less. This is the wrong way to teach. We need to develop people who will think well of themselves. People who think well of themselves are in turn able to think well of others. This is essential to the complete human being.

We need to develop people who will think well of their teachers. This can be achieved only by having teachers who deserve to be held in confidence and respect. This cannot be achieved by the double-cross, by the surprise test, by asking questions whose answers are to be found only in the footnotes of some textbook, or by any other of the multitudinous methods that have been developed by many teachers. It is not possible for learners to respect a person who is waiting to trick them.

We need people who will see their stake in others, since that is the stuff of which we are built. It is difficult for us to be much better than the stuff of which we are built. This again may be the answer to the age-old question, "Am I my brother's keeper?"

We need people who will see themselves as part of a becoming world, rather than a static world. Thus will not only change be expected, but it will be welcomed. The fact that we do not know what tomorrow will bring should be an exciting thing, a thing that adds interest to life, not something to be dreaded and viewed with apprehension. This view of the universe will add much to the way in which life is held.

We need people who are naturally optimistic. There is no point in being purposive unless we think that the next spot we are in will be better than the one we now occupy. This is essentially what optimism means.

We need people who possess moral courage. I do not mean to limit this to the old set of morals, but to include much more than that. It is a call for people who are nonconformist in the ways that really matter. Thus the moralist can be thwarted in ways that will disturb him most. It is not the little things so many do that are the mark of the real nonconformist. I do not think I need spell these things out in any more detail; let the reader supply the specifics.

We need people who value what a human being is above the outside values so common in our society. This is my concept of what materialism is. What do we care most about? Do we care most about how another human being feels—what is happening to him—or do we care more about a raise in pay, a better automobile, a finer home, a better standing with our neighbors?

It would be easy to say that open selves are produced by having a chance to live the life that is good to live. But this calls for some explanation. The life that is good to live is primarily one in which the individual is loved and is able to feel it. By love I do not mean the sort of love that is accompanied by soft music and moonlight. That is all right too, but the love of an adult for a child is quite another matter. It is more a matter of caring, of concern for the feelings of the child. Nobody can be without this kind of love and grow into anything that is truly human.

The unloved grow into a different kind of people altogether. They do not have the usual capacity for relating to other people. Their handshake is quite noticeably withdrawn. These and many other symptoms reveal the fact that in their infancy and during their childhood they have lacked this most important ingredient.

We have known for a long time that rich environments produce increased intelligence and that poor environments reduce it. By this it is meant that the environment has to be rich not in the material things of life, but rather in the human things. Some of the richest homes from the material point of view are actually the poorest places for children to inhabit, and some of the poorest places materially are filled with love and companionship, the very best places for children to be. We have been slow to recognize this, probably because it has contradicted the precepts so many of us hold dear. The general public has assumed that a wealthy home is a good home, and it has been difficult to persuade people that the opposite may be true.

Each person in our world is different from any other person who has been or will be. This uniqueness is a fact of life which we need to come to value, rather than trying to decry it and counteract it. This fact of life has been provided for by the action of the chromosomes in the cells from which the individual is conceived and it cannot be altered. There is one partial exception in the case of identical twins, but even here it is impossible to give identical experiences. Even when both are paddled, it makes a great deal of difference which one is paddled first. I have dealt at some length with this in "The Significance of Being Unique," published first in *ETC.* I will not, therefore, devote much space to it now, except to say that if teachers took this into account it would reduce or eliminate the despair that so many teachers feel when, at the end of a course, not everybody knows the same things exactly as the teacher thinks he taught them. Actually, it is because of the very nature of people that they cannot come up with identical answers. Each has to interpret what he sees and hears in the light of his own experience and purpose. Thus differences should be expected and welcomed, rather than decried.

Students need to be involved in what they are doing. This involvement has to be planned for by the teacher or by the students themselves. It will not come about by itself. Of course the student does not have to have his own way about everything, but even if his involvement is actually planned by his fellows, he needs to have a feeling that he had a say in the planning. It makes a great deal of difference whether or not one has been consulted. Few people, and certainly not the ones we can have the most confidence in for the future, do anything with much verve or enthusiasm just because they are told to do it by someone in authority. This is the old teacher-pupil planning about which so much has been said and written, and so little has been done.

In order to live the life that is good to live, one needs to be respected as a person. One can hardly be a whole person unless he is respected by others. The word "respect" is a most interesting one. *Spect* comes from the word which means "to look" and *re* means to repeat, to do again. Thus to be respected means to be looked at again. In order to be looked at again one has to be worth more than a passing glance.

All these factors help to build courage, which is essential to all humanness. For without courage one becomes a mere shadow of a human being. Courage makes it possible to attack many of the problems of life in a truly human and functional way. It makes all the difference between the craven and the bold.

But what do we teachers see as we look out upon the world which we have had a large hand in creating? We see threats taking the place of positive action. We see that we still believe in the theory that "getting tough" will solve problems instead of making them worse and perhaps driving them underground. Or we see students acting as though they were forced to strike and to make demands which, at least to us, seem unreasonable and impossible to comply with. We have left them no choice but to rebel, and, in their frenzy, they make demands which cannot be met. This is the only outlet left to them.

We see fear actually being used as a teaching technique. Fear is an emotion that has no place in the student-teacher relationship. It provokes all kinds of adverse behaviors. It is the cause of many of the evil happenings in our social structure. And to think that we knowingly and deliberately use it!

We see whole people taught piecemeal. Somehow the learner is supposed to put all the pieces together, but he seldom does. The old system of teaching subjects separately, which might have had some validity when schools started centuries ago, still holds us in its grip. The thought of approaching our environment as a whole seems never to have occurred to most educators.

We see many forms of rejection in teaching practice. There are so many ways which even well-meaning teachers have of rejecting people that it is almost impossible to count them. I once had a doctoral student who proposed to do a two-semester-hour study of rejection by visiting schools. In about two weeks he came back and said this was no two-hour study; it was so vast it would make a doctoral dissertation.

I do not think that we have the right to reject anybody. This does not mean that I would admit anybody to any class regardless of his preparation to do what the class was set up to do. I am thinking mostly of our captive audiences in our elementary and secondary schools. If we are going to require that they be there, it is then also essential that we have something to do which has meaning to them—and that we have the freedom to do it. Rejection leads to alienation from self and others, and it is indeed a poor reason for requiring people to be there.

We will have to give up our faith in violence as a method. Violence never has made anyone better or more educable. Our faith in violence has come full circle now, and we are suffering the consequences.

What we need in this land of ours is better people; and if we are to have better people, the teachers of the nation will have to produce them. The parents and other adults who have influence over our young are products of the old system and have no way of knowing any better. What we need is a revolution among teachers, not in salaries and working conditions, but in attitude and emotion. This would bring about conditions in which our young would have no need for revolt.

The Psychological Basis of Human Values

DONALD SNYGG

THE RELATION OF PSYCHOLOGY TO ECONOMICS

In a rapidly changing society like our own, social and economic situations never repeat themselves exactly. Every situation has something new about it. As a result, no economic, business, or political planning is possible except as the planners have a concept of causation which enables them to make some guess about what people will do under circumstances which have never before arisen. This is true whether we are planning individually as businessmen or consumers or collectively as citizens. The faster the society changes, the more its members have to depend on theory.

One of the major obstacles in the way of getting more dependable concepts for predicting economic behavior is our limited knowledge of psychology. Economic or political behavior is behavior by people. When economists analyze and interpret economic behavior, when they forecast the outcome of this or that economic policy or trend, they are forecasting what people will do. To do this an accurate concept of human nature is essential. Any theories or predictions about what people will do are certain to be inaccurate if they are based on false concepts of the people whose behavior is predicted.

This places economists and other social scientists in an awkward situation. Human beings are complex organisms and there are a great many conflicting theories about them. In choosing among those theories we

From A. Dudley Ward, ed., *Goals of Economic Life*. Copyright 1953 by The Federal Council of the Churches of Christ in America. Reprinted by permission of Harper & Row, Publishers, Inc.

cannot safely trust our limited personal experience, which may have been with a special kind of people. The social or economic theorist who bases his theories of what people will do on his personal version of human nature is quite likely to get a theory which is applicable only to his own generation of his society or to his own social class. He is in danger of getting a theory which is applicable only to himself.

If he protects himself against this provincialism by basing his economic theories on current psychological concepts, he can still get into difficulties. The conceptual systems of professional psychologists are in the process of development and some of them, including some which psychologists are very hopeful about, are still too specialized to be applicable to the behavior of human beings outside the laboratory. The social scientist who uses a theory of this type without understanding its sources is in danger of building his picture of society on a theory which in its current incomplete form is applicable only to the maze behavior of the white rat.

And no matter which conceptual framework he adopts, he will find many of its concepts unconvincing because they are contrary to what he and his readers have always thought to be common sense.

COMMON–SENSE CONCEPTS OF HUMAN NATURE

One of the main obstacles in the way of our learning more about human nature is the fact that we already "know" so many things about it that are not true. Most people can recognize their ignorance of such subjects as entomology or cultural anthropology or nuclear physics, but few people except professional psychologists feel ignorant about human nature. Psychology, it is generally believed, is just common sense—what everybody knows. Some may doubt that redheaded people are quick tempered, but it is generally held to be "common sense" that *the* basic human needs are for food, shelter, and clothing; that practice makes perfect; and that the way to cure people of bad habits is to punish them. We delude ourselves, however, when we believe that these generalizations are dependable or that we learned them by experience. "Common sense" about human nature all too often turns out to be an author's epigram or an academic theory, now disproved, which was proposed so long ago that our grandparents heard about it in time to teach it to our parents.

The Fiction of Economic Man

One of the most prominent of the "common sense" barriers to better understanding of human nature is the widespread belief that economic motives are the only ones that matter in the economic realm. Studies of employee aspirations in American industry do not confirm the idea that pay is the only incentive or even the most important one. Wage incentive systems frequently result in slowdowns by the more efficient workers, who do not wish to outproduce their associates. Among American industrial workers, desire for group membership and approval has usually proved more potent than desire for money when the two are in conflict.

Katona[1] has recently reported that businessmen have a tendency to aim at increased volume rather than increased profits. He believes that economic motives are changing and lists, among others, professional pride and desire for prestige, for power, and for approbation.[2]

Competition as a Motive of Behavior

Another common-sense idea which does not stand up in practice is the idea that people are inevitably competitive. It is quite true that most people measure their achievements by the achievements of their neighbors, and Katona has justifiably concluded that "the more money other people have the more a person wants." [3] As used in many schools and factories, however, competition is a comparatively ineffective way of getting people to work harder. People do not compete actively unless they think they have a chance to win. This causes a large part of any group to withdraw from competition early. These people then exert pressure on the others to drop out of the competition with them. In addition, more people are unwilling to compete when competing means the loss of friends, as it often does. Forced competition, in which people are obliged to compete against their friends, is a threat to the individual and therefore unpleasant. It is not surprising that workers or departments which have been involved in contests frequently drop their output to below normal as soon as the contest is over.[4] As a rule teachers who depend on competition as a means of motivation are able to get the majority

1. G. Katona, *Psychological Analysis of Economic Behavior* (New York: McGraw-Hill, 1951).
2. The fiction of complete economic determinism, set up by the early economists as a convenient way of delimiting their field, has been mistaken by a great many people for a demonstrated scientific fact. As such it has had a profound effect on popular thinking about human nature and about our society. At a time when our way of life is under heavy attack, when many of the members of the society have lost faith in its ability to deal with the problems of human need, it is unfortunate that the simplest and most understandable analysis that many educated people are apt to encounter is based on the assumption that our economic system is a mechanism for the satisfaction of greed. Such a picture is not likely to attract converts or to strengthen the loyalty of the present members of the society. Nor does it lead to the effective functioning of the institutions which are caricatured and misunderstood.
3. Katona, *Psychological Analysis of Economic Behavior*.
4. T. W. Harrell, *Industrial Psychology* (New York: Rinehart, 1949), p. 280.

of their students to compete only when they "choose up sides" and appeal to group loyalties.

PSYCHOLOGICAL CONCEPTS OF HUMAN NATURE

Although a great deal of progress has been made during the three quarters of a century that psychology has been an experimental science, psychologists are continually reminded of the tentative nature of their generalizations by the fact that competent psychologists may still differ from one another in their preference among the various conceptual frameworks and types of explanation that are used. The truth is that human behavior is so many-sided, so complex, and so variable that there is no single point of view yet discovered by which we can understand it all. The problem is to find a point of view which will enable us to see the whole disorderly mass of phenomena in order and regularity, and, it is hoped, to make it predictable. In looking for a conceptual system which will make human behavior more understandable, present-day psychologists are following a number of different leads.

The Stimulus-Response Approach to Behavior

The most obvious approach is to attempt to explain behavior by the known principles of the physical sciences. Such a conceptual system was made quite plausible by the discovery of the reflex arc in 1832. It was discovered that the stimulation of a given nerve always resulted in the contraction of the same muscles, provided the spinal cord had been severed above the point where the nerve entered it. This fixed stimulus-response unit, which could be explained plausibly by several different principles of the physical sciences, was assumed to be the basic unit of behavior.

Following this assumption, the next problem was to discover how these fixed "basic" reflexes combine and interact with one another to produce the more variable and coherent behavior which is characteristic of an undamaged organism, animal or human.

The most important difficulty confronting this concept of behavior is the problem of stimulus selection. There are in any given physical situation great numbers of physical stimuli to which the organism makes no apparent response. A stimulus which sets off a response in one situation or at one time may have no effect at another time or in another situation. Or it may elicit a completely different response. And the stimulus which does elicit the response is not necessarily the strongest one in terms of physical energy.

This variability is ascribed either to changes in the conductivity of the nervous system or to tensions and imbalances which require (drive) the organism to behave so as to relieve them.

This latter concept has diverted the emphasis in physiologically oriented theories of motivation from the external physical stimulus which "triggers" the act to the internal conditions that determine which of the great number of potential factors present in the physical environment will be selected as the objects of the organism's behavior. A number of these conditions, personified as "drives" for food, water, avoidance of injury, rest, elimination, air, and constant body temperature, have been taken over from physiology.

Since the behavior supposedly motivated by these physiological drives or "needs" is essential to the survival of the organism, they are commonly assumed to be the basic drives from which all other "drives" or "needs" are derived. These physiological drives, at least, operate in all living individuals. They are often considered to constitute a single drive for physical survival or for homeostasis, that is, for the maintenance of the organism's physiological balance.

Homeostasis as an Explanation of Behavior

This is not a mere change of words. The concept of homeostasis enables us to visualize and use a completely different concept of living organisms from the machine concept of the stimulus-response theorists. It even leads to a different system of ethics.

Thinking in terms of the physics of their own day, the physiologists who a century ago adopted the reflex arc as their conceptual unit of behavior were taking a machine as their model. The motive power of their conceptual man was supplied from the outside in the form of a stimulus, i.e., a spur.

The newer concept of homeostasis, which also originated in physiology, assumes, on the other hand, that the living organism is an organized dynamic field and that, like all organized fields, it must behave so as to maintain its organization. Thus the organized nature of our behavior, the explanation of which has caused the stimulus-response theorists so much trouble, is simply an aspect of our nature as living organisms. An individual's behavior, from this point of view, is both the result of his physical organization and the means by which it is maintained. The physiological evidence in favor of this concept is overwhelming and does not need to be given here. The essential thing is that this point of view leads us to conceive of human beings, not as passive machines which have to be pushed into action, but as living organisms actively exploring their environments for the means of maintaining their own integrity. They actively seek the satisfaction of need and, if we consider them as whole organisms, they have free will. Choices between food and water, for instance, are determined by the physiological state of the organism itself.

All of this, so far, is completely in harmony with the known principles of physics and chemistry and fits into the present framework of the physical sciences.

It is too bad that it is not quite adequate. A large part of human behavior and even some animal behavior cannot be explained by or even reconciled with the purely physiological needs. It is not uncommon for people to eat when they have already eaten more than they need or can comfortably contain. It is not uncommon for them to refuse food when they are famished. People drive too fast for safety, they mutilate themselves for beauty, they give their lives as heroes, as martyrs, and as suicides, all activities which are hardly consonant with maintaining the physiological balance. In the wartime experiment [5] on the effects of semistarvation, the thirty-six men who were the subjects lost an average of 25 per cent of their body weight. With it they lost interest in almost everything but food. They dreamed of food; thought constantly about food. Life became, as one expressed it, merely "passing time from one meal to the next." Another reported: "Stayed up till 5:00 A.M. last night studying cookbooks. So absorbing I can't stay away from them."

This extreme preoccupation with food would seem at first glance to be an ideal example of the effect of an urge toward organic homeostasis. But, in spite of the fact that food could easily have been purchased or stolen, only a few of the participants violated their pledge to eat only the prescribed diet. When shopping they did not purchase the food needed by their bodies. Instead they bought cookbooks, cooking utensils, and "bargains." One man hoarded *National Geographic* magazines. Two men stole. But only one stole food. The other stole china cups.

If this is homeostasis, it is not homeostasis in a purely physiological sense.

Even lower animals not infrequently show behavior which is hard to reconcile with a demand for bodily maintenance. The writer once had to remove a white rat from a laboratory activity wheel because of extreme loss of weight. She had been going without food and water in order to keep her cagemates from using the wheel. As soon as she was removed from the cage one of the other animals began behaving in the same way. Homeostasis can explain dominating behavior which results in the individual's getting more food, but when a poorly nourished animal abstains from food and water in order to dominate its cagemates,

5. H. S. Guetzkow and P. H. Bowman, *Men and Hunger* (Elgin, Ill.; Brethren Publishing House, 1946).

an explanation of the act as an effort to maintain a constant physiological state seems a little farfetched.

The Concept of Psychological Needs

One way of handling this difficulty is to postulate the existence of additional nonorganic drives or needs, usually called psychological needs. Among the psychological needs proposed by various writers are needs for activity *and* for relaxation, for security *and* for new experience, for self-assertion *and* for self-abasement, for imitativeness *and* for creative self-expression, for work *and* for leisure, for beauty *and* for practicability, for protection *and* for independence, for emotional security *and* for excitement, for superiority, for dominance, for status, for possession of children, for recognition, for achievement, for affection, for value, for ownership, for knowledge, for power, for prestige, and for "value-in-general."

It should be obvious that this conceptual scheme gets into difficulties since it leads to the postulation of contradictory goals. If we are free to postulate a new psychological need to explain any act otherwise inexplicable, the list will grow and grow. As someone has said, this method could lead to the postulation of a psychological need for pumpkin pie in October.

In spite of the way this theory of mixed physiological-psychological needs frays out into confusion and conflict, it is popular at the present time. For one thing, it provides a convenient formula for explaining anything that anyone has ever done. If none of the many conflicting drives can explain an act, a new drive can easily be added to the list. But it is impossible to predict by this method what an individual is going to do because it offers us no way of knowing which of the many conflicting hypothetical drives will be operating. As a result, applied psychologists, whose planning often requires a fairly accurate prediction of what an individual will do in a particular situation, do not find it helpful.

This puts the psychologist in the same awkward position as the other social scientists. Economists could go about their work with more confidence if the psychologists could give them a reliable psychology to work with; but the psychologists cannot solve their problem of prediction of individual human behavior by the physical-science methods most of them have been taught to prefer. Until the physiologists give them a better base to work on they cannot even begin to attack the problem.

In the meantime we are confronted with pressing problems of education, rehabilitation, and social reconstruction and planning for which a better understanding of human nature is essential. Without it we cannot be sure of our techniques or our goals. It is not safe to try to fit these problems into a theoretical framework which, no matter how bright its prospects for the future, is inadequate for that purpose now. Because they are expected to deal with human beings now and cannot wait for the physiological approaches to be perfected, many educational, clinical, and social psychologists are exploring the possibilities of other points of view.

The Group as a Determiner of Behavior

Two different and, to some extent, complementary approaches seem to be developing. The first uses the principle which Professor Emerson has rather happily called social homeostasis. Like physical organisms and other dynamic fields, the social group exists independently of any of its individual parts. It may exist long after all of its individual parts have been replaced; in fact it may continue to exist *because* some of its parts have been sacrificed or discarded. We can predict that so long as the society exists someone will be carrying out the functions required for its existence. As long as the society exists we can be confident that someone is playing these required roles. In an authoritarian society we can expect to find, for instance, leaders, followers, and the scapegoat minority or foreign enemies which are necessary to keep the followers in willing obedience to the leaders. If all of these roles, and many subsidiary ones, were not played the society would collapse.

Another characteristic that human societies and living organisms share with other dynamic fields is that their response to their external environment is selective. The type of response evoked by an environmental change depends upon the nature of the society or the organism; and changes which evoke a violent response from one society will elicit no response from another. A frequently cited example of this selectivity in the social field is Linton's study of the Tanala-Betsileo.[6] These two Madagascar tribes apparently shared the same culture until the Betsileo shifted from dry rice culture to wet rice culture. The wet rice culture has a number of economic advantages since it gives a higher yield, provides for better conservation of the soil, and can be carried out by single families. Since the system does not require frequent removal to new land

6. A. Kardiner and R. Linton, *The Individual and His Society* (New York: Columbia University Press, 1939). Also in T. Newcomb and E. Hartley, *Readings in Social Psychology* (New York: Henry Holt and Company, 1947).

it has the further advantage of enabling families engaged in wet rice culture to live in better and more permanent homes. Nevertheless, one of the Tanala clans which took up the new method soon abandoned it because it interferred with their religious ceremonies.

This same study furnishes other examples of the way in which societies function as dynamic fields. Because of the interdependent character of the organization in such a field, changes in one part of the field will affect, sometimes drastically, all other parts of the field. Once the Betsileo took up wet rice culture a profound change in their society followed. The fact that the land suitable for such cultivation was scattered and in small plots which could be cultivated more or less permanently made private ownership of the land desirable. Since the cultivation was by families rather than by clans (as it had been before), the ownership was by families. Class distinctions began to appear as a result of differences in family wealth. Slaves acquired economic value. Because the limiting factor in production was water, a strong central power to control irrigation became essential. The result was that the Betsileo developed a "rigid caste system with a king at the head, nobles, commoners, and slaves." In consequence the individual Betsileo has a different style of behavior and different behavior goals from the individual Tanala.

The recent studies of social class in American communities abound with examples of the ways in which class membership helps determine the values, goals, and aspirations of individual Americans. In "Yankee City," [7] in the early 'thirties, the typical upper-class member believed in heredity and manners as determinants of worth and status. He wanted money, not as an end in itself, but as a means of living "properly" in the family house, surrounded by symbols of the family position in the community, which it was his goal to maintain. The members of the middle class, on the other hand, believed in the power of money and education and wanted them both in order to gain higher status. The typical member of the 25 per cent of the population who constituted the lower-lower class cared little for education and looked on money as something to be spent for immediate satisfactions. The different social classes thus seem to obey different laws of economics. Kinsey[8] has similarly called attention to the difference in attitude toward sex among the different social classes.

Man is fundamentally a social animal. As an isolated individual he does not amount to much and he seems to know it. In spite of the accusations often made that the group holds its members back from progress and self-fulfillment, the truth is that, whatever our role, we can

7. W. L. Warner, *The Social System of a Modern Community* (New Haven: Yale University Press, 1941).

8. A. C. Kinsey, *Sexual Behavior in the Human Male* (Philadelphia: W. B. Saunders, 1948).

achieve it only in cooperation with others. Lewin[9] demonstrated that people change their ways of living faster in groups than they can individually. They also seem to think more effectively when they do it together. In one experiment[10] Shaw gave three reasoning problems to each of twenty-one individuals and to five groups of four people each. The individuals, working alone, arrived at correct solutions to only 8 per cent of the problems, the groups to 56 per cent. Group membership is important. Sobel,[11] in studying the psychiatric breakdown of army personnel in combat, found that after men had lost interest in defending their country, had forgotten to hate the enemy, were too tired to care about the immediate military objective and too frightened to pretend courage, they were still kept going by their loyalty to their immediate group. The effect of group membership on behavior in schools and factories has already been mentioned. As Murphy[12] puts it, ". . . so that we know his age, sex, subculture, and economic position . . . we can go a long way toward safely describing his personality." If we want to predict what a person will probably do in a given situation, the fastest way is to find what groups he feels part of and what his role is in the groups.

And yet the assumption that an individual behaves as he does because he is a member of a group which requires such behavior leaves a great many questions unanswered. Suppose that a man is a member of many different groups, as most people are nowadays. If the interests of these groups conflict, what will he do? The group-determinant hypothesis cannot tell us.

It is necessary to distinguish, at this point, between the rough hypothesis that the behavior of an individual will be that which is required by his social role and the more sophisticated principle of social homeostasis advanced by Professor Emerson. In a static society[13] like that of the social insects the difference can be ignored. The fact that a society has existed unchanged for a reasonable period of time indicates that it has developed the techniques necessary for its survival. As long as its environment remains unchanged such a society will continue to maintain

9. K. Lewin, "Group Decision and Social Change," in T. Newcomb and E. Hartley, eds., *Readings in Social Psychology* (New York: Henry Holt and Company, 1947), pp. 314–315.

10. M. E. Shaw, "A Comparison of Individuals and Small Groups in the Rational Solution of Complex Problems," *Am. Jour. Psychol.* 44, 1932: 491–504. Also in Newcomb and Hartley, *Readings in Social Psychology*.

11. R. Sobel, "Anxiety-Depression Reactions after Prolonged Combat Experience—The Old Sergeant Syndrome," *Bull. U.S. Army Medical Dept., Combat Psychiatry Supplement* (November 1949): 137–146.

12. G. Murphy, *Personality* (New York: Harper & Brothers, 1947).

13. A static society can survive only in a static environment. For reasons which will appear later it is unlikely that man will ever have such an environment. (He keeps changing it.)

itself, provided that its members continue to play their required roles.[14] But in human societies, even the most ancient of which are now being forced into constant change by the changes in their social and physical surroundings, the survival of the society is often possible only if the members break out of the traditional pattern and abandon their old roles for new ones.

This places us in an uncomfortable dilemma. If we follow the social-role hypothesis we are unable to explain social change or to predict its course or even its direction because social change requires a change in roles, which the theory does not explain. If we adopt the more subtle and inspiring concept of social homeostasis we cannot explain why some societies and groups fail to make the changes required for successful self-maintenance. Neither concept gives us much help in predicting the behavior of specific persons. Neither one explains why new groups are formed or what happens in situations which the social sanctions do not cover. They do not explain why some people disregard the sanctions of their native society to identify with and accept the sanctions of another.

Effective as they may be for other purposes, it does not seem that any of the psychological approaches we have described so far can give a clear picture of human purposes or human value. The physiological theories seem to imply that a society is good to the extent that it produces and distributes the goods necessary for the physical health of its members; but the fact that "psychological" needs have to be invoked to supplement the purely physiological needs indicates that people need something more than the physical necessities of life. It is hard to say just what this is, because the alleged psychological needs are so diverse and conflicting.

The social-determinant theories of behavior give a picture of value which is even more disconcerting because it seems to disregard completely the fate of the individual human being. The successful society, this approach implies, is the society which survives. Whether or not this society satisfies the need or helps fulfill the destiny of human beings in general or of specific persons in particular is not pertinent to this point of view. It is reasonable to suppose that societies will have better chances for survival if their institutions and customs tend to keep their members alive, maintain their loyalty, and attract new adherents. In other words, the successful society must to some extent satisfy human need. But by itself the group approach, whose basic dynamism is the maintenance and extension of the group organization, gives us no inkling about what people need. The basic problem which must be solved before we can understand group dynamics thus turns out to be the problem of basic human values. What is the motivating purpose of human behavior?

14. In insect societies the role is determined by the physical structure and the individual is physically incapable of changing its role. This is, except for some sex roles, not true of human beings.

THE INDIVIDUAL-FIELD APPROACH

At the present time a number of psychologists[15] appear to be more or less independently converging on a purely psychological theory of behavior which is more capable of dealing with the problems of human purpose and human values than the physiological and group approaches we have already discussed. These people do not form a school or group and do not share a formally organized body of theory, so that what follows is only my personal analysis of the general approach. The basic assumptions appear to be these:

1. The behavior of human beings, although it is often not appropriate to the immediate physical environment, is always appropriate to what is variously called the individual's psychological field, behavioral field, private world, assumptive world, perceptual field, or phenomenal field.

   This is the crucial assumption of the approach. Instead of abandoning field dynamics because in the guise of organic homeostasis it is not adequate to explain all behavior, the individual-field psychologists keep the principle and move it to a conceptual causal field where it does work.

   In terms of what we know about living organisms some such field is biologically necessary to animals with distance perception. Among those animals which remain small and live in the water or in a host organism, getting their food by drifting into contact with it or having it drift into contact with them, behavior is purely homeostatic. The only part of the physical environment which affects the animal or its behavior is that part which is in close contact with its surface. Such an animal lives in a behavioral field one molecule thick, and anything nutritive or noxious within that area is automatically dealt with. The individual has no choice of action and all animals of the species would respond in the same way.

   An animal of this kind is unable to perceive food at a distance and move toward it, or to perceive danger at a distance and avoid it. It is completely at the mercy of its environment. If such a species is to survive one of two things has to happen. As one alternative its individual members might develop a high rate of reproduction and enough motility to scatter them so widely that a few, at least, would always

15. I hesitate to name individuals because there are so many, but the following should be listed: in social psychology, G. W. Allport, Cantril, Coutu, Crutchfield, Klee, Krech, Lewin, Murphy, and Sherif; in clinical psychology, Combs, Lecky, Raimy, and Rogers; in education, Hopkins, Kelley, and Woodruff; and in the psychology of economic behavior, Hayes and Katona. The point of view owes much to the work of the Gestalt psychologists, particularly Kohler and Wertheimer; to the writings of L. K. Frank, A. Maslow, and R. H. Wheeler; and to the perceptual studies of Ames, Bruner, Murphy, Postman, and many others. See D. Snygg and A. W. Combs, *Individual Behavior* (New York, Harper & Brothers, 1949).

be blundering into a favorable environment. Or, after developing motility, the individual organism might increase its chances for survival by developing distance perception[16] so that it could perceive food or danger at a distance and behave accordingly. But this presents a new problem. An animal able to perceive objects at a distance is now exposed to stimuli from a tremendous number of food and danger foci. An organism which responded simultaneously to all of the physical stimuli which bombard it from these sources would tear itself to pieces. In order to maintain its organization it must trim the confusing, stunning, incoherent field with which it is now in contact down to manageable size. It has to pick out that part of the physical field which is most important to the maintenance of its own organization at the moment and deal with that, more or less ignoring the rest.[17] This "cut-down" field is the individual (or psychological) field.[18]

One important feature of the "cut-down" psychological field is that it has a time dimension. It includes a past and a future. For the organism whose behavioral world is limited to its immediate surface nothing exists except what is here and now; but the acquisition of distance perception automatically gives the field a time dimension. Food at a distance is not, for the organism, food now. If it is perceived at all as food it is food-in-the-future. As a result of this development great individual differences and apparent irrationalities in behavior begin to appear. The degree of choice required by the simplest type of distance perception results in wide differences between the individual fields of different individuals in the same physical situation.[19] And when an organism like man is able to symbolize and introduce into its psychological field objects and concepts not physically present, the range of possible behavior becomes tremendous. The behavior of individuals would be completely unpredictable if it were not for the next principle.

2. The psychological field is an organized dynamic field. The immediate

16. This would necessitate a larger organism and therefore a slower rate of reproduction.
17. When a man is being chased by a bull he is not likely to notice the mosquitoes.
18. To realize in a small way how few of the stimuli physically present actually get into the individual's perceptual field, listen for the "s" sounds the next time someone speaks to you. They are so prevalent in English that many foreigners think of English as the "hissing language," but English-speaking people rarely hear them. They are too busy listening for the sense of what is being said.
19. The irrationalities are only apparent. Behavior is judged irrational when it is not appropriate to the perceptual field of the observer. The sequence of plays chosen by a quarterback who is trying to coax the defense out of position to set up a breakaway play for a touchdown will appear foolish to a spectator who sees the situation in a shorter time perspective and thinks only in terms of maximum gain on the next down. And the spectator's choices would appear irrational to the quarterback.

purpose of all of an individual's behavior, including his behavior as a perceiver, is the maintenance of organization in his individual field. If the field organization should disintegrate his physical organization could not be maintained.[20] If he loses faith in his perceptions organized behavior becomes impossible.[21]

The meaning and value of perceived objects and events are determined by the individual's field organization at the time. As examples we can take the different meaning and value to an individual of food before and after a heavy meal.[22] Our perceptions seem to follow dynamic-field principles in that events and objects are always interpreted in the way which will require the least change in the field. Suppose, for instance, that a large part of my perceptual field is organized around the belief that a certain man is an enemy. Then on an important occasion he treats me with kindness and generosity. The odds are that I will perceive his behavior as a subtle insult or a deliberate attempt to deceive. If he were unimportant to me, I would be able to change my perception of him as a result of his kind act; bus since his supposed enmity plays an important role in my field organization, it will be easier to distort my perception of his act than to change the rest of my field to conform to the act. Many of the demonstrations devised by Ames and his associates at the Hanover Institute illustrate this principle.

3. The perceptual self is the part of the field which is perceived as behaving. As a result it is the focal part of the field. The only aspects of the cosmos which seem important, indeed the only aspects which can enter the field at all, are those which are related to the self. If the principle of field organization is too abstract to be useful, we can paraphrase it by saying that the immediate purpose of all behavior

20. The nausea of seasickness is a minor example of the breakdown of physical organization which occurs in a disorganized perceptual field. Workers at the Hanover Institute (See H. Cantril, *The "Why" of Man's Experience* (New York, The Macmillan Company, 1950); and E. C. Kelley, *Education for What Is Real* (New York: Harper & Brothers, 1948) report that subjects exposed to perceptual phenomena which they are unable to reconcile with one another frequently become nauseated.

21. Cf. the difficulty of mirror drawing, as a mild example.

22. The economic implications of this illustration are interesting. If the individual is satiated the food has no immediate value to him. In fact it may have a negative value if he has to dispose of it. However, if his field includes a perception of the future as one in which he will want to eat the food or in which he can exchange it for something else which he will want, it will be perceived as having value and he may save it. If he has a pressing immediate problem not relating to food, it is not likely that he will be aware of the food at all. If he has gone through experiences which have caused him to feel that food is always valuable, he may seek it out and eat it or hoard it even if it causes him physical discomfort to do so. Value depends upon the pyschological field of the individual, and concepts of "true value" and "fair price" are psychologically unreal.

is the maintenance of the behaver's perceptual field, particularly of his perceptual self.

This takes care of the probems of marytrdom and suicide, which are inexplicable by physiological principles and, in the case of suicide in our society where it is socially disapproved, by the concept of group role. It is not the physical self but the self-as-perceived, the perceptual self, which we are trying to perserve. A man who has come to think of himself as selfless and devoted to duty or to others will act so as to maintain that perception of himself, even at the expense of his life. There are strong connotations for character education here. A person who has been taught to perceive himself as an outsider will behave like an outsider, with no feeling of responsibility to the group. A person who has been taught to regard himself as a criminal has to maintain and enhance that concept of himself by believing that "only suckers work."

4. Because human beings are aware of the future, at least of its existence and uncertainties, it is not enough to maintain the perceptual self for the present moment. It has to be maintained in the future, built up and enhanced so that the individual feels secure for the future. And since the future is uncertain and unknown, no enhancement of the individual's experience of personal value,[23] no degree of self-actualization, is enough. Human beings are, by nature, insatiable. This should be an important point for the economists.

   The ideal sought is a state in which the individual feels so much in harmony with the universe, so much a part of it, that he does not have to defend himself against any other part.[24]

Ways of Satisfying Need

Seen in this way, the many conflicting physiological and psychological "needs" which were discussed earlier turn out to be alternative ways of satisfying the individual's basic need for enhancement of his experience of personal worth and value. A more convenient classification of these alternative ways of satisfying need is given below. Since behavior is always determined by the individual field of the behaver, the method used by any individual in any situation will be one which is appropriate to

23. Terminology modified from H. Cantril, *The "Why" of Man's Experience.* (New York: Macmillan, 1950).

24. It is significant that this state is said to have been achieved, at least in moments of ecstasy, by some of the saints. It probably involves the perception of the universe as one completely pervaded with infinite love and compassion for all living things. From this point of view the higher religions represent man's greatest insight in their recognition of the ultimate goal of human endeavor and their audacious attempt to move directly toward it.

his perceptions of himself and of the external situation at that particular time.[25]

Means of Maintaining and Enhancing the Self

A. Change in body state leading to change in the perceptions of the self.

1. Restoration of the body balance by eating, breathing, elimination, rest, etc.
2. Blocking off organic sensations of failure, pain, or tensions indicative of personal inadequacies by the use of alcohol or drugs.
3. Elicitation of an organic mobilization and increase in body strength by entering a dangerous or irritating situation; speeding, gambling,[26] etc.

B. Self-reassurance by demonstration of mastery, control, or superiority.

1. Over people: Competition leading to victory over worthy opposition.[27] Other demonstrations of superiority by gossip, practical joking, scapegoating, making gifts, etc.
2. Demonstration of control over material objects.
   a. Creative. Doodling to art.
   b. Destructive. Nailbiting to vandalism.[28]
3. Accumulation of property, hoarding.

C. Reassurance and enhancement by association and identification with respected individuals and groups. Evidence of respect and love by respected persons. Feeling of identity with a great cause, of being part of a great movement.

D. By change in the nonself part of the field which places the self in a less threatened position.

25. This concept is capable of bringing back the group role in a new form. It is now the individual's concept of what is required to maintain his picture of himself as a member of the group. If he does not perceive himself as a true member of the group his obligations, not being recognized, will have to be enforced, if at all, by police action. In a growing society the members seek and embrace their roles as means of self-enhancement. That is the reason the society is growing. This point of view supports Toynbee's hypothesis that a society whose members have to be held to their posts by coercion is disintegrating.
26. Gambling also provides foundations for more convincing daydreams (D2).
27. Even if the individual is defeated he has enhancement through increase in body strength during the competition.
28. Creative activities provide more permanent symbols of self-value than destructive activities, but they usually take longer and require more skill. Destructive acts therefore are more apt to be committed by an immature person or a person under great stress provided that they are not inconsistent with the perceptual self he is trying to enhance.

1. By change in the physical environment. Travel, moving, redecorating, etc.
2. By daydreaming or fantasy, including that done by professionals. Radio, television, theater, fiction, etc.[29]

The Basis of Human Values

Looking at the problem of value from this point of view we can come to the following conclusions:

1. The basic goal of all individuals is for a feeling of increased worth, of greater value.
2. This goal is never completely reached. Given one success, one degree of self-enhancement, human beings will always aspire to more.
3. Satisfaction of the need for greater personal value can be and is sought in a number of alternative ways. Goods and experiences are of value to the individual only as they contribute to the feeling of personal worth.

We are now in a position to make some judgments about values. Since the individual can strive, with some success, for self-enhancement in a number of different ways, no single way is indispensable.[30]

THE SPECIAL STATUS OF ECONOMIC ACTIVITY

Although economic activity is only one of many ways by which the individual strives for an increased feeling of worth, value, and belonging, it is likely to demand a major portion of his time and attention. *Economic activity* takes a great deal of time because it is concerned with the control of "scarce" goods, that is, with materials and services that

29. Many activities help to satisfy the need for enhancement in several ways. The most satisfying sex experiences associate means A and C. Cigarette smoking, particularly for smokers who inhale, supplies a tissue irritant which causes a rise in blood pressure and an increase in heartbeat and amount of blood sugar (A2 and A3). The smoker also secures reassurance from manipulating an object and blowing smoke (B2). (Many smokers report that they get less pleasure from smoking in the dark.) He may also use smoking as a way of demonstrating membership in social groups (C) and gain a feeling of value by offering cigarettes and matches to people without them. It is small wonder that so many millions of dollars a year are spent for tobacco.

30. The only qualification is that if the individual fails to use the methods for seeking enhancement which also result in maintaining the body balance, he will die. As a usual thing he will use such methods because any marked physical disorganization results in such a change in the psychological field. See F. A. Beach, "Body Chemistry and Perception," in R. R. Blake and G. V. Ramsey, *Perception and Approach to Personality* (New York, Ronald Press, 1951) that the individual does act so as to restore the body balance. But this is not always the case.

require conscious effort to get. Many of the scarce materials would be helpful to their possessor even if they were not scarce. Food and clothing, for instance, may be used to maintain or restore the body balance and increase the consumer's perception of body strength. An automobile may be used to increase the driver's feeling of power and value, by helping him to earn his living, or by giving him a chance to exhibit skill and good judgment or daring. But objects or services do not have to be useful in such a direct fashion to be valuable. Scarcity alone can make an object valuable because the mere possession of a scarce object, provided it is sought by others, can be a constant and reassuring symbol of dignity, worth, and power. Air is necessary for self-maintenance but no one will derive the fullest possible satisfaction from air until it is bottled under expensive brand names and sold at such high prices that the consumers (and hoarders) are impressed by their own wealth, extravagance, and good taste. As things stand now we do a great deal of breathing but devote little attention to it. Since air is not scarce, breathing ordinarily presents no problems and therefore no opportunity for self-enhancement by overcoming obstacles.

At a social level in which the minimal physical necessities are so easily obtained that their possession arouses no pride, a great deal of time may be devoted to the economic struggle for such symbols of worth as modern kitchen equipment, antique (or ultramodern) furniture, mink coats, or a private office with its own water cooler, any of which would lose much of their value if they became more plentiful or if people quit competing for them. As long as such objects are scarce, it takes quite a bit of effort and ability or power to get them. As a result they have come to be, in the eyes of many, reassuring symbols of self-worth and status. Such people will sacrifice a great deal to get them. Superficially each individual has a large number of alternative symbolic goals available, but actually he can strive with hope and satisfaction only for the goals which are appropriate to his concept of himself and the situation. Failure to achieve the goals by which he has chosen to measure himself results in humiliation and anguish, which are not lessened by his power to achieve other ends which are not appropriate to his self-concept and are therefore not regarded as enhancing.[31]

31. This gives additional importance to money or liquid assets whose possession appears to give assurance of ability to reach goals the individual has not yet thought of. The accumulation of money can thus become an important goal in itself.

At the present time, however, the relative importance of this goal is probably declining due to inflation, high income taxes, and the divorce of ownership from control in the large corporations. In this type of organization the distinction between economic and political activities becomes very thin, as the struggle is not only for scarce objects but for scarce titles and positions, an increasing number of which require such special technical skills that their acquisition by outright purchase would be regarded as unethical.

The Psychological Function of Trade

This point of view, if it should come to be accepted as common sense, would lead to a better appreciation of the role played by the businessman in the production of values. It is sometimes assumed that value is an intrinsic property of the object and that anyone who buys an object for less than that value gets a bargain and anyone who pays more is a loser. This leads to the belief that neither the buyer nor the seller has produced anything. A business transaction, from this point of view, is a contest between two parties each of whom is trying to victimize the other by buying goods for less or selling them for more than their intrinsic worth. From this point of view business is attempted cheating and the model transaction is the purchase of Manhattan Island from the Indians.

From the individual-field point of view, however, both parties to a transaction may, and usually do, profit from it. Objects are valuable to people if they assist them in the satisfaction of their individual need for self-maintenance and enhancement. Since different people strive for satisfaction of this need in different ways, objects and experiences will have different values for different people, and both parties to an exchange which is free from coercion can be expected to profit by it. A model transaction, from this point of view, might be one between a starving man with a keg of water and a man suffering from thirst who has a surplus of food.

The Process of Choice

This approach also provides a conceptual framework for dealing with the process of choice. Lacking such a framework, economists have had to assume that anyone's choice of goals is perfectly free, limited only by the possibilities of the physical environment. In any actual situation the choice is much more narrowly limited since in order to be chosen an object or experience has to be perceived as a means by which the individual can approach closer to his goal. What will be chosen is thus determined by the nature and organization of the chooser's field at the instant of choice. People in the same physical situation will make different choices because they have different goals, or because they are in different stages of their progress toward their goals, or for a number of other reasons. A person under strong pressure, for instance, is likely to concentrate so strongly on his immediate goal that he will fail to perceive opportunities to by-pass it when they occur. When he feels threatened by intense and immediate loss of self-respect, the future aspects of his private field fade into the background and he acts "without foresight."

There is reason to believe that what people call "foresight" is related to the individual's concept of himself. The person who feels relatively secure in his feelings of personal worth does not need to concentrate so completely on the immediate problem and therefore has a better chance to see it in a broad perspective.

All of this seems to negate another assumption frequently made by economists, which is that the chooser is a completely rational and highly informed being capable of action in his own best interests.[32]

SELF–INTEREST AND ALTRUISM

The fact that man is potentially able to strive for satisfaction of need in many different ways gives us an answer to an important question, which may be stated in two different ways:

"Is man naturally good or evil?" or "Is man essentially altruistic or essentially selfish?"

Since we believe that a man's behavior may be either good or evil, it seems to follow that a good society will help and encourage him to strive for enhancement in ways which further not only his own experience of personal value but the value experiences of others as well. The self-enhancement which accrues from an experience of being needed, from feeling part of a great movement, from contributing to something nobler and more important than our own lives, is just as natural and probably more lasting than the self-enhancement gained through successful aggression. In the long run it is better for the individual himself if he uses the socially desirable ways of seeking enhancement because such methods are not so apt to incite other people to thwart and resist him. There is no necessary conflict between the basic aspirations of the individual and the basic aspirations of others. There is no inevitable conflict between the individual and society.

Failure of Identification with Others

Let us consider, however, one way in which man may fall into antihuman behavior. The person who does not feel part of a social group will not behave as a member of the group. Even though a concept of himself as a just or honorable man may keep him from consciously self-seeking behavior at the expense of the people with whom he does not identify, his feelings and, as a result, his behavior toward them will be essentially

32. Advertisers know better and so do economists, but they have been forced into this position by a dearth of psychological knowledge. Since the psychologists have not furnished the kind of information about people that the economists have needed, the economists have had to go ahead and predict what a simplified hypothetical man would do.

selfish. Since the organization of our individual field is largely determined by our own need for a feeling of self-worth, it is easy for such a "good citizen" who does not feel one with his victims to commit great acts of aggression against people "for their own good" or in the name of justice, of patriotism, of economic law, or of preservation of the faith, and to do it in all sincerity and with a great feeling of rectitude. Law and ethics can help prevent injustice that we can recognize, but the best insurance against injustice is complete identification with the potential victim so that injury to the victim is injury to the self. The man who loves his neighbor as himself has not abandoned self-interest. He still seeks for self-maintenance and enhancement, but his self now includes his neighbor.

Identification with Others as the Basis of Ethics

It is on this base that human ethics seem to have developed best. It is true that on logical grounds it is to almost everyone's advantage to work together on the basis of "You scratch my back and I'll scratch yours." But attempts to explain existing systems of ethics or create new ones on the basis of enlightened self-interest seem to be psychologically unrealistic. For a society to survive it must receive from some of its members sacrifices, sometimes of their lives, for which it cannot compensate them in a material sense. A system of ethics based on *quid pro quo* could in no way command the degree of self-sacrifice required and secured in all societies. This self-sacrifice seems to be a manifestation of identification, love and faith in something more important than our own lives.

There is a growing feeling among psychologists that self-acceptance is necessary before we can accept or love others. Rogers[33] has concluded on the basis of his clinical experience and research that a person who feels so threatened that he is preoccupied with the necessity for defending himself has little sympathy to give to others. Murphy[34] believes that to love others we have to love (accept) ourselves first.

The degree to which men can attain brotherhood with all men is still unknown. Professor Emerson,[35] looking at the problem against the background of millions of years of biological development, sees it as a goal

33. C. R. Rogers, *Client-Centered Therapy* (Boston: Houghton-Mifflin, 1951). See also A. H. Maslow, "Self-Actualizing People: A Study in Psychological Health," *Personality Symposia* 39 (1); *Values in Personality Research,* W. Wolff, ed. (New York: Grune and Stratton, 1950).
34. G. Murphy, *Personality.*
35. Chapter 10.

which is almost assured. From a psychological point of view it does not seem impossible, given enough time. Man is certainly not averse to identifying himself with others. But he tends to identify most completely with comparatively small groups, probably because he can more clearly perceive his value to such a group.

The greatest obstacle in the way of universal brotherhood at the present time is not man's unregenerate selfishness and individualism. It is the fact that to give their lives meaning and dignity the people of the world have identified themselves with a great number of conflicting groups and causes for which many of them are prepared to sacrifice themselves *and others.*

Limitations of Individual Experience

It is not yet safe to assume that the process of identification with larger and larger groups can go on indefinitely. The individual field is at best only a limited version of reality, and as the group becomes larger and more complex it is more and more difficult for the individual to perceive his value and function in it and consequently to seek identification with it. Education can help; but no matter how highly educated we are, there are physiological and psychological limits to our ability to comprehend and identify with a complex society and many people in our society may already have approached those limits. There is something suspicious about the way one civilization after another gets to the point where there is a high degree of interdependence between people who are not personally acquainted and then goes into a decline.

Even if we should succeed in getting a better conception of our relation to others, the resulting feeling of brotherhood might be disappointingly mild. The "cut-down" nature of the perceptual field makes it impossible for us ever to achieve as warm a feeling of identification with all as we now have with some. The more people we identify with, the less time and interest we can give to each. It may follow that a man who loves all of mankind equally will not love any one person much.

This brings us to the second source of evil in human nature. It lies in our inability to recognize or accept the limited nature of our perceptual fields. As has been pointed out earlier, the individual's personal field is a limited and often distorted version of reality. Nevertheless, it is the only version he has and he has to trust it. This naïve assurance that our private experience is a valid representation of reality is dangerous. It breeds atrocities. Most of the great enormities of human history have been committed in the name of what the perpetrators believed to be noble causes. They would have been ashamed to commit such atrocities for purely selfish reasons.[36]

There is no reason to suppose that human beings will ever become omniscient, so this source of evil seems certain to remain with us permanently. However, there are reasons for believing that its effects may be alleviated. In a society of people better able to accept themselves and therefore better able to accept others, there would be a greater respect for and acceptance of the corrective insights of others and less disposition to seize on a worthy cause as an excuse for aggression against others.

COMPARISONS BETWEEN SOCIETIES

Since there are many ways in which people can secure some degree of self-actualization, it is reasonable to suppose that there can be many different "good" societies. However, if we judge a society by its contribution to the value experience of individual human beings, a society is good to the extent that it enables its members and neighbors to live with health, security, self-respect, and dignity. It is good to the extent that it enables its members and neighbors to feel adequate to live with reality and, in consequence, to perceive it without distortion. Such a society will institutionalize and encourage techniques of production and cooperation among its members. Each member will have "an opportunity to work, to feel personally successful, and to sacrifice for some cause which to him is important. Each person must have opportunity to feel that his life has meaning, importance, and purpose." [37] Such a society will be continually changing. "No successes and no recognition can be enough to give anyone the permanent feeling of adequacy and self-assurance that he needs. Further achievement and growth are always necessary. As a result no society which attempts to remain static can adequately satisfy the needs of its members. A 'good society' must provide its members with opportunities for self-enhancement by pioneering in new fields and at ever more difficult problems." [38]

36. Compare the mannered observance of the "laws of war" in the admittedly selfish dynastic wars of the eighteenth century with the savagery and ferocity of the religious wars of the sixteenth and seventeenth centuries and the "wars for humanity" of the twentieth.
37. D. Snygg and A. W. Combs, *Individual Behavior* (New York: Harper & Brothers, 1949), p. 200.
38. Ibid. To the writer the approach which has been described seems to argue against the planned society, particularly if the goal of that society is a static state of perfection. It seems to be a valid corollary of the individual-field approach that planning for other people is ineffective because each has his own individual organization of values and goals which are relatively unrecognized by others. In addition planning by a few for the many is sure to be less realistic than the active explorations of the many because it is based on fewer points of view about nature

From this point of view there is nothing inevitable about the direction of social change. The Marxist ideas of inevitable communism and the Greek idea of inevitable cycles, both of which seem to have been based on the short-time trends of a single civilization, are equally mistaken. No two societies develop in exactly the same direction because when a "hitch" develops in a society the possibilities for solving it are limited by the character of its individual members and the potentialities of its physical and social environment. These differ in all societies.

In human societies, particularly in civilizations, people are constantly pushing against the frontiers for better ways of satisfying their individual need. Sometimes (frequently in our own society) such a push [39] is so successfull that it opens up a whole new field of possibilities and problems and creates a crisis because the society has no established practice for dealing with them. In such a situation, with social precedents vague or absent, each member of the society has to make his own decision and in doing so he helps to change his society for the better or for the worse. This is a ticklish moment because there are opportunities for disaster if the attempted solutions are based on false analogies with problems which have already been solved or if they are otherwise based on false concepts of reality. In our own society an increasingly large proportion of our problems have to do with people both in our society and outside of it. In this situation erroneous concepts of human nature are particularly dangerous.

---

and about people. Planning by a few in authority is especially dangerous because by reason of their authority and responsibilities they are certain to have developed goals and aspirations not shared by the other members of the society. The result is, all too often, a solution which does not win cooperation and which has to be enforced, if at all, by force, thus splitting the society and destroying its unity.

39. The temper tantrums of a baby and the discovery of nuclear energy both represent such pushes. One difference is that our society has already developed techniques for dealing with temper tantrums.

Human Life Goals in the Humanistic Perspective

CHARLOTTE BUHLER

INTRODUCTION

With the psychologists' attention having been concentrated for some time entirely on the need aspect of human motivation, the goal aspect has been almost completely neglected. Yet psychologists are beginning to realize the great importance of this aspect, especially within the frame of reference of psychotherapy. "All I hear is questions about goals," a psychoanalytically-oriented therapist said in a recent discussion in admitting that the handling of goals and values was an unresolved problem.

Research related to goals has been scarce and haphazard. There is no systematic description nor theory of the constituent and contributory *factors* to goalsetting.

From Narziss Ach's studies (1905) on "determining tendencies" at the beginning of this centruy, over Kurt Lewin's (1926) "aspiration levels," to more recent studies of decision making, of achievement, and of success, we have investigations of special aspects of goalsetting. Development aspects of goalsetting were discussed by the author (1962) in a study on "Genetic Aspects of the Self." Goal patterns of healthy, essentially happy, and effective individuals were demonstrated by A. Maslow (1954), while H. Otto (1963) found, on the other hand, that the majority of people who answered his questionnaire on personality strength and personal resources had never given any thought or time to an assessment or evaluation of their potentialities. In accordance with this, I find in my therapy groups that very few of these people chose careers or entered

This paper was read as the Presidential Address at the Fourth Annual Convention of the American Association for Humanistic Psychology in New York, 1966. Reprinted from *Journal of Humanistic Psychology* (Spring 1967): 36–52, by permission of the author and the publisher.

personal relationships under the aspect of their own potentialities or their self-actualization.

Everett Shostrom (1963) found, while standardizing his "Inventory for the Measurement of Self-Actualization," that the most self-actualizing person is the one who "is able to tie the past and the future to the present in meaningful continuity." His study throws some light on the healthy and unhealthy relationships of the individual to time.

But little is known about the continuity of pursuits of those who, in the end, found their lives to be fulfilled as against those who ended in failure. In fact, we know the barest minimum about what people seek in life and what they do with themselves. The whole field is full of speculation.

While this address cannot be the occasion for a systematic investigation of all factors entering goalsetting, I want to point to certain behavioral as well as experiential patterns which in the developmental progression seem to indicate advance in goalsetting. The twelve points which I will discuss are considered very tentative formulations and are not claimed to be final nor necessarily complete. The organizing principle for the twelve points is *developmental;* that is to say, I will enumerate them as I see them coming up in the individual's development.

ACTIVITY

The first behavior contributing to and involving, already from the start, certain characteristics of the individual's goalsetting is the *activity* with which the individual begins his existence even in the prenatal stage.

As Eiduson, Eiduson, & Geller (1962) establish in a careful survey of the most recent literature, the individual starts with a given genetic setup acting in and on a given environment. While this environment's influence becomes immediately a co-determinant of the individual's behavior, there is from the start selectivity in the way the individual responds to all given stimuli.

Some interesting details may be mentioned briefly with respect to the nature of the individual's primary activity.

This primary activity is known to occur in different *levels,* as M. Fries (1953) called it. She distinguished five activity levels, starting from very passive up to overactive behavior. Also some very recent observers, Thomas *et al.* (1963), establish consistency in the infant's activity level.

The activity level seems more or less coordinated with passivity and aggressiveness of approach. This passivity and aggressiveness is seen by L. W. Sontag (1950) as representing the infant's earliest approaches to working out the basic problem of dependency versus independence. This implies a very important assumption: namely, that the natural tendency to be passive or aggressive predisposes the baby, from birth on, to two fundamentally opposed human relationships. They are the *acceptance of dependency* or the *struggle for independence*. Of course, it must be said at once that passivity and aggressiveness could not possibly be the sole determinants of dependent or independent behavior, nor are passivity and aggressiveness themselves completely unalterable. But within limits, Sontag's theory, for which he brings considerable experimental evidence from the Fels Institute's research projects, impresses this writer as sound. Kagan & Moss (1962) pursued this Fels Institute research study on a longitudinal range from infancy into adulthood. They found that the continuity of the previously mentioned traits was later influenced by the individual's sex role standard.

Another characteristic of the infant's primary activity is what the writer (1958) called degrees of curiosity or lack of it, and what Thomas *et al.* (1963) establish as consistently accepting or rejecting responses to new stimuli and experiences. In this we can see roots of later preferences for adventure as against preference for familiar situations. Also creativity and non-creativity—the interest in, or lack of interest in, discovering and doing something new—may have here one of its roots.

SELECTIVE PERCEPTION

The second behavior, contributing also from the start to the individual's later goalsetting, is his selective perception.

Sensory perception, which begins in the intrauterine life, is for quite some time partly vague, partly very specified, and becomes only gradually organized. R. Spitz (1965) has, in continuing our earlier Viennese research, brought systematic evidence for the way in which the awareness of an object is gradually built up during the first year of life.

All during this process, the infant responds in a very individual way to the world of stimuli that he perceives. His responsiveness is selective from the start, as is now widely acknowledged. Stirnimann (1940) brings comprehensive data proving this selectivity. Tinbergen (1948) speaks of an "innate perceptual pattern." Hilgard (1951) speaks of the pursuit of "innate preferences."

Apart from preferences, there are also such individual features as degrees of sensitivity in response to environmental stimuli. Hypersensitivity is one of the most generally acknowledged inborn characteristics. The vulnerability of the hypersensitive child is one of those conditions which are apt to induce neurotic development.

To what degree and in what way goalsetting is linked up with perception first, and later with imagery or phantasy, is still undecided. Undoubtedly when a person decides to get an orange out of his refrigerator, he must focus his imagination on an object which he knows from his perception.

But when a person has a vague urge for some activity—he may have imagined only vaguely one or another situation—he may fantasize about it, but the main thing in him may be this urge and a variety of feelings. In the creative process, as described by some writers and musicians, there may be a phase in which fleeting images pass through the mind in colors and in a variety of feelings.

There we find a selective imagination brought to life under the directive of an active mind which sets and pursues a goal.

In the two, the ability of *directive activity,* operating in unison with a *selective perception and imagination,* I see the core of the person or the individual's "rudimentary self." With this I mean the beginning of a system of purposeful behavior in the direction of the development of the individual's own potentials.

REACTIONS TO CARE AND CONTACT

A basic goal, from the start, is *psychophysical needs.* However, this satisfaction seems only to be beneficial if brought about in what R. Spitz (1965) called the right "emotional climate." This emotional climate depends on the type of personal care which the mother or her substitute gives to the infant. While subconsciously so, the infant's need seems to be for psychophysical satisfactions received in an atmosphere of love and care. This shows us from the beginning an unconscious intent in the direction of human closeness.

There is more proof of that. We know that as early as from about three to six weeks on, the infant responds with a smile to another person's smile and that it initiates sounds. Piaget (1951) observed, the same as I did, a behavior which must be called "strenuous efforts" at imitating sounds and mouth movements. Here we find rudimentary stages of understanding and of identification.

Thus the earliest tendency to need-satisfaction is, from the start, one in which not only satiation is wanted, but care as well as contact.

WILL, CONSCIENCE, IDENTITY

The fourth behavior contributing to goalsetting becomes conscious in the experiences: *I want.* This getting into conflicts with the experiences, *I must, I should,* results in the two to four-year-old child's first inquiry into *who am I?*—an inquiry which from then on will plague the individual sometimes far into his adulthood or even all through his life.

In his first "I want to" behavior, the child is quite arbitrary regarding his objective. He may say "yes" and "no" in short succession to the same offer or request. He tries out how it feels to make choices and decisions of his own. And he discovers himself, if allowed by his environment, as a person in his own right.

Here, then, is where the autonomous ego is set up, and where the child begins to discover his own self and the possibility of giving himself a direction of his own. Erikson (1959) speaks of the happenings of this period as of the "battle for autonomy."

But clinical studies show more recently how very individually different this period is being experienced. There are some children who, while having tantrums and resisting their environment, do not really set up goals of their own. They just fight submission, but remain in the end just as dependent on their environment as they were before. All they want to do is to be opposite of what their environment wants.

Some of my patients who are now in their thirties or forties, or even older, remember that all they ever wanted was to do the opposite of what was suggested to them. This, then, is the beginning of a completely neurotic self-determination. There are children who are set on neurotic love relationships with a parent and who do not want autonomy but possessive domination.

Besides this neurotic outcome of the battle for autonomy, there are also healthy solutions. Partly depending on the specific environment, partly on the child, the outcome may be a voluntary submission and identification with the adults' goals.

The opposite type, the child with much of a creative potential, begins at this point with his first attempts toward self-realization. The more or less creative child will, in this period, already have ideas of his own of how to set up his identity. This child may feel that she does not want to be like her mother, but like her aunt, whom she admires; or she may want to do things as the neighbor lady does, who can teach her something she wants to learn (Buhler, 1962a).

These tentative early goals show us beginnings of the child's conscious attempts to identify with certain persons and with certain objectives in the humanistic perspective of values.

These first goals may have to do with aptitudes or with moral considerations, "Is he a good boy or is he a bad boy?" asks Peter, two, in talking thoughtfully to himself. "No, he is a bad boy," he concludes with a certain glee. Peter is too young to even speak of himself as "I," yet already conceives of a moral goal for himself. Of course, all this is partly playful, but still it is astonishing how many valid, lasting decisions are being made in this period.

Besides evaluation and identification there is, however, something more to be noted. Vacillating in their directives as these children's self-expression may be, there is definitely the evidence of a degree of intentionality in them. They are not yet sure what exactly they want or should do with themselves, but they know vaguely there is something to be realized in some distant future.

If we jump from this age to the young adolescents whom Getzels & Jackson (1962) examined, we find a fully established self-awareness and dependently conforming or independently self-responsible identities. In this excellent study of "Creativity and Intelligence," we meet adolescents during their high school years who have very clear ideas about themselves.

There are those like Mary, a high IQ but non-creative girl, who has a positive image of her family and who states in her autobiography that she has "internalized" her mother's ideas and is very close to her (p. 163).

And these are those who, like John, declare, "If I could achieve one thing during my lifetime, I would want it to be 'independence.' "

And his equally original sister, Joan, says, "that, although she thinks of her parents as being pleasant enough, she has no intention of identifying with them. As to her mother, she feels that she need only make an assertive statement on the question of identification: 'When they try to get me to be like my mother, I . . . tell them that I am me.' And that is that" (p. 191).

These identity concepts go along with elaborate self-evaluations. Here we see the beginnings of certain features of long-range goalsetting.

The cases of this study will also serve as examples for the next factor determining goalsetting. That is the factor of potentialities in terms of abilities and aptitudes.

MASTERY

The experience in this area begins with "I can" or "I cannot."

I agree with Lois Murphy (1962) that this "I can" or "I cannot" belongs to the earliest experiences of infancy. This four- to five-month-old baby who swings his rattle under good control, as against that one who hits himself or loses hold of the rattle—this $1\frac{1}{2}$-year-old who successfully puts one block on the other so that it stands, as against that child whose towers always tumble before they are finished—of course these babies do not have a conscious awareness of their being able or unable to master these materials, but semiconsciously they have first realizations of success and of failure. Proofs of this are the happy smiles of the one and the unhappy rages of the other. Observations of the despair and helplessness of these failing children have been made thus far only in an incidental way. They are usually children with brain injuries or childhood schizophrenia, children who are uncoordinated and unintegrated.

Experiences in coping and in mastery contribute essentially to the setting up of a child's personality, as L. Murphy showed (1962) in her extensive observations.

Already, then, the more adaptively and the more creatively coping individual can be distinguished. This difference becomes very pronounced in Getzels & Jackson's studies (1962). And here we already see some distinctive characteristics of life goals.

In these well-known studies of creative versus highly intelligent, non-creative high school students, great pains were taken to establish all relevant variables that could codetermine the subjects' behavior.

The findings show us the creative and the high-achievement though non-creative type associated with different motivational patterns. The non-creative, moving toward conventional standards and conforming with what is expected of them, show themselves in dependency relationships with their environment. The creative group, on the other hand, who move away from models provided by teachers and who seek out careers that do not conform with what is expected of them, show themselves in independence relationships with their environment.

There are further related results regarding the social and moral orientation of these two groups. While both groups participate in activities that are expected and approved by the social order, the adaptive, non-creative group tends more to be what one usually calls socially "adjusted." They are "insiders"; they seem

> to prefer social interaction to individual achievement, to seek experiences that are immediately enjoyable as against those that promise more remote gratification, to find more satisfaction in experiencing with others than in asserting their own autonomy, to be willing to sacrifice moral commitment in the interest of interpersonal harmony (p. 159).

The highly creative show the reverse of these trends. They tend to be "outsiders" and stand up individualistically for highly moral principles.

All the described findings are suggestive of different innate tendencies of these two groups. But the possible role of environmental influence is not neglected by Getzels & Jackson ". . . irrespective of the possible role of genetic factors." To quote them further: The findings in this direction are that the high-IQ family "is one in which individual divergence is limited and risks minimized, and the overall impression of the high-creativity family is that it is one in which individual divergence is permitted and risks are accepted" (p. 76).

The cautious conclusion from all these findings would be that in his eventual goal structure and goal development, an individual's inherent tendencies to be more creative and independent or more non-creative and dependent are codetermined by the environment's goals and values. These enhance that "openness to experiences" and that willingness to take risks which were found in the creative child, as they also enhance that orientation toward security and success which are found in the non-creative child.

The question of how the child who is not creative and not so adaptive as the family might expect will fare under these influences has not as yet been established in correspondingly thorough studies.

But from other studies, such as B. Eiduson's (1962) investigation on "Scientists," we gather how extremely complicated the picture becomes, as soon as the dynamics of very different individual lives are compared.

CONSTRUCTIVENESS AND DESTRUCTIVENESS

From the beginning, the infant is under the impact of his environment. Parents, siblings, peers, and other persons contribute essentially to the child's goalsetting by information, guidance, and by all social relationships that are being established. We already mentioned dependency and independence. But apart from these, there is a host of feelings of love and fear, of frustration and hostility, of acceptance, security—or the opposite—of belonging or being a loner and an outsider, of rivalry and jealousy, of submission and domination, of cooperation and opposition, friendships and crushes, and many more.

Apart from the impact which the child receives from his environment, he becomes increasingly aware of how the others—his elders and his peers—are handling themselves and their affairs. He begins to interpret their intents, their selfishness or their kindness. In responding to them and in coping with them, their demands, their rebuffs, their beatings, the eight- to twelve-year child develops ideas, methods, and directions of his own. He becomes an essentially constructive person who handles himself and his social relationships in the direction of goals that benefit him and others, as against the essentially destructive person, who is full of hostilities and whose mind is set on damaging others or even himself.

In introducing the concepts of constructiveness and destructiveness, I want to emphasize that I think of them as complex motivational patterns. Constructiveness is not a simple entity such as activity, but a complex unit, such as achievement. There may be the instinctual element of building in it. But constructiveness and destructiveness, as understood here, are developed under the influence of a person's interaction with his environment. Everybody probably harbors both constructive as well as destructive attitudes. But similar to the achievement attitude, constructiveness or destructiveness may under circumstances be all-pervasive.

Studies on this aspect of constructiveness or destructiveness as basic attitudes to life are not as yet available. Fritz Redl & David Wineman's (1951) studies on "Children Who Hate" come the closest to it in describing and analyzing an all-pervasive destructiveness of a group of pre-adolescent youngsters.

The definition of the term constructiveness would be that this is the basic orientation of a person who tries to work out things for himself and for others in such a way that there is a beneficial result. Beneficial might be a result that gives pleasure or is helpful or educational or contributory to any kind of growth and development. The opposite orientation of destructiveness is that of persons who harbor much hostility and who try to damage others or themselves. Such damaging might be consciously, or unconsciously, planned and might range from preventing happiness and success of others, or oneself, to actually trying to injure, to ruin, to eliminate people.

Harmful aggression with a destructive intent may be observed even in nursery school children. As a basic attitude of malevolence, it seems to begin to dominate a child from about eight to ten or twelve years on, the age in which some of the conflicts between children and their parents culminate.

In criminal adolescents and adults there is often evidence of a predominant orientation toward destructiveness.

At this point, the two basic goals, to be constructive or to be destructive, can only be introduced as concepts with the hope of later availability of appropriate evidence.

ACHIEVEMENT MOTIVATION

In this period, all foregoing experiences of being able to master things and being successful against failures converge to generate an individual attitude to and concept of achievement. The idea of achievement as a goal has by then become more or less clearly established in the child's mind. Many factors contribute to how it is being conceived by the individual.

In the studies of D. McClelland and his collaborators (1953), the enormous impact of the parental attitude to achievement has not only been established, but also analyzed in its various characteristics.

Achievement styles are established which often remain the same all through life, styles in terms of work habits, of dependence or independence in goalsetting, orientation toward success or failure, and, particularly, attitudes to values and beliefs.

Evidence as accumulated by the McClelland group, by Getzels & Jackson (1962), by Eiduson (1962), by Goertzel & Goertzel (1962), show attitudes to achievement in their consistency and show them almost always linked up with beliefs and values.

BELIEFS AND VALUES

In the eight- to twelve-year-old period, in which a child begins to have some overview over his various personal relationships as well as his competence in life, he consolidates beliefs and values for himself. The constructive or destructive attitudes which he starts building, result from the experiences and evaluations which crystallize now to opinions and convictions. Eight- to twelve-year-old children often debate with others or with themselves issues such as honesty, fairness, popularity, power, being important, being accomplished, and being the best in everything.

In these beliefs and values, the growing child establishes ordering principles for himself. Like some other goal-determining principles which we see at work from the start—namely, need-satisfaction, self-limiting adaptation, creative expansion—the ordering principle is also noticeable from the infant's first attempts at coordination and organization on. I consider all these as basic tendencies and call this last one *tendency to the upholding of the internal order* (C. Buhler, 1959).

LOVE AND OTHER COMMITTING RELATIONSHIPS

We said previously that, from the beginning, the infant's need-satisfaction depends on care given within the framework of a warm, human relationship. Very early in life the infant not only responds to the "emotional climate" which the adult creates, but he also strains himself toward a contact of understanding.

In adolescence, two new goals of human relationships are discovered and aspired. They are intimacy and commitments. Healthy intimacy and commitments may be defined as freely chosen bonds. Their free choice distinguishes them from unfree dependency on the one hand, while on the other hand they represent a voluntary reduction of independence.

Intimacy and commitment in a sex and love-relationship, if shared by both partners, develop it beyond functional enjoyment to something new: namely, the ecstatic experience of a unity. The goal of achieving this is, as everybody knows, one of the, if not *the* most essential, life goals of the maturing person.

Maslow cites it among his peak experiences. Also psychoanalysis recognizes in this a new step in the development of object relations. It is called the development of genitality. "Genitality," says Erikson (1959,

p. 96), "is the potential capacity to develop orgastic potency in relation to a loved partner of the opposite sex."

This sex-love unity is probably the most essential of the uniting experiences and goals of the person willing to commit himself, to give and to share. But in the same period, commitments to friends, to groups, to causes, become also freely chosen goals. These commitments bring the beliefs which the eight- to twelve-year-old child began to conceive of, into the sphere of reality.

The development in this whole area is, as we all know, full of problems and perils for the majority of youths. The degree to which they want to allow themselves the pleasure of sexual excitement is one of their problems. The finding of and commitment to a love-partner is a second, the accomplishment of self-dedication through intercourse a third. And the question to what degree these goals may preoccupy them in comparison with achievement goals and with the dedication to groups and causes is perhaps the most difficult to resolve. The pursuit of sexual and other pleasureable excitements easily becomes, for the adolescent, a goal which conflicts with other goals of life, especially achievement goals.

A great deal of conflict concerning the hierarchy of the different values that were developed up to this point is practically unavoidable. A hierarchical order and integration of all the directions which we encountered up to now is a task of younger adulthood, if not of the rest of life.

INTEGRATION

We mentioned the word integration. All during childhood and adolescence, we saw goalsetting being developed in various and increasing directions. In this development, several factors are obviously of decisive influence. The complexity of the process of goalsetting is extraordinary, and the integrative task required is tremendous.

Very little research has been dedicated, up to now, to this whole question of integration. Thomas French (1952) has devoted a comprehensive investigation to this principle of integration. He has particularly dwelt on the factor of hope as an integrating principle. Hope is undoubtedly of fundamental importance in holding a person together and in keeping a person going.

However, before it comes to hope, there are problems regarding the inner organization of our goals. One principle of organizing seems to be given in the individually varying roles of different values and beliefs. G. Allport (1961) also sees a hierarchy of values as the organizing principles of the self. But what determines that hierarchy of values?

In the first instance, we must think of it as changing in time and being determined by age.

A second codeterminant is obviously the genetic factor, about which we know least of all. But, undoubtedly, a person's dispositions—his gifts and aptitudes, as well as his deficiencies—are codetermining the hierarchy of values and with it the structure of his goalsetting.

Thirdly, there is the host of environmental influences.

Emotional dynamics are nowadays the best-known factor of all which influence a person. However, as far as goalsetting is concerned, here, also, only recent clinical studies give us relevant information regarding the environmental impact.

The same is true of socio-cultural influences on goalsetting, a factor which recent social psychological studies have explored (Strodtbeck, 1958).

While we have increasing knowledge of all these factors, little is known regarding the integrating procedure by means of which the individual evaluates and orders all these codeterminants of his goalsetting. While much of this may take place in the unconscious, it still remains a question of how it is done.

How do people choose? Or how does it come about that in one case the impact of a mother's ambition—in another case a cultural prejudice acquired in a group—plays a decisive role in what a person believes and wants? It does not explain anything to say one factor was "stronger." Obviously, it is the individual who reacts more strongly to one or the other factor. And what determines his choices and decisions? A discussion of these factors of goalsetting has been prepared by the author and collaborators (in press).

Little has been done to investigate integration in its early stages. A. Weil (1956), who specialized in the study of childhood schizophrenias, comes to the conclusion that the unevenness of these children's maturational patterning, apart from their peculiarities, is the reason why their development lacks integration at all times. In this, she sees their basic pathology. And, indeed, the inability of integration seems part of the basic pathology of schizophrenia at any age.

But correspondingly, then, is an even and regular maturational progress a guarantee of successful integration?

It seems to me that we know far too little about people's inner organization, about decisions between preferences, about what ultimate needs they have as against more visible or more pressuring ones.

Very few people know themselves in this respect. Most subjects or patients whom I ask: What do you want ultimately? What is ultimately important to you? will give vague answers. "I wish I knew myself," they will say.

DIRECTION, PURPOSE, AND MEANING

The problem of integration entails the factor of direction, purpose, and meaning in a way, because it seems that we integrate ourselves with the view of certain goals in mind. These goals may be closer or farther away, shortsighted or seen under a big perspective; whatever they are, they have an influence on the way an individual organizes his behavior. The integrative process of the person who wants the "here and now" will undoubtedly be different from the one who has a long-range plan. Some concrete answers as to how a great variety of determining factors may be absorbed and integrated into a specific way of life, with specific goals and purposes, result from B. Eiduson's study of *Scientists* (1962).

In this study, the development and personalities of forty scientists were examined by means of tests and interviews. All of these men, says Eiduson,

> whose early determining factors show a great variety, seem to have in common that their excellent intellectual abilities lead them to early concentration on intellectual interests, and they all turn away from their families during adolescence or when starting college (p. 66).

This independence factor which we found associated with creative abilities in earlier studies, also becomes apparent here.

These scientists show, as Eiduson (1962) states in summarizing her findings, "a great diversity of sources that fed the investment in the intellectual" (p. 89). Yet they are all men whose life goals, to an extraordinary degree, are identified with, and related to, their creative research.

From this and other research it appears that the creative person finds it easier to set a direction and goals for himself. Also, they are goals which lead the creative person in a more natural way to transcend himself, which V. Frankl (1966), as well as Maslow (1964), considers a specifically human accomplishment. It becomes increasingly evident that in dedicating himself to a self-transcending goal, a person feels his life to be meaningful, as V. Frankl pointed out. But to be meaningful, and, with this, to fulfill a basic existential human need, this goal must be chosen in accordance with a person's own best potentialities.

This concept of meaningfulness, which has a long history regarding its definition, occupied many thinkers, historically speaking, since Brentano and Husserl, W. Dilthey, E. Spranger, and K. Buhler, my own work—then in existentialistic writings like Paul Tillich's and recently V. Frankl's (1966)—in its application to psychotherapy. This concept seems to refer to the development of an existential quality of life which I think is best defined by two characteristics, one emphasized by K. Buhler (1927), who says, what is meaningful is a contributory constituent to a teleological whole; the other by P. Tillich (1952), whose discourse on the despair of meaningfulness calls for an act of faith by which to accept oneself in a meaningful act.

As for creative work, it also usually enhances a person's enthusiasm for life and his self-esteem. It helps him more quickly to find his identity and to establish himself as a person in his own right.

For all these reasons, the humanistic psychologist is greatly interested in awakening and increasing people's creative potentials. H. Otto (1962) has recently started systematic work with older persons in this direction. And, luckily, schools and parents begin to become aware of the fundamental importance of this factor of creativity, the existence of which, as Guilford (1950) observed, had been almost forgotten in psychology and education.

However, not everybody is primarily creative. What about the direction of those people who are primarily non-creative?

In Getzels & Jackson's previously mentioned studies, it is very apparent how the non-creative youngsters whom they examined and who were essentially healthy, non-neurotic persons, found it easy and natural to fall in with their families' and their teachers' guidance and ideas for their futures. That means they allowed their elders to help them find their direction in life.

A mutually satisfactory development under this kind of influence does, however, not only depend on the willingness and adaptability of the child. It depends perhaps even more on the wisdom and adequate understanding of the grown-up environment.

The questions that pose themselves at this point will be taken up from a different angle when we discuss our last factor.

FULFILLMENT AND FAILURE

What is a human being living toward? The presumable end result has been described in different terms. Some think of no result at all and see only a growth and decline process with a peak somewhere in the earlier part of the middle. Some never see any other goal than the attainment or restoring of equilibrium. Some think of the full development of the self as the ultimate satisfaction. The humanistic psychologists, as you know, usually speak of self-realization as the goal.

I personally considered this concept at about the same time as K. Horney (1950) first introduced it into the literature. In discussing it, I rejected it in favor of the concept of fulfillment. I find that, while a good objective description of a very important aspect of a fulfilled life, self-realization is only one aspect, and, at that, it is one that only relatively few people are fully aware of.

What do people want to get out of their lives? Naïve people, as you know, speak of happiness and various goods that they think will bring it to them. More materialistic and/or ambitious people may speak of the success they want to end up with. But if one talks with older people, as I did in a study I am presently engaged in, one hears quite other things.

If not very analytical, the essentially fulfilled people may say: they had a good life and they would not want it any different or much different if they had to live it all over again.

In the opposite case of complete failure, they may say, "It all came to nothing," or they are tired and glad it is all over. Or as Sonja Kowalewska expressed it in the title of a drama she left after her suicidal death: "As it was and as it could have been."

In the case of a resigned ending, they may say, there were so many disappointments.

All this is to say people have, toward their end, inclusive feelings of fulfillment or failure or a kind of resignation in between. Even people who in earlier years lived with short-range goals or from day to day, seem to have toward the end an inclusive reaction to their life as a whole.

If, in talking with more analytically-minded people, one tries to let them specify the main aspects of their fulfillment or failure feelings, four major considerations could be distinguished.

The first is the aspect of *luck*. Practically always people mention that they had much luck, or lack of luck, in meeting the right persons or getting the right opportunities at the right time. This factor seems to contribute most to happiness or unhappiness, to the feeling of being a fortunate or an unfortunate person. In religious persons, this is an area where they see, most of all, God's hand.

The second may be called the aspect of the realization of *potentialities*. This is usually referred to in terms as these: "I did most of what I wanted to do," or "I did what was right for me," or "I did many things that were wrong for me," or "I could not really make the best out of myself."

The third is the aspect of *accomplishment*. Most people I talked with feel strongly about this aspect. They feel that their life should amount to something; it should have borne fruit; it should represent an accomplishment of some kind. There should be "something to show" for the past life. This factor contributes greatly to their ultimate satisfaction or dissatisfaction with their lives.

Finally, a fourth factor is that of a *moral* evaluation. Often persons emphasized that they had lived *right,* meaning in terms of their moral and/or religious convictions. Many persons mentioned objectives they had lived for in some form of self-dedication, be it the family or social groups, mankind, or progress in some field of endeavor.

The four aspects correspond essentially to the goals of the four tendencies all of which I had assumed to be basic tendencies toward fulfillment.

The most successful lives in terms of fulfillment I found to be those who were rather conscious of their life being something they ought to do something with and they were responsible for—be it in religious terms of relationship to a God, or in existential terms in relationship to the universal order, or simply in ethical terms of non-metaphysical convictions.

Religion, philosophy, and moral convictions are, of course, as we know, not sufficient to help a person live a healthy life and conquer his destructive neurotic tendencies. The essentially fulfilled lives that I studied seem to have been able to be essentially successful in sustaining an individually balanced equilibrium between their basic tendencies to *need-satisfaction, self-limiting adaptation, creative expansion,* and *upholding of the internal order,* and to be constructive under whichever aspect they believed in.

Summary

Human goalsetting is, as you see, a very complex process emerging from a multiplicity of ingredients. I pointed out twelve main developmental advances on different levels and in different areas of personality functioning. Briefly summarized, they are: (1) *Activity* with a more passive or more aggressive approach; (2) selective *Perception;* (3) *Care and Contact;* (4) *Identity* and *Intentionality* beginnings with choice and direction of the person who feels he wants or he must or he should; (5) *Mastery* beginnings based on the experience "I can" or "I cannot," with success and failure, adaptive and creative behavior; (6) *Constructiveness* and *Destructiveness* developed in the dynamic interrelationships with the environment; (7) *Achievement* motivation; (8) *Beliefs and Values* with opinions and convictions; (9) *Love* and other committing relationships; (10) *Integration* of factors; (11) *Direction, Purpose, and Meaning;* (12) *Fulfillment, Resignation, and Failure.*

One of the results of the studies (in preparation) of lives which accomplished essential fulfillment as against lives ending in the resignation of a heap of unordered experiences, many disappointments, or in the despair of failure, is this:

Fulfillment seems to result primarily from a constructive and thoughtful way of living; constructive to the degree that even major tragedies as well as great misfortunes are overcome and used beneficially; thoughtful in the use of even mediocre potentialities for accomplishments and meaningful self-dedication; thoughtful also in attempting to look repeatedly backwards and forward at the whole of one's existence and to assess it in whatever terms one believes in.

References

Ach, N. *Uber die Willenstätigkeit und das Denken* (About Will and Thinking). Göttingen: Vandenhock & Ruzprecht, 1905.

Allport, G. *Pattern and Growth in Personality*. New York: Harper, 1961.

Buhler, C. "Earliest Trends in Goalsetting." *Rev. Psychiat. Infantile,* 25 (1958): 1–2, 13–23.

———. "Theoretical observations about life's basic tendencies." *Amer. J. Psychother.,* 13 (1959): (3), 561–581.

———. *Genetic Aspects of the Self*. New York: Academic Sciences, 1962. (a)

———. *Values in Psychotherapy*. Glencoe, Ill.: Free Press, 1962. (b)

———. *Intentionality and Fulfillment*. San Francisco: Jossey-Bass, in press.

———, and Massarik, F., eds. *The Course of Human Life. A Study of Life Goals in the Humanistic Perspective*. New York: Springer, 1968.

Buhler, K. *Die Krise der Psychologie*. Jena: G. Fischer, 1927. (Transl. *The Crisis of Psychology*. Cambridge: Schekman Publishing Co., in press.)

Eiduson, B. *Scientists*. New York: Basic Books, 1962.

———, Eiduson, S.; and Geller, E. "Biochemistry, Genetics and the Nature-Nurture Problem." *Amer. J. Psychiat.,* 58 (1962).

Erikson, E. *Identity and the Life Cycle*. New York: International University Press, 1959.

Frankl, V. "Self-Transcendence as a Human Phenomenon." *J. Humanistic Psychol.,* 6 (2), (1966): 97–106.

French, T. *The Integration of Behavior*. Chicago: University of Chicago Press, 1952, 1954, 1956 (3 vols.).

Fries, M., and Woolf, P. "Some Hypotheses on the Role of the Congenital Activity Type in Personality Development." *The Psychoanalytic Study of the Child*. New York: International University Press, 1953, vol. 8.

Getzels, J., and Jackson, P. *Creativity and Intelligence, Explorations with Gifted Students*. New York: Wiley, 1962.

Goertzel, V., and Goertzel, M. *Cradles of Eminence*. Boston: Little, Brown, 1962.

Guilford, J. P. *Fields of Psychology*. New York: Van Nostrand, 1950.

Hilgard, E. "The Role of Learning in Perception." In R. R. Blake and G. V. Ramsey, eds., *Perception*. New York: Ronald Press, 1951.

Horney, K. *Neurosis and Human Growth*. New York: W. W. Norton, 1950.

Kagan, J. "Acquisition and Significance of Sex Typing and Sex Role Identity." *Child Development Research, Russell-Sage Foundation*. Philadelphia: Wm. F. Fell, 1964.

———, and Moss, H. A. *Birth to Maturity*. New York: Wiley, 1962.

Lewin, K. "Vorsatz, Wille und Bedürfris" (Intention, Will and Need). *Psychol. Forschg.,* 7 (1926): 330–385.

Maslow, A. *Motivation and Personality*. New York: Harper, 1954.

———. *Religions, Values, and Peak-Experiences*. Columbus: Ohio State University Press, 1964.

McClelland, D. Atkinson; Clark, W. R.; and Lowell, E. *The Achievement Motive.* New York: Appleton-Century-Crofts, 1953.

Murphy, L. *The Widening World of Childhood.* New York: Basic Books, 1962.

Otto, H. "The Personal Resource Development Research—The Multiple Strength Perception Effect. *Proceedings of Utah Acad. Sci., Arts, & Letters,* 38 (1961–1962).

——— Self-Perception of Personality Strengths by Four Discrete Groups." *J. Human Relations,* 12 (4) (1963).

Piaget, J. *Dreams and Imitation in Childhood.* New York: W. W. Norton, 1951.

Redl, F., and Wineman, D. *Children Who Hate, the Disorganization and Breakdown of Behavior Controls.* Glencoe, Ill.: Free Press, 1951.

Shostrom, E. "Personal Orientation Inventory." San Diego: Educational and Industrial Test Service, 1963.

Sontag, L. "The Genetics of Differences in Psychosomatic Patterns in Childhood." *Amer. J. Orthopsychiat.,* 20 (3) (1950).

Spitz, R. "Genèse des premières relations objectales," *Rev. franç. Psychanal.,* Paris, 1954.

Spitz, R. *The First Year of Life.* New York: International University Press, 1965.

Stirnimann, F. *Psychologie des neugeborenen Kindes.* Zurich und Leipzig: Rascher Verl., 1940.

Stirnimann, F. Psychologie des neugeborenen Kindes. In E. Schachtel, ed., *Metamorphosis.* New York: Basic Books, 1959.

Strodtbeck, F.; McClelland, D.; et al. *Talent and Society.* Princeton: Van Nostrand, 1958.

Thomas, A., et al. *Behavioral individuality in early childhood.* New York: New York University Press, 1963.

Tillich, P. *The Courage to Be.* New Haven: Yale University Press, 1952.

Tinbergen, N. "Social Releases and the Experimental Method Required for Their Study." *Wilson Bull.,* 60 (1948): 6–51.

Weil, A. "Some Evidences of Deviational Development in Infancy and Early Childhood." vol. 11. *Psychoanalytic Study of the Child.* New York: International University Press, 1956.

4
THE HELPING PROCESS

In this part of the Sourcebook, *we are concerned with the essence of helping: the process and the helper. The articles presented here have been chosen for the insights their authors give into the helping process and the problems helpers must face in practicing their profession.*

The article by Carl Rogers makes the very important point that all helping relationships are essentially learning situations. This point has also been made by the authors of this sourcebook in another book, Helping Relationships: Basic Concepts for the Helping Professions,[1] *and we believe that it is an important one. An unwarranted distinction is often made between one kind of helping and another with regard to the type of variables, goals, and processes involved as, for example, between teaching and counseling. Because they are viewed as having quite different functions, counselors and teachers often misunderstand each other. As a consequence, both tasks may fail.* All *helping relationships are learning situations. This common element must be understood as the basis for the design of effective practice in whatever form the helping process may be used.*

Most helping relationships are temporary and terminal. Their purpose is not to support and sustain a person throughout one's life, as is a drug such as insulin. Rather, their purpose is to

1. Arthur W. Combs, Donald L. Avila, and William W. Purkey, *Helping Relationships: Basic Concepts for the Helping Professions* (Boston: Allyn and Bacon, Inc., 1971).

begin a growth process that will assist a person toward eventually solving his or her own problems successfully without help. In his article, "Fostering Self-Direction," Combs deals with this major goal of all helping processes. He suggests some things helpers must do if they are to contribute to the development of self-sufficient human beings.

The remaining papers in Part IV pertain to the process of helping as well as with the helper. The readers are asked to analyze their own behavior as helpers. What helpers should be as well as what they should not be is discussed.

William Purkey directs his attention to some positive qualities of a good helper. He points out that one of the most important aspects of being a good helper has to do with what one thinks of oneself as a person and as a professional worker. George Lawton points out some common mistakes a helper can make in attempting to satisfy his or her own needs. Not unlike Purkey, he makes it clear that helpers must know themselves as well as their clients lest, unwittingly, they satisfy their own needs while sabotaging their clients.

David Aspy, in a short but poignant paper, brings us sharply face-to-face with a human failing we all have been guilty of and that would be a particularly devastating characteristic for helpers to possess. "How Did He Get There?" is a striking portrait of personal envy.

David Campbell takes a new and different look at an old bugaboo. Many people believe that competition is the foundation of our society. They also believe that it is nurturing, healthy, and necessary. Campbell, along with the editors of this volume, see it quite differently. He explains why in this dramatic statement.

The Interpersonal Relationship in the Facilitation of Learning

CARL R. ROGERS

It is in fact nothing short of a miracle that the modern methods of instruction have not yet entirely strangled the holy curiosity of inquiry; for this delicate little plant, aside from stimulation, stands mainly in need of freedom; without this it goes to wrack and ruin without fail.

ALBERT EINSTEIN

I wish to begin this paper with a statement which may seem surprising to some and perhaps offensive to others. It is simply this: Teaching, in my estimation, is a vastly overrated function.

Having made such a statement, I scurry to the dictionary to see if I really mean what I say. Teaching means "to instruct." Personally I am not much interested in instructing another. "To impart knowledge or skill." My reaction is, why not be more efficient, using a book or programmed learning? "To make to know." Here my hackles rise. I have no wish to *make* anyone know something. "To show, guide, direct." As I see it, too many people have been shown, guided, directed. So I come to the conclusion that I *do* mean what I said. Teaching is, for me, a relatively unimportant and vastly overvalued activity.

But there is more in my attitude than this. I have a negative reaction to teaching. Why? I think it is because it raises all the wrong questions. As soon as we focus on teaching, the question arises, what shall we teach? What, from our superior vantage point, does the other person need to know? This raises the ridiculous question of coverage. What shall

From *Humanizing Education: The Person in the Process,* Robert R. Leeper, ed. Washington, D.C.: Association for Supervision and Curriculum Development, 1967, pp. 1–18. Reprinted with permission of the author and publisher.

the course cover? (Here I am acutely aware of the fact that "to cover" means both "to take in" and "to conceal from view," and I believe that most courses admirably achieve both these aims.) This notion of coverage is based on the assumption that what is taught is what is learned; what is presented is what is assimilated. I know of no assumption so obviously untrue. One does not need research to provide evidence that this is false. One needs only to talk with a few students.

But I ask myself, "Am I so prejudiced against teaching that I find no situation in which it is worthwhile?" I immediately think of my experience in Australia only a few months ago. I became much interested in the Australian aborigine. Here is a group which for more than 20,000 years has managed to live and exist in a desolate environment in which a modern man would perish within a few days. The secret of his survival has been teaching. He has passed on to the young every shred of knowledge about how to find water, about how to track game, about how to kill the kangaroo, about how to find his way through the trackless desert. Such knowledge is conveyed to the young as being *the* way to behave, and any innovation is frowned upon. It is clear that teaching has provided him the way to survive in a hostile and relatively unchanging environment.

Now I am closer to the nub of the question which excites me. Teaching and the imparting of knowledge make sense in an unchanging environment. This is why it has been an unquestioned function for centuries. But if there is one truth about modern man, it is that he lives in an environment which is *continually changing.* The one thing I can be sure of is that the physics which is taught to the present day student will be outdated in a decade. The teaching in psychology will certainly be out of date in 20 years. The so-called "facts of history" depend very largely upon the current mood and temper of the culture. Chemistry, biology, genetics, sociology, are in such flux that a firm statement made today will almost certainly be modified by the time the student gets around to using the knowledge.

We are, in my view, faced with an entirely new situation in education where the goal of education, if we are to survive, is the *facilitation of change and learning.* The only man who is educated is the man who has learned how to learn; the man who has learned how to adapt and change; the man who has realized that no knowledge is secure, that only the process of *seeking* knowledge gives a basis for security. Changingness, a reliance on *process* rather than upon static knowledge, is the only thing that makes any sense as a goal for education in the modern world.

So now with some relief I turn to an activity, a purpose, which really warms me—the *facilitation of learning.* When I have been able to transform a group—and here I mean all the members of a group, myself included—into a community of *learners,* then the excitement has been almost beyond belief. To free curiosity; to permit individuals to go charging off in new directions dictated by their own interests; to unleash curiosity; to open everything to questioning and exploration; to recognize that everything is in process of change—here is an experience I can never forget. I cannot always achieve it in groups with which I am associated but when it is partially or largely achieved then it becomes a never-to-be forgotten group experience. Out of such a context arise true students, real learners, creative scientists and scholars and practitioners, the kind of individuals who can live in a delicate but ever-changing balance between what is presently known and the flowing, moving, altering, problems and facts of the future.

Here then is a goal to which I can give myself wholeheartedly. I see the facilitation of learning as the aim of education, the way in which we might develop the learning man, the way in which we can learn to live as individuals in process. I see the facilitation of learning as the function which may hold constructive, tentative, changing, process answers to some of the deepest perplexities which beset man today.

But do we know how to achieve this new goal in education, or is it a will-of-the-wisp which sometimes occurs, sometimes fails to occur, and thus offers little real hope? My answer is that we possess a very considerable knowledge of the conditions which encourage self-initiated, significant, experiential, "gut-level" learning by the whole person. We do not frequently see these conditions put into effect because they mean a real revolution in our approach to education and revolutions are not for the timid. But we do find examples of this revolution in action.

We know—and I will briefly describe some of the evidence—that the initiation of such learning rests not upon the teaching skills of the leader, not upon his scholarly knowledge of the field, not upon his curricular planning, not upon his use of audio-visual aids, not upon the programmed learning he utilizes, not upon his lectures and presentations, not upon an abundance of books, though each of these might at one time or another be utilized as an important resource. No, the facilitation of significant learning rests upon certain attitudinal qualities which exist in the personal *relationship* between the facilitator and the learner.

We came upon such findings first in the field of pyschotherapy, but increasingly there is evidence which shows that these findings apply in the classroom as well. We find it easier to think that the intensive relationship between therapist and client might possess these qualities, but we are also finding that they may exist in the countless interpersonal interactions (as many as 1,000 per day, as Jackson [1966] has shown) between the teacher and his pupils.

What are these qualities, these attitudes, which facilitate learning? Let me describe them very briefly, drawing illustrations from the teaching field.

REALNESS IN THE FACILITATOR OF LEARNING

Perhaps the most basic of these essential attitudes is realness or genuineness. When the facilitator is a real person, being what he is, entering into a relationship with the learner without presenting a front or a facade, he is much more likely to be effective. This means that the feelings which he is experiencing are available to him, available to his awareness, that he is able to live these feelings, be them, and able to communicate them if appropriate. It means that he comes into a direct personal encounter with the learner, meeting him on a person-to-person basis. It means that he is *being* himself, not denying himself.

Seen from this point of view it is suggested that the teacher can be a real person in his relationship with his students. He can be enthusiastic, he can be bored, he can be interested in students, he can be angry, he can be sensitive and sympathetic. Because he accepts these feelings as his own he has no need to impose them on his students. He can like or dislike a student product without implying that it is objectively good or bad or that the student is good or bad. He is simply expressing a feeling for the product, a feeling which exists within himself. Thus, he is a person to his students, not a faceless embodiment of a curricular requirement nor a sterile tube through which knowledge is passed from one generation to the next.

It is obvious that this attitudinal set, found to be effective in psychotherapy, is sharply in contrast with the tendency of most teachers to show themselves to their pupils simply as roles. It is quite customary for teachers rather consciously to put on the mask, the role, the facade, of being a teacher, and to wear this facade all day removing it only when they have left the school at night.

But not all teachers are like this. Take Sylvia Ashton-Warner, who took resistant, supposedly slow-learning primary school Maori children in New Zealand, and let them develop their own reading vocabulary. Each child could request one word—whatever word he wished—each day, and she would print it on a card and give it to him. "Kiss," "ghost," "bomb," "tiger," "fight," "love," "daddy"—these are samples. Soon they were building sentences, which they could also keep. "He'll get a licking." "Pussy's frightened." The children simply never forgot these self-initiated learnings. Yet it is not my purpose to tell you of her methods. I want instead to give you a glimpse of her attitude, of the passionate realness which must have been as evident to her tiny pupils as to her readers. An editor asked her some questions and she responded: " 'A few cool facts' you asked me for. . . . I don't know that there's a cool fact in me, or anything else cool for that matter, on this particular subject. I've got only hot long facts on the matter of Creative Teaching, scorching both the page and me" (Ashton-Warner, 163, p. 26).

Here is no sterile facade. Here is a vital *person,* with convictions, with feelings. It is her transparent realness which was, I am sure, one of the elements that made her an exciting facilitator of learning. She does not fit into some neat educational formula. She *is,* and students grow by being in contact with someone who really *is.*

Take another very different person, Barbara Shiel, also doing exciting work facilitating learning in sixth graders.[1] She gave them a great deal of responsible freedom, and I will mention some of the reactions of her students later. But here is an example of the way she shared herself with her pupils—not just sharing feelings of sweetness and light, but anger and frustration. She had made art materials freely available, and students often used these in creative ways, but the room frequently looked like a picture of chaos. Here is her report of her feelings and what she did with them.

> I find it (still) maddening to live with the mess—with a capital M! No one seems to care except me. Finally, one day I told the children . . . that I am a neat, orderly person by nature and that the mess was driving me to distraction. Did they have a solution? It was suggested they could have volunteers to clean up. . . . I said it didn't seem fair to me to have the same people clean up all the time for others—but it *would* solve it for me. "Well, some people *like* to clean," they replied. So that's the way it is (Shiel 1966).

I hope this example puts some lively meaning into the phrases I used earlier, that the facilitator "is able to live these feelings, be them, and able to communicate them if appropriate." I have chosen an example of negative feelings, because I think it is more difficult for most of us to visualize what this would mean. In this instance, Miss Shiel is taking the risk of being transparent in her angry frustrations about the mess. And what happens? The same thing which, in my experience, nearly always happens. These young people accept and respect her feelings, take them into account, and work out a novel solution which none of us, I believe, would have suggested in advance. Miss Shiel wisely comments, "I used to get upset and feel guilty when I became angry—I finally realized the children could accept *my* feelings, too. And it is important for them to know when they've 'pushed me.' I have limits, too" (Shiel 1966).

Just to show that positive feelings, when they are real, are equally effective, let me quote briefly a college student's reaction, in a different course. ". . . Your sense of humor in the class was cheering; we all felt

1. For a more extended account of Miss Shiel's initial attempts, see Rogers, 1966a. Her later experience is described in Shiel, 1966.

relaxed because you showed us your human self, not a mechanical teacher image. I feel as if I have more understanding and faith in my teachers now. . . . I feel closer to the students too." Another says, ". . . You conducted the class on a personal level and therefore in my mind I was able to formulate a picture of you as a person and not as merely a walking textbook." Or another student in the same course,

> . . . It wasn't as if there was a teacher in the class, but rather someone whom we could trust and identify as a "sharer." You were so perceptive and sensitive to our thoughts, and this made it all the more "authentic" for me. It was an "authentic" *experience,* not just a class (Bull 1966).

I trust I am making it clear that to be real is not always easy, nor is it achieved all at once, but it is basic to the person who wants to become that revolutionary individual, a facilitator of learning.

PRIZING, ACCEPTANCE, TRUST

There is another attitude which stands out in those who are successful in facilitating learning. I have observed this attitude. I have experienced it. Yet, it is hard to know what term to put to it so I shall use several. I think of it as prizing the learner, prizing his feelings, his opinions, his person. It is a caring for the learner, but a non-possessive caring. It is an acceptance of this other individual as a separate person, having worth in his own right. It is a basic trust—a belief that this other person is somehow fundamentally trustworthy.

Whether we call it prizing, acceptance, trust, or by some other term, it shows up in a variety of observable ways. The facilitator who has a considerable degree of this attitude can be fully acceptant of the fear and hesitation of the student as he approaches a new problem as well as acceptant of the pupil's satisfaction in achievement. Such a teacher can accept the student's occasional apathy, his erratic desires to explore byroads of knowledge, as well as his disciplined efforts to achieve major goals. He can accept personal feelings which both disturb and promote learning—rivalry with a sibling, hatred of authority, concern about personal adequacy. What we are describing is a prizing of the learner as an imperfect human being with many feelings, many potentialities. The facilitator's prizing or acceptance of the learner is an operational expression of his essential confidence and trust in the capacity of the human organism.

I would like to give some examples of this attitude from the classroom situation. Here any teacher statements would be properly suspect, since many of us would like to feel we hold such attitudes, and might have a biased perception of our qualities. But let me indicate how this attitude of prizing, of accepting, of trusting, appears to the student who is fortunate enough to experience it.

Here is a statement from a college student in a class with Morey Appell.

> Your way of being with us is a revelation to me. In your class I feel important, mature, and capable of doing things on my own. I want to think for myself and this need cannot be accomplished through textbooks and lectures alone, but through living. I think you see me as a person with real feelings and needs, an individual. What I say and do are significant expressions from me, and you recognize this (Appell 1959).

One of Miss Shiel's sixth graders expresses much more briefly her misspelled appreciation of this attitude, "You are a wounderful teacher period!!!"

College students in a class with Dr. Patricia Bull describe not only these prizing, trusting attitudes, but the effect these have had on their other interactions.

> . . . I feel that I can say things to you that I can't say to other professors . . . Never before have I been so aware of the other students or their personalities. I have never had so much interaction in a college classroom with my classmates. The climate of the classroom has had a very profound effect on me . . . the free atmosphere for discussion affected me . . . the general atmosphere of a particular session affected me. There have been many times when I have carried the discussion out of the class with me and thought about it for a long time.

> . . . I still feel close to you, as though there were some tacit understanding between us, almost a conspiracy. This adds to the in-class participation on my part because I feel that at least one person in the group will react, even when I am not sure of the others. It does not matter really whether your reaction is positive or negative, it just *is.* Thank you.

> . . . I appreciate the respect and concern you have for others, including myself. . . . As a result of my experience in class, plus the influence of my readings, I sincerely believe that the student-centered teaching method does provide an ideal framework for learning; not just for the accumulation of facts, but more important, for learning about ourselves in relation to others. . . . When I think back to my shallow awareness in September compared to the depth of my insights now, I know that this course has offered me a learning experience of great value which I couldn't have acquired in any other way.

> . . . Very few teachers would attempt this method because they would feel that they would lose the students' respect. On the contrary. You gained our respect, through your ability to speak to us on our level, instead of ten miles above us. With the complete lack of communication we see in this school, it was a wonderful experience to see people listening to each other and really communicating on an adult, intelligent level. More classes should afford us this experience (Bull 1966).

As you might expect, college students are often suspicious that these seeming attitudes are phony. One of Dr. Bull's students writes:

> . . . Rather than observe my classmates for the first few weeks, I concentrated my observations on you, Dr. Bull. I tried to figure out your motivations and purposes. I was convinced that you were a hypocrite. . . . I did change my opinion, however. You are not a hypocrite, by any means. . . . I do wish the course could continue. "Let each become all he is capable of being." . . . Perhaps my most disturbing question, which relates to this course is: When will we stop hiding things from ourselves and our contemporaries? (Bull 1966).

I am sure these examples are more than enough to show that the facilitator who cares, who prizes, who trusts the learner, creates a climate for learning so different from the ordinary classroom that any resemblance is, as they say, "purely coincidental."

EMPATHIC UNDERSTANDING

A further element which establishes a climate for self-initiated, experiential learning is empathic understanding. When the teacher has the ability to understand the student's reactions from the inside, has a sensitive awareness of the way the process of education and learning seems *to the student,* then again the likelihood of significant learning is increased.

This kind of understanding is sharply different from the usual evaluative understanding, which follows the pattern of, "I understand what is wrong with you." When there is a sensitive empathy, however, the reaction in the learner follows something of this pattern, "At last someone understands how it feels and seems to be *me* without wanting to analyze me or judge me. Now I can blossom and grow and learn."

This attitude of standing in the other's shoes, of viewing the world through the student's eyes, is almost unheard of in the classroom. One could listen to thousands of ordinary classroom interactions without coming across one instance of clearly communicated, sensitively accurate, empathic understanding. But it has a tremendously releasing effect when it occurs.

Let me take an illustration from Virginia Axline, dealing with a second grade boy. Jay, age 7, has been aggressive, a troublemaker, a slow of speech and learning. Because of his "cussing" he was taken to the principal, who paddled him, unknown to Miss Axline. During a free work period, he fashioned a man of clay, very carefully, down to a hat and a handkerchief in his pocket. "Who is that?" asked Miss Axline. "Dunno," replied Jay. "Maybe it is the principal. He has a handkerchief in his pocket like that." Jay glared at the clay figure. "Yes," he said. Then he began to tear the head off and looked up and smiled. Miss Axline said, "You sometimes feel like twisting his head off, don't you? You get so mad at him." Jay tore off one arm, another, then beat the figure to a pulp with his fists. Another boy, with the perception of the young, explained, "Jay is mad at Mr. X because he licked him this noon." "Then you must feel lots better now," Miss Axline commented. Jay grinned and began to rebuild Mr. X. (Adapted from Axline 1944.)

The other examples I have cited also indicate how deeply appreciative students feel when they are simply *understood*—not evaluated, not judged, simply understood from their *own* point of view, not the teacher's. If any teacher set herself the task of endeavoring to make one nonevaluative, acceptant, empathic response per day to a pupil's demonstrated or verbalized feeling, I believe he would discover the potency of this currently almost nonexistent kind of understanding.

Let me wind up this portion of my remarks by saying that when a facilitator creates, even to a modest degree, a classroom climate characterized by such realness, prizing, and empathy, he discovers that he has inaugurated an educational revolution. Learning of a different quality, proceeding at a different pace, with a greater degree of pervasiveness, occurs. Feelings—positive and negative, confused—become a part of the classroom experience. Learning becomes life, and a very vital life at that. The student is on his way, sometimes excitedly, sometimes reluctantly, to becoming a learning, changing being.

THE EVIDENCE

Already I can hear the mutterings of some of my so-called "hard-headed" colleagues. "A very pretty picture—very touching. But these are all self reports." (As if there were any other type of expression! But that's another issue.) They ask, "Where is the evidence? How do you know?" I would like to turn to this evidence. It is not overwhelming, but it is consistent. It is not perfect, but it is suggestive.

First of all, in the field of psychotherapy, Barrett-Lennard (1962) developed an instrument whereby he could measure these attitudinal qualities: genuineness or congruence, prizing or positive regard, empathy or understanding. This instrument was given to both client and therapist, so that we have the perception of the relationship both by the therapist and by the client whom he is trying to help. To state some of the findings very briefly it may be said that those clients who eventually showed more therapeutic change as measured by various instruments, perceived *more* of these qualities in their relationship with the therapist than did those who eventually showed less change. It is also significant that this difference in perceived relationships was evident as early as the fifth interview, and predicted later change or lack of change in therapy. Furthermore, it was found that the *client's* perception of the relationship, his experience of it, was a better predictor of ultimate outcome than was the perception of the relationship by the therapist. Barrett-Lennard's original study has been amplified and generally confirmed by other studies.

So we may say, cautiously, and with qualifications which would be too cumbersome for the present paper, that if, in therapy, the client perceives his therapist as real and genuine, as one who likes, prizes, and empathically understands him, self-learning and therapeutic change are facilitated.

Now another thread of evidence, this time related more closely to education. Emmerling (1961) found that when high school teachers were asked to identify the problems they regarded as most urgent, they could be divided into two groups. Those who regarded their most serious problems, for example, as "Helping children think for themselves and be independent"; "Getting students to participate"; "Learning new ways of helping students develop their maximum potential"; "Helping students express individual needs and interests"; fell into what he called the "open" or "positively oriented" group. When Barrett-Lennard's Relationship Inventory was administered to the students of these teachers, it was found that they were perceived as significantly more real, more acceptant, more empathic than the other group of teachers whom I shall now describe.

The second category of teachers were those who tended to see their most urgent problems in negative terms, and in terms of student deficiencies and inabilities. For them the urgent problems were such as these: "Trying to teach children who don't even have the ability to follow directions"; "Teaching children who lack a desire to learn"; "Students who are not able to do the work required for their grade"; "Getting the children to listen." It probably will be no surprise that when the students of these teachers filled out the Relationship Inventory they saw their teachers as exhibiting relatively little of genuineness, of acceptance and trust, or of empathic understanding.

Hence we may say that the teacher whose orientation is toward releasing the student's potential exhibits a high degree of these attitudinal qualities which facilitate learning. The teacher whose orientation is toward the shortcomings of his students exhibits much less of these qualities.

A small pilot study by Bills (1961, 1966) extends the significance of these findings. A group of eight teachers was selected, four of them rated as adequate and effective by their superiors, and also showing this more positive orientation to their problems. The other four were rated as inadequate teachers and also had a more negative orientation to their problems, as described above. The students of these teachers were then asked to fill out the Barrett-Lennard Relationship Inventory, giving their perception of their teacher's relationship to them. This made the students very happy. Those who saw their relationship with the teacher as good were happy to describe this relationship. Those who saw an unfavorable relationship were pleased to have, for the first time, an opportunity to specify the ways in which the relationship was unsatisfactory.

The more effective teachers were rated higher in every attitude measured by the Inventory: they were seen as more real, as having a higher level of regard for their students, were less conditional or judgmental in their attitudes, showed more empathic understanding. Without going into the details of the study it may be illuminating to mention that the total scores summing these attitudes vary sharply. For example, the relationships of a group of clients with their therapists, as perceived by the clients, received an average score of 108. The four most adequate high school teachers as seen by their students, received a score of 60. The four less adequate teachers received a score of 34. The lowest rated teacher received an average score of 2 from her students on the Relationship Inventory.

This small study certainly suggests that the teacher regarded as effective displays in her attitudes those qualities I have described as facilitative of learning, while the inadequate teacher shows little of these qualities.

Approaching the problem from a different angle, Schmuck (1963) has shown that in classrooms where pupils perceive their teachers as understanding them, there is likely to be a more diffuse liking structure among the pupils. This means that where the teacher is empathic, there are not a few students strongly liked and a few strongly disliked, but liking and affection are more evenly diffused throughout the group. In a later study he has shown that among students who are highly involved in their classroom peer group, "significant relationships exist between actual liking status on the one hand and utilization of abilities, attitude toward self, and attitude toward school on the other hand" (1966, p. 357–58). This seems to lend confirmation to the other evidence by indicating that in an understanding classroom climate every student tends to feel liked by all the others, to have a more positive attitude toward himself and toward school. If he is highly involved with his peer group (and this appears probable in such a classroom climate), he also tends to utilize his abilities more fully in his school achievement.

But you may still ask, does the student actually *learn* more where these attitudes are present? Here an interesting study of third graders by Aspy (1965) helps to round out the suggestive evidence. He worked in six third-grade classes. The teachers tape-recorded two full weeks of their interaction with their students in the periods devoted to the teaching of reading. These recordings were done two months apart so as to obtain an adequate sampling of the teacher's interactions with her pupils. Four-minute segments of these recordings were randomly selected for rating. Three raters, working independently and "blind," rated each segment for the degree of congruence or genuineness shown by the teacher, the degree of her prizing or unconditional positive regard, and the degree of her empathic understanding.

The Reading Achievement Tests (Stanford Achievement) were used as the criterion. Again, omitting some of the details of a carefully and rigorously controlled study, it may be said that the children in the three classes with the highest degree of the attitudes described above showed a significantly greater gain in reading achievement than those students in the three classes with a lesser degree of these qualities.

So we may say, with a certain degree of assurance, that the attitudes I have endeavored to describe are not only effective in facilitating a deeper learning and understanding of self in a relationship such as psychotherapy, but that these attitudes characterize teachers who are regarded as effective teachers, and that the students of these teachers learn more, even of a conventional curriculum, than do students of teachers who are lacking in these attitudes.

I am pleased that such evidence is accumulating. It may help to justify the revolution in education for which I am obviously hoping. But the most striking learnings of students exposed to such a climate are by no means restricted to greater achievement in the three R's. The significant learnings are the more personal ones—independence, self-initiated and responsible learning; release of creativity, a tendency to become more of a person. I can only illustrate this by picking, almost at random, statements from students whose teachers have endeavored to create a climate of trust, of prizing, of realness, of understanding, and above all, of freedom.

Again I must quote from Sylvia Ashton-Warner one of the central effects of such a climate.

> . . . The drive is no longer the teacher's, but the children's own. . . . The teacher is at last with the stream and not against it, the stream of children's inexorable creativeness (Ashton-Warner, p. 93).

If you need verification of this, listen to a few of Dr. Bull's sophomore students. The first two are mid-semester comments.

> . . . This course is proving to be a vital and profound experience for me. . . . This unique learning situation is giving me a whole new concept of just what learning is. . . . I am experiencing a real growth in this atmosphere of constructive freedom. . . . The whole experience is very challenging. . . .

> . . . I feel that the course has been of great value to me. . . . I'm glad to have had this experience because it has made me think. . . . I've never

been so personally involved with a course before, especially *outside* the classroom. It's been frustrating, rewarding, enjoyable and tiring!

The other comments are from the end of the course.

. . . This course is not ending with the close of the semester for me, but continuing. . . . I don't know of any greater benefit which can be gained from a course than this desire for further knowledge. . . .

. . . I feel as though this type of class situation has stimulated me more in making me realize where my responsibilities lie, especially as far as doing required work on my own. I no longer feel as though a test date is the criterion for reading a book. I feel as though my future work will be done for what *I* will get out of it, not just for a test mark.

. . . I have enjoyed the experience of being in this course. I guess that any dissatisfaction I feel at this point is a disappointment in myself, for not having taken full advantage of the opportunities the course offered.

. . . I think that now I am acutely aware of the breakdown in communications that does exist in our society from seeing what happened in our class. . . . I've grown immensely. I know that I am a different person than I was when I came into that class. . . . It has done a great deal in helping me understand myself better. . . . Thank you for contributing to my growth.

. . . My idea of education has been to gain information from the teacher by attending lectures. The emphasis and focus were on the teacher. . . . One of the biggest changes that I experienced in this class was my outlook on education. Learning is something more than a grade on a report card. No one can measure what you have learned because it's a personal thing. I was very confused between learning and memorization. I could memorize very well, but I doubt if I ever learned as much as I could have. I believe my attitude toward learning has changed from a grade-centered outlook to a more personal one.

. . . I have learned a lot more about myself and adolescents in general. . . . I also gained more confidence in myself and my study habits by realizing that I could learn by myself without a teacher leading me by the hand. I have also learned a lot by listening to my classmates and evaluating their opinions and thoughts. . . . This course has proved to be a most meaningful and worthwhile experience. . . . (Bull 1966).

If you wish to know what this type of course seems like to a sixth grader, let me give you a sampling of the reactions of Miss Shiel's youngsters, misspellings and all.

. . . I feel that I am learning self abilty. I am learning not only school work but I am learning that you can learn on your own as well as someone can teach you.

. . . I have a little trouble in Socail Studies finding things to do. I have a hard time working the exact amount of time. Sometimes I talk to much.

. . . My parents don't understand the program. My mother say's it will give me a responsibility and it will let me go at my own speed.

. . . I like this plan because thire is a lot of freedom. I also learn more this way than the other way you don't have to wate for others you can go at your on speed rate it also takes a lot of responsibility (Shiel 1966).

Or let me take two more, from Dr. Appell's graduate class.

. . . I have been thinking about what happened through this experience. The only conclusion I come to is that if I try to measure what is going on, or what I was at the beginning, I have got to know what I was when I started—and I don't. . . . So many things I did and feel are just lost . . . scrambled up inside. . . . They don't seem to come out in a nice little pattern or organization I can say or write. . . . There are so many things left unsaid. I know I have only scratched the surface, I guess. I can feel so many things almost ready to come out . . . maybe that's enough. *It seems all kinds of things have so much more meaning now than ever before.* . . . This experience has had meaning, has done things to me and I am not sure how much or how far just yet. I think I am going to be a better me in the fall. *That's one thing I think I am sure of* (Appell 1963).

. . . You follow no plan, yet I'm learning. Since the term began I seem to feel more alive, more real to myself. I enjoy being alone as well as with other people. My relationships with children and other adults are becoming more emotional and involved. Eating an orange last week, I peeled the skin off each separate orange section and liked it better with the transparent shell off. It was jucier and fresher tasting that way. I began to think, that's how I feel sometimes, without a transparent wall around me, really communicating my feelings. I feel that I'm growing, how much, I don't know. I'm thinking, considering, pondering and learning (Appell 1959).

I can't read these student statements—6th grade, college, graduate level—without my eyes growing moist. Here are teachers, risking themselves, *being* themselves, *trusting* their students, adventuring into the existential unknown, taking the subjective leap. And what happens? Exciting, incredible *human* events. You can sense persons being created, learnings being initiated, future citizens rising to meet the challenge of unknown worlds. If only one teacher out of one hundred dared to risk, dared to be, dared to trust, dared to understand, we would have an infusion of a living spirit into education which would, in my estimation, be priceless.

I have heard scientists at leading schools of science, and scholars in leading universities, arguing that it is absurd to try to encourage all students to be creative—we need hosts of mediocre technicians and workers and if a few creative scientists and artists and leaders emerge, that will be enough. That may be enough for them. It may be enough to suit you. I want to go on record as saying it is *not* enough to suit me. When I realize the incredible potential in the ordinary student, I want to try to release it. We are working hard to release the incredible energy in the atom and the nucleus of the atom. If we do not devote equal energy—yes, and equal money—to the release of the potential of the individual person, then the enormous discrepancy between our level of physical energy resources and human energy resources will doom us to a deserved and universal destruction.

I'm sorry I can't be coolly scientific about this. The issue is too urgent. I can only be passionate in my statement that people count, that interpersonal relationships *are* important, that we know something about releasing human potential, that we could learn much more, and that unless we give strong positive attention to the human interpersonal side of our educational dilemma, our civilization is on its way down the drain. Better courses, better curricula, better coverage, better teaching machines, will never resolve our dilemma in a basic way. Only persons, acting like persons in their relationships with their students can even begin to make a dent on this most urgent problem of modern education.

I cannot, of course, stop here in a professional lecture. An academic lecture should be calm, factual, scholarly, critical, preferably devoid of any personal beliefs, completely devoid of passion. (This is one of the reasons I left university life, but that is a completely different story.) I cannot fully fulfill these requirements for a professional lecture, but let me at least try to state, somewhat more calmly and soberly, what I have said with such feeling and passion.

I have said that it is most unfortunate that educators and the public think about, and focus on, *teaching*. It leads them into a host of questions which are either irrelevant or absurd so far as real education is concerned.

I have said that if we focused on the facilitation of *learning*—how, why, and when the student learns, and how learning seems and feels from the inside, we might be on a much more profitable track.

I have said that we have some knowledge, and could gain more, about the conditions which facilitate learning, and that one of the most important of these conditions is the attitudinal quality of the interpersonal relationship between facilitator and learner. (There are other conditions, too, which I have tried to spell out elsewhere [Rogers, 1966b]).

Those attitudes which appear effective in promoting learning can be described. First of all is a transparent realness in the facilitator, a willingness to be a person, to be and to live the feelings and thoughts of the moment. When this realness includes a prizing, a caring, a trust and respect for the learner, the climate for learning is enhanced. When it includes a sensitive and accurate empathic listening, then indeed a freeing climate, stimulative of self-initiated learning and growth, exists.

I have tried to make plain that individuals who hold such attitudes, and are bold enough to act on them, do not simply modify classroom methods—they revolutionize them. They perform almost none of the functions of teachers. It is no longer accurate to call them teachers. They are catalyzers, facilitators, giving freedom and life and the opportunity to learn, to students.

I have brought in the cumulating research evidence which suggests that individuals who hold such attitudes are regarded as effective in the classroom; that the problems which concern them have to do with the release of potential, not the deficiencies of their students; that they seem to create classroom situations in which there are not admired children and disliked children, but in which affection and liking are a part of the life of every child; that in classrooms approaching such a psychological climate, children learn more of the conventional subjects.

But I have intentionally gone beyond the empirical findings to try to take you into the inner life of the student—elementary, college, and graduate—who is fortunate enough to live and learn in such an interpersonal relationship with a facilitator, in order to let you see what learning feels like when it is free, self-initiated and spontaneous. I have tried to indicate how it even changes the student-student relationship—making it more aware, more caring, more sensitive, as well as increasing the self-related learning of significant material.

Throughout my paper I have tried to indicate that if we are to have citizens who can live constructively in this kaleidoscopically changing world, we can *only* have them if we are willing for them to become self-starting, self-initiating learners. Finally, it has been my purpose to show that this kind of learner develops best, so far as we now know, in a growth-promoting, facilitative, relationship with a *person*.

References

Appell, M. L. "Selected Student Reactions to Student-Centered Courses." Mimeographed manuscript, 1959.

———. "Self-Understanding for the Guidance Counselor." *Personnel and Guidance Journal,* 42 (2), (October 1963): 143–148.

Ashton-Warner, S. *Teacher.* New York: Simon and Schuster, 1963.

Aspy, D. N. "A Study of Three Facilitative Conditions and Their Relationship to the Achievement of Third Grade Students." Ed.D. diss., University of Kentucky, 1965.

Axline, Virginia M. "Morale on the School Front." *Journal of Educational Research,* 38 (1944): 521–533.

Barrett-Lennard, G. T. "Dimensions of Therapist Response as Causal Factors in Therapeutic Change. *Psychological Monographs,* 76 (1962): 562.

Bills, R. E. Personal correspondence, 1961, 1966.

Bull, Patricia. Student reactions, Fall 1965. State University College, Cortland, New York. Mimeographed manuscripts, 1966.

Emmerling, F. C. "A Study of the Relationships Between Personality Characteristics of Classroom Teachers and Pupil Perceptions." Ph.D. diss., Auburn University, Auburn, Ala., 1961.

Jackson, P. W. "The Student's World." University of Chicago. Mimeographed, 1966.

Rogers, C. R. "To Facilitate Learning." In Malcolm Provus, ed., NEA Handbook for Teachers, *Innovations for Time to Teach.* Washington, D.C.: Department of Classroom Teachers, NEA, 1966a.

Rogers, C. R. "The Facilitation of Significant Learning." In L. Siegel, ed., *Contemporary Theories of Instruction.* San Francisco, Calif.: Chandler, 1966b.

Schmuck, R. "Some Aspects of Classroom Social Climate." *Psychology in the Schools,* 3 (1966) : 59–65.

———. "Some Relationships of Peer Liking Patterns in the Classroom to Pupil Attitudes and Achievement." *The School Review,* 71 (1963) : 337–359.

Shiel, Barbara J. "Evaluation: A Self-Directed Curriculum, 1965." Mimeographed, 1966.

Fostering Self-Direction

ARTHUR W. COMBS

Schools which do not produce self-directed citizens have failed everyone—the student, the profession, and the society they are designed to serve. The goals of modern education cannot be achieved without self-direction. We have created a world in which there is no longer a common body of information which everyone must have. The information explosion has blasted for all time the notion that we can feed all students the same diet. Instead, we have to adopt a cafeteria principle in which we help each student select what he most needs to fulfill his potentialities. This calls for student cooperation and acceptance of major responsibility for his own learning.

As Earl Kelley has suggested, the goal of education in the modern world must be the production of increasing uniqueness. This cannot be achieved in autocratic atmospheres where all decisions are made by the teachers and administration while students are reduced to passive followers of the established patterns. Authoritarian schools are as out of date in the world we live in as the horse and buggy. Such schools cannot hope to achieve our purposes. Worse yet, their existence will almost certainly defeat us.

The world we live in demands self-starting, self-directing citizens capable of independent action. The world is changing so fast we cannot hope to teach each person what he will need to know in twenty years. Our only hope to meet the demands of the future is the production of intelligent, independent people. Even our military establishment, historically the most authoritarian of all, has long since discovered that fact. For twenty years the armed forces have been steadily increasing the de-

Reprinted from *Educational Leadership* 23, 1966, 373–376, by permission of the author and the publisher.

gree of responsibility and initiative it expects of even its lowest echelons. The modern war machine cannot be run by automatons. It must be run by *thinking* men.

Much of the curriculum of our current schools is predicated on a concept of learning conceived as the acquisition of right answers and many of our practices mirror this belief. Almost anyone can pick them out. Here are a few which occur to me:

> Preoccupation with right answers; insistence upon conformity; cookbook approaches to learning; overconcern for rules and regulations; preoccupation with materials and things instead of people; the solitary approach to learning; the delusion that mistakes are sinful; emphasis on memory rather than learning; emphasis on grades rather than understanding and content details rather than principles.

Meanwhile, psychologists are telling us that learning is a *personal* matter; individual and unique. It is not controlled by the teacher. It can only be accomplished with the cooperation and involvement of the student in the process. Providing students with information is not enough. People rarely misbehave because they do not know any better. The effectiveness of learning must be measured in behavior change: whether students *behave differently* as a consequence of their learning experience. This requires active participation by the student. So learning itself is dependent upon the capacity for self-direction.

TOWARD SELF–DIRECTION

What is needed of us? How can we produce students who are more self-directed?

1. We Need to Believe This Is Important

If we do not think self-direction is important, this will not get done. People are too pressed these days to pay much attention to things that are not important. Everyone does what seems to him to be crucial and urgent. It seems self-evident that independence and self-direction are necessary for our kind of world. Why then has self-direction been given such inadequate attention? It is strange we should have to convince ourselves of its importance.

Unfortunately, because a matter is self-evident is no guarantee that people will really put it into practice. It must somehow be brought into clear figure in the forefront of our striving if it is to affect behavior. Everyone knows it is important to vote, too, yet millions regularly fail to vote. To be effective as an objective, each of us must hold the goal of self-direction clear in our thinking and high in our values whenever we are engaged in planning or teaching of any kind.

This is often not easy to do because self-direction is one of those goals which *everyone* is supposed to be working for. As a result, almost no one regards it as urgent! For each person, his own special duties are so much clearer, so much more pressing and his derelictions so much more glaring if he fails to produce. The goals we hold in common do not redound so immediately to our credit or discredit. They are therefore set aside while we devote our energies to the things that *really* matter to us.

To begin doing something about self-direction we must, therefore, begin by declaring its importance; not as a lofty sentiment, but as an absolute essential. It must be given a place of greater concern than subject matter itself, for a very simple reason: It is far more important than subject matter. Without self-direction no content matters much. It is not enough that it be published in the handbook as a "Goal of Education." Each of us at every level must ask himself: Do I really think self-direction is important and what am I doing about it?

2. Trust in the Human Organism

Many of us grew up in a tradition which conceived of man as basically evil and certain to revert to bestial ways if someone did not control him. Modern psychologists tell us this view is no longer tenable. From everything we can observe in humans and animals the basic striving of the organism is inexorably toward health both physical and mental. It is this growth principle on which doctors and psychotherapists depend to make the person well again. If an organism is free to do so—it can, will, it *must* move in positive ways. The organism is not our enemy. It wants the same things we do, the achievement of adequacy. Yet alas, how few believe this and how timid we are to trust our students with self-direction.

A recent best selling book, *Summerhill,* by A. S. Neill has fascinated many educators. In it Neill describes the absolute trust he placed in the children under his care. Many teachers are shocked by his unorthodox procedures and the extreme behavior of some of the children. But whether one approves of Neill's school or not, the thing which impressed me most was this: Here was a man who dared to trust children far beyond what most of us would be willing to risk. Yet, all the things we are so afraid might happen if we did give them such freedom, never happened! For forty years the school continued to turn out happy, effective citizens as well as, or better than, its competitors. It is time we give up fearing the human organism and learn to trust and use its built-in drives toward self-fulfillment. After all, the organism has had to be pretty tough to survive what we have done to it through the ages.

Responsibility and self-direction are learned. They must be acquired from experiences, from being given opportunities to be self-directing and responsible. You cannot learn to be self-directing if no one permits you to try. Human capacities are strengthened by use but atrophy with disuse. If young people are going to learn self-direction, then it must be through being *given* many opportunities to exercise such self-direction throughout the years they are in school. Someone has observed that our schools are operated on a directly contrary principle. Children are allowed more freedom of choice and self-direction in kindergarten (when they are presumably least able to handle it) and each year thereafter are given less and less, until, by the time they reach college, they are permitted practically no choice at all! This overdraws the case, to be sure, but there is enough truth in the statement to make one uncomfortable. If we are to produce independent, self-starting people we must do a great deal more to produce the kinds of experiences which will lead to these ends.

3. The Experimental Attitude

If we are going to provide young people with increased opportunity for self-direction, we must do it with our eyes open *expecting* them to make mistakes. This is not easy, for the importance of "being right" is in our blood. Education is built on right answers. Wrong ones are regarded as failures to be avoided like the plague. Unfortunately, such attitudes stand squarely in the way of progress toward self-direction and independence.

People too fearful of mistakes cannot risk trying. Without trying, self-direction, creativity and independence cannot be discovered. To be so afraid of mistakes that we kill the desire to try is a tragedy. Autonomy, independence and creativity are the products of being willing to look and eager to try. If we discourage these elements we do so at our peril. In the world we live in, victory is reserved only for the courageous and inventive. It is possible we may lose the game by making mistakes. We will not even get in the game if we are afraid to try.

Experimentation and innovation must be encouraged everywhere in our schools, in teachers as well as students. Each of us needs to be engaged in a continuous process of trying something new. The kind of experimentation which will make the difference to education in the long run is not that produced by the professional researcher with the aid of giant computers but by the everyday changes in goals and processes brought about by the individual teacher in the classroom.

To achieve this, teachers need to be freed of pressures and details by the administration for the exercise of self-direction and creativity. In addition, each of us must accept the challenge and set about a systematic search for the barriers we place in the path of self-direction for ourselves, our colleagues and our students. This should suggest all kinds of places for experimentation where we can begin the encouragement of self-direction. One of the nice things about self-direction is that it does not have to be taught. It only needs to be encouraged and set free to operate.

4. The Provision of Opportunity

The basic principle is clear. To produce more self-directed people it is necessary to give more opportunity to practice self-direction. This means some of us must be willing to give up our traditional prerogatives to make all the decisions. Education must be seen, not as providing right answers, but as confrontation with problems; not imaginary play problems either, but *real* ones in which decisions count.

Experiences calling for decision, independence and self-direction must be the daily diet of children, including such little decisions as what kinds of headings and margins a paper should have and big ones like the courses to be taken next year. They must also include decisions about goals, techniques, time, people, money, meals, rules, and subject matter.

If we are to achieve the objective of greater self-direction, I see no alternative to the fuller acceptance of students into partnership in the educative endeavor. Our modern goal for education, "the optimal development of the individual," cannot be achieved without this. Such an aim requires participation of the student and his wholehearted cooperation in the process. This is not likely to be accomplished unless students have the feeling they matter and their decisions count. Few of us are deeply committed to tasks imposed upon us; and students are not much different. Self-direction is learned from experience. What better, more meaningful experience could be provided than participation in the decisions about one's own life and learning?

The basic belief of democracy is that when people are free they can find their own best ways. Though all of us profess our acceptance of this credo, it is distressing how few of us dare to put it to work. Whatever limits the capacity of our young people to accept both the challenge and the responsibilities of that belief is destructive to all of us. It is time we put this belief to work and to expression in the education of our young as though we really meant it.

The Task of the Teacher

W. W. PURKEY

Let people realize clearly that every time they threaten someone or humiliate or hurt unnecessarily or dominate or reject another human being, they become forces for the creation of psychopathology, even if these be small forces. Let them recognize that every man who is kind, helpful, decent, psychologically democratic, affectionate, and warm, is a psychotherapeutic force even though a small one.

ABRAHAM H. MASLOW, *Motivation and Personality*

In this book you have been introduced to a body of theory about the self. We have considered some of the self's major characteristics, analyzed how the self and scholastic success are related, and reviewed the creation of the self. Now we turn our attention to the task of the teacher: to help each student gain a positive and realistic image of himself as a learner.

Before we consider the process of building positive and realistic self concepts in students, it is necessary to point out the need to avoid instilling negative ones. The self is remarkably conservative, and once a child has formed a negative image of himself as a learner, the task of the teacher becomes extremely difficult. Therefore, the *prevention of negative self concepts is a vital first step in teaching.* The unfavorable features of some schools, which we discussed in the previous chapter, can be modified by teachers who are aware of the need and who want to make changes.

Several studies have shown that it is possible to develop a curriculum

From W. W. Purkey, *Self Concept and School Achievement.* Englewood Cliffs, N.J.: Prentice-Hall, Inc., 1970, pp. 43–65. Reprinted with permission of the author and publisher.

in which the expected academic learning takes place while positive self concepts are being built. Frankel (1964) studied the effects of a special program of advanced summer study on the self-perceptions of academically talented high school students. He concluded that the self concepts of the group showed significant gains after attending the program, particularly in the areas of self-reliance and special talents. In a somewhat similar study of the effects of a pre-kindergarten on the self concept, Crovetto, Fischer, and Boudreaux (1967) developed a modified Head Start curriculum specifically designed to affect the child's self concept in a positive direction. When the experimental group of students was compared with a control group, it was found that the experimental class members showed gains on the *Draw-A-Man Test,* while the control group did not. The experimental curriculum appeared to be effective in helping to develop a more positive self concept in children.

Beneath program arrangements and curricular innovations lies the teacher's personal role. What part do teachers play in the development of the child's self? Can teachers change the child's self-image if they try to do so? If they can, what methods of teaching produce what kinds of self-image? Is it possible to distinguish between teachers in the frequency and kind of comment which they make about the child's self? To answer these questions, Staines (1958) conducted a study involving careful observation, recording, and analyzing of data from teacher-child and child-child interaction in four elementary school classrooms. Data were collected on the educational outcomes of the interaction between personalities in the atmosphere of the classroom, particular attention being given to identifying those teachers who could be reliably distinguished by the frequency of their use of words and kinds of situational management which, in the opinion of competent judges who served as observers, are likely to be positive influences on the self concepts of students.

The investigation showed marked differences between teachers in the frequency of references about the child in their comments, particularly in their positive or negative comments on the child's performance, status, and self-confidence or potency. Also, it was found that it is possible to teach so that, while aiming at the normal results of teaching, specific changes can be made in the child's self-image. Staines concluded that changes in the child's self concept do occur as an outcome of the learning situation, and that the self must be recognized as an important factor in learning. Teaching methods can be adapted so that definite changes of the kind sought for will occur in the self without injury to the academic program in the process.

Teachers want to be significant forces in the lives of their students. As Moustakas (1966) declared, every teacher wants to meet the student on a significant level, every teacher wants to feel that what he does makes a difference. Yet in order to influence students it is necessary to become a *significant other* in their lives. We are seldom changed by people whom we see as insignificant or unimportant. The way the teacher becomes significant seems to rest on two forces: (1) what he believes, and (2) what he does.

WHAT THE TEACHER BELIEVES

No printed word nor spoken plea
Can teach young minds what men should be,
Not all the books on all the shelves
But what the teachers are themselves.

ANONYMOUS

A basic assumption of the theory of the self concept is that we behave according to our beliefs. If this assumption is true, then it follows that the teacher's beliefs about himself and his students are crucial factors in determining his effectiveness in the classroom. Available evidence (Combs 1969) indicates that the teacher's attitudes toward himself and others are as important, if not more so, than his techniques, practices, or materials. In fact, there do not seem to be any techniques which are always associated with people who are effective in the helping relationship. Rogers (1965) reported that personality changes in therapy come about not because of such factors as professional qualifications and training, or knowledge or skill, or ideological orientation, but primarily because of the attitudinal characteristics of the relationship. Attitudes play an important role, and so we need to examine the teacher's beliefs about himself and his students in some detail.

WHAT THE TEACHER BELIEVES ABOUT HIMSELF

There seems to be general agreement that the teacher needs to have positive and realistic attitudes about himself and his abilities before he is able to reach out to like and respect others. Numerous studies (Berger 1953; Fey 1954; Luft 1966) have reported that there is a marked relation between the way an individual sees himself and the way he sees others. Those who accept themselves tend to be more accepting of others (Trent 1957) and perceive others as more accepting (Omwake 1954). Further, according to Omwake, those who reject themselves hold a correspondingly low opinion of others and perceive others as being self-rejecting. From these studies it seems clear that the teacher needs to see himself in essentially positive ways. The manner in which this can be accomplished needs further investigation, but Jersild and Combs have given us some clues.

Jersild (1952, 1960, 1965) has been a pioneer in emphasizing the importance of the attitudes that teachers hold about themselves. He argues that the self-understanding of teachers is a necessary factor in coping with their feelings and in becoming more effective in the classroom. The personal problems of teachers often interfere with their effectiveness in teaching, and an understanding of the influence of these and other attitudes and emotions is vital in working with students. Jersild has suggested that we need to encourage in-service group counseling situations for teachers, in which their attitudes and feelings can be safely explored with others. This, it is hoped, would result in increased understanding of and sensitivity to oneself, and to more effective teaching in the classroom.

A similar view is reported by Combs and his associates (1963, 1964, 1965, 1969) in their research on the perceptual organization of effective helpers. They found that effective teachers, counselors, and priests could be distinguished from ineffective helpers on the basis of their attitudes about themselves and others. Such findings as these have long-range implications for the professional education of teachers. In fact, the suggestion that teacher preparation should be based on a perceptual, self concept approach has already appeared in Combs' *The Professional Education of Teachers* (1965), and an experimental program of teacher training using the perceptual approach was introduced at the University of Florida in 1969.

The way the evidence points is that each teacher needs to view himself with respect, liking, and acceptance. When teachers have essentially favorable attitudes toward themselves, they are in a much better position to build positive and realistic self concepts in their students.

WHAT THE TEACHER BELIEVES ABOUT STUDENTS

The ways significant others evaluate the student directly affects the student's conception of his academic ability. This in turn establishes limits on his success in school. Teachers, in their capacity of significant others, need to view students in essentially positive ways and hold favorable expectations. This is particularly important at the elementary level, but is vital in all grades. Several studies bear directly on the importance of what the teacher believes about students.

Davidson and Lang (1960) found that the student's perceptions of the teacher's feelings toward him correlated positively with his self-perception. Further, the more positive the children's perceptions of their teacher's feelings, the better their academic achievement and the more desirable their classroom behavior as rated by the teacher. Clarke (1960) reported a positive relationship between a student's academic performance and his perception of the academic expectations of him by significant others.

One of the most comprehensive studies of the self concept of ability and school success was that of Brookover and his associates (1965, 1967) which we considered, in part, earlier. Brookover and his associates conducted a six-year study of the relation between the self concept of academic ability and school achievement among students in one school class while in the seventh through the twelfth grades. A major purpose of the study was to determine whether improved self concept results from the expectations and evaluations held by significant others as perceived by the students. As Brookover, Erickson, and Joiner conclude: "The hypothesis that students' perceptions of the evaluations of their academic ability by others (teachers, parents, and friends) are associated with self concepts of academic ability was confirmed" (1967, p. 110). The almost unavoidable conclusion is that the teacher's attitudes and opinions regarding his students have a significant influence on their success in school. In other words, when the teacher believes that his students can achieve, the students appear to be more successful; when the teacher believes that the students cannot achieve, then it influences their performance negatively. This self-fulfilling prophecy has been illuminated by the research of Rosenthal and Jacobson (1968a, b).

The basic hypothesis of Rosenthal and Jacobson's research was that students, more often than not, do what is expected of them. To test this hypothesis, the two researchers conducted an experiment in a public elementary school of 650 students. The elementary-school teachers were told that, on the basis of ability tests administered the previous spring, approximately one-fifth of the students could be expected to evidence significant increases in mental ability during the year. The teachers were then given the names of the high-potential students. Although in fact the names had been *chosen at random* by the experimenters, when intelligence tests and other measures were administered some months later, those identified as potential spurters tended to score significantly higher than the children who had not been so identified. Also, Rosenthal and Jacobson found that these children were later described by their teachers as happier, more curious, more interesting, and as having a better chance of future success than other children. The conclusion drawn by Rosenthal and Jacobson is that the teacher, through his facial expressions, postures, and touch, through what, how, and when he spoke, subtly helped the child to learn. This may have been accomplished, according to the researchers, by modifying the child's self concept, his expectations of his own behavior, and his motivations, as well as his cognitive style. They summarized their study by stating that the evidence suggests strongly that "children who are expected by their teachers to gain intellectually in fact do show greater intellectual gains after one year than do children of whom such gains are not expected" (1968b, p. 121). The full educational implications of the self-fulfilling prophecy remain to be explored, but it seems certain that the ways the teacher views the student have a significant influence on the student and his performance.

WHAT THE TEACHER DOES

As we have seen, the key to building positive and realistic self-images in students lies largely in what the teacher *believes* about himself and his students. These beliefs not only determine the teacher's behavior, but are transmitted to the students and influence their performance as well. Yet we cannot ignore what the teacher *does* in the classroom, for the behavior he displays and the experiences he provides, *as perceived by students,* have a strong impact in themselves. In this section we will consider two important aspects of the teacher's role: (1) *the attitudes he conveys;* and (2) *the atmosphere he develops.*

THE ATTITUDE THE TEACHER CONVEYS

It is difficult to overestimate the need for the teacher to be sensitive to the attitudes he expresses toward students. Even though teachers may have the best intentions, they sometimes project distorted images of themselves. What a person believes can be hidden by negative habits picked up long ago. Therefore, teachers need to ask themselves:

- *Am I projecting an image that tells the student that I am here to build, rather than to destroy, him as a person?* (Spaulding 1963, reported that there is a significant relationship between a student's positive self concept as reported, and the degree to which teachers are calm, accepting, supportive, and facilitative, and a negative relationship between a student's self concept and teachers who are threatening, grim and sarcastic.)
- *Do I let the student know that I am aware of and interested in him as a unique person?* (Moustakas 1966, maintains that every child wants to be known as a unique person, and that by holding the student in esteem, the teacher is establishing an environmental climate that facilitates growth.)
- *Do I convey my expectations and confidence that the student can accom-*

plish work, can learn, and is competent? (Rosenthal and Jacobson 1968b, have shown that the teacher's expectations have a significant influence on the student's performance.)

- *Do I provide well-defined standards of values, demands for competence, and guidance toward solutions to problems?* (Coopersmith 1967, has provided evidence that self-reliance is fostered by an environment which is well-structured and reasonably demanding, rather than unlimitedly permissive.)
- *When working with parents, do I enhance the academic expectations and evaluations which they hold of their children's ability?* (Brookover et al. 1965, has illustrated that this method yields significant results in enhancing self concept and improving academic achievement.)
- *By my behavior, do I serve as a model of authenticity for the student?* (Both Jourard 1964, and Rogers 1965, suggest that a most important factor in the helping relationship is the helper serving as a model of genuineness, without "front.")
- *Do I take every opportunity to establish a high degree of private or semi-private communication with my students?* (Spaulding 1963, found a high relationship between the pupil's self concept and the teacher's behavior when it involved personal and private talks with students.)

The above questions are samples of how the teacher may check himself to see if he is conveying his beliefs in an authentic and meaningful fashion. As Gill reported, teachers' attitudes toward students are vitally important in shaping the self concepts of their students. Gill summarized his study by saying that "teachers should consider self concept as a vital and important aspect of learning and development which the school, through its educational process, should seek to promote and foster in every child" (1969, p. 10).

THE ATMOSPHERE THE TEACHER CREATES

Six factors seem particularly important in creating a classroom atmosphere conducive to developing favorable self-images in students. These are (1) challenge; (2) freedom; (3) respect; (4) warmth; (5) control; and (6) success. A brief discussion of each of these may be helpful.

Challenge

Because of the focus of this book, little has been said about high standards of academic accomplishment. This omission should not be taken to mean that achievement should be minimized. As we have seen, high academic expectations and a high degree of challenge on the part of teachers have a positive and beneficial effect on students. A good way to create challenge is to wait until the chances of success are good, and then say: "This is hard work, but I think that you can do it." The teacher chooses the right moment to put his trust on the line with students. Of course, an important part of challenge is relevance. If the required learning is relevant to the student's world of experience and has some personal meaning to him, then he is likely to work hard—*if* he feels free to try. This brings us to the question of freedom.

Freedom

It is difficult for self-esteem to grow in an environment where there is little or no freedom of choice. If the student is to grow and develop as an adequate human being, he needs the opportunity to make meaningful decisions for himself. This also means that he must have the freedom to make mistakes, and even to laugh at his inadequacies. Carlton and Moore (1966, 1968) have shown that the freedom of self-directed dramatization improved the reading ability and enhanced the self concept of elementary-school youngsters. This general emphasis on freedom has been highlighted by Moustakas, who wrote: "Self values are in jeopardy in any climate where freedom and choice are denied, in a situation where the individual rejects his own senses and substitutes for his own perceptions the standards and expectations of others" (1966, pp. 4*f*). When the student has a say in his own development and is given personal decisions to make, he develops faith in his own judgments and thoughts.

Closely related to the notion of freedom of choice is the idea of freedom from threat. Children seem to learn and develop best in an atmosphere characterized by much challenge and little threat. Kowitz has noted, for example, that if the child feels evaluation takes place with "vicious assault upon his self concept" (1967, p. 163), there can be little real freedom. In fact, some students fear failure so much that they avoid achievement whenever they can and, when they cannot, do not try to succeed. In this way, they can avoid the task of trying to achieve. A comprehensive study of the person who fears failure is provided by Birney, Burdick, and Teevan (1969).

What this means to the teacher is that students will learn, provided the material appears to be relevant to their lives and provided they have the freedom to explore and to discover its meaning for themselves. We know that exploration is curtailed in an atmosphere in which one must spend most of his time avoiding or reducing the experience of anxiety brought about by threat to the self. Sarason (1961) has reported that a poor performance by anxious subjects occurred only when the task was presented as a threat. When anxious subjects were told that failure was normal and expected, they actually outperformed subjects who were less anxious. The freedom to try without a tiger springing at you if you fail is essential to a healthy atmosphere in the classroom.

In considering the factors of freedom and challenge, the classroom teacher can ask himself:

- *Do I encourage students to try something new and to join in new activities?*
- *Do I allow students to have a voice in planning, and do I permit them to help make the rules they follow?*
- *Do I permit students to challenge my opinions?*
- *Do I teach in as exciting and interesting a manner as possible?*
- *Do I distinguish between students' classroom mistakes and their personal failure?*
- *Do I avoid unfair and ruthless competition in the classroom?*

Questions like these can help the teacher evaluate himself and the classroom climate he creates.

Respect

A basic feeling by the teacher for the worth and dignity of students is vital in building self concepts in them. No aspect of education is more important than the feeling on the part of the teacher that the individual student is important, valuable, and *can* learn in school. Sometimes teachers forget the importance of respect and run roughshod over the personal feelings of students. Using both the official and unofficial school practices which we cataloged in Chapter 3, teachers sometimes lower the feelings of worth of many young people. One of my students told me why he could never get along with his previous English teacher. It was because, although his name is Cribbidge, "She always called me cabbage whenever she called roll, and then laughed." The rule seems to be that whenever we treat a student with respect, we add to his self-respect, and whenever we embarrass or humiliate him, we are likely to build disrespect in him both for himself and others.

If the teacher genuinely values and respects students, it will be reflected in everything he does. Davidson and Lang (1960) found that when students feel that teachers value and respect them, they are likely to value and respect themselves. Moustakas summed it up this way: "By cherishing and holding the child in absolute esteem, the teacher is establishing an environmental climate that facilitates growth and becoming" (1966, p. 13).

The need for respect is particularly important in working with culturally disadvantaged students. These are the children whose behavior makes them most difficult to respect, but who probably need respect the most. Teachers must make an extra effort to communicate to these young people a feeling of trust, positive regard, and respect. Closely related to respect is the concept of warmth.

Warmth

There is considerable evidence to support the assumption that a psychologically safe and supportive learning situation encourages students to grow academically as well as in feelings of personal worth. Cogan (1958) reported that students with warm, considerate teachers produced unusual amounts of original poetry and art. Christensen (1960) found the warmth of teachers significantly related to their students' vocabulary and achievement in arithmetic. Reed (1962) concluded that teachers characterized as considerate, understanding, and friendly, and with a tolerance for some release of emotional feeling by students, had a favorable influence on their students' interest in science.

Relating more directly to the task of building favorable self concepts, Spaulding's research (1964) supported the findings of previous investigators regarding positive attitudes toward the self. He found significant correlations between the height of the self concept and the degree to which the teachers in his study were calm, accepting, supportive, and facilitative. It is interesting to note that significant negative correlations with the height of pupils' self concepts were found when teachers were dominating, threatening, and sarcastic.

An important part of warmth is commitment. Teaching has been described as a delicate relationship, almost like a marriage, where, in a sense, the teacher and student belong to each other. The student says "There is *my* teacher" and the teacher says "These are *my* students." The process of commitment is illustrated by the story of the chicken and pig who were walking down a country lane: The chicken excitedly told the portly pig of his latest business idea. "We'll prepare and franchise the best tasting ham 'n eggs money can buy, and we'll make a fortune." The pig thought it over for a moment and replied: "It's easy for you to get enthused. For you it's an occupation, but for *me* it means *total* commitment!" Perhaps total commitment is asking too much of teachers, but certainly they need to feel that their work with students is more than an occupation. A warm and supportive educational atmosphere is one in which each student is made to feel that he belongs in school and that teachers care about what happens to him. It is one in which praise is used in preference to punishment, courtesy in preference to sarcasm, and consultation in preference to dictation.

Some practical questions about respect and warmth which the teacher might ask himself are:

- *Do I learn the name of each student as soon as possible, and do I use that name often?*
- *Do I share my feelings with my students?*
- *Do I practice courtesy with my students?*
- *Do I arrange some time when I can talk quietly alone with each student?*
- *Do I spread my attention around and include each student, keeping special watch for the student who may need extra attention?*
- *Do I notice and comment favorably on the things that are important to students?*
- *Do I show students who return after being absent that I am happy to have them back in class, and that they were missed?*

It is in ways such as these that we tell the student that he is important to us.

Control

Coopersmith (1967) has suggested that children who are brought up in a permissive environment tend to develop less self-esteem than those reared in a firmer and more demanding atmosphere. The assumption that clearly established and relatively firm guidance produces more self-esteem in children can also be applied to the classroom. It is important for the teacher to maintain discipline, for the type of control under which a child lives has considerable effect on his self-image. It is yet another way of telling the student that the teacher cares about him and what he does. Classroom control does not require ridicule and embarrassment. The secret seems to be in the leadership qualities of the teacher. When he is prepared for class, keeps on top of the work and avoids the appearance of confusion, explains why some things must be done, and strives for consistency, politeness, and firmness, then classroom control is likely to be maintained. When punishment is unavoidable (and often it *can* be avoided), then it is best to withdraw the student's privileges. Of course, this means that teachers must be sure that there *are* some privileges in school which can be withdrawn. Poor control procedures would include punishing the entire class for the transgressions of a few, using corporal punishment, or using school work as punishment.

In considering classroom control, teachers might ask themselves:

- *Do I remember to see small disciplinary problems as understandable, and not as personal insults?*
- *Do I avoid having "favorites" and "victims"?*

- *Do I have, and do my students have, a clear idea of what is and what is not acceptable in my class?*
- *Within my limits, is there room for students to be active and natural?*
- *Do I make sure that I am adequately prepared for class each day?*
- *Do I usually make it through the day without punishing students?*

Questions such as these help the teacher to estimate his ability to handle students in a way which maintains discipline and, at the same time, builds positive and realistic self concepts in students.

Some teachers believe that warmth and firmness are in opposition to each other, but this is not so. Warmth is more than the obvious display of affection, it is also expressed by firmness which says to the student, "You are important to me and I care about the ways in which you behave."

Success

Perhaps the single most important step that teachers can take in the classroom is to provide an educational atmosphere of success rather than failure. Reviewing over a dozen experiments, Wylie (1961) made the tentative statement that students are likely to change their self-evaluations after experimentally induced success or failure. This statement has been echoed in more recent studies. Costello (1964) found that overall, regardless of the task or the ability of the students, praise produces more improvement in performance than blame. Ludwig and Maehr (1967) showed that the approval of significant others caused an increase in self-ratings and an increased preference for activities connected with the criterion task, and that disapproval resulted in a lowered self-rating and a decreased preference for related activities. Moreover, the reaction to the evaluation was followed by a spread of effect, from the areas directly approved by the significant others to related areas of self-regard.

A number of writers have pointed out some of the steps involved in giving honest experiences of success. Page's (1958) research showed that pupils' performance improved significantly when teachers wrote encouraging comments on their written work. A control group, given conventional grades without comment, lost ground. Walsh (1956) explains that it is helpful to show students that they have mastered even the smallest step, rather than vaguely saying "That's nice" about everything.

The sensitive teacher points out areas of accomplishment, rather than focusing on mistakes. Continuing awareness of failure results in lowered expectations, not learning. According to Combs and Snygg (1959) a positive view is learned from the ways people treat the learner. People learn that they are able, not from failure but from success. Questions about success which the teacher might ask himself when he thinks about success experiences for students include:

- *Do I permit my students some opportunity to make mistakes without penalty?*
- *Do I make generally positive comments on written work?*
- *Do I give extra support and encouragement to slower students?*
- *Do I recognize the successes of students in terms of what they did earlier?*
- *Do I take special opportunities to praise students for their successes?*
- *Do I manufacture honest experiences of success for my students?*
- *Do I set tasks which are, and which appear to the student to be, within his abilities?*

What all of this discussion hopes to say to teachers is that a backlog of challenge, freedom, respect, warmth, control, and success develops positive self-images in students and encourages academic achievement. The absence of these factors makes for the person who is crippled psychologically.

THE SENSITIVITY THE TEACHER DEVELOPS

> *You can know me truly only if I let you, only if I want you to know me. . . . If you want me to reveal myself, just demonstrate your good will—your will to employ your powers for my good, and not for my destruction.*
>
> SIDNEY JOURARD, *The Transparent Self*

"Sensitivity" is a term which is used to serve many purposes and to describe various processes. In this book it is defined as the ability to sense what an individual feels about himself and the world. Sensitivity first requires the honest *desire* to become aware of how others are experiencing things. This sounds simple, but the fact is that many people don't take the necessary time and trouble to be sensitive to others. After the desire must come the habit of really listening, and listening for meanings rather than words. For instance, a student might say that he does not wish to try, when he means that it is better not to try than to try and be proved wrong.

Entering a person's private world in order to understand how he is seeing things is difficult, for the individual self can only be approached through the perceptions of some other person, perceptions filled with all sorts of prejudices, aspirations, and anxieties. Fortunately, however, most teachers have a great supply of sensitivity, as do most humans. It's just a matter of applying this sensitivity more deliberately to teaching. To the degree to which a teacher is able to predict how his students are viewing themselves, their subject, and the world, to that degree he is in a position to become a successful teacher.

Throughout this book the idea has been stressed over and over that the teacher must give the self concepts of students far greater emphasis than is presently given. The purpose of this section is to assist teachers to become more competent in assessing the self concepts of the students with whom they work. For a long time, many of us in education and psychology have been saying that theory about the self has a vital role to play in the educative process and that teachers should be made more aware of the importance of how students view themselves. Yet little has been done to equip teachers and counselors with simple clinical techniques and instruments which would enable them to be more sensitive to their students. It would seem that we in education have the responsibility, within the limits of our training, to investigate, to understand, and to utilize the self concept as a means of facilitating scholastic success. What a person says about himself, and the influences we draw from his behavior, are valuable data for teachers. However, these are problems in understanding how students view themselves, as we shall see.

PROBLEMS IN EVALUATING THE SELF

"First of all," he said, "if you can learn a simple trick, Scout, you'll get along a lot better with all kinds of folks. You never really understand a person until you consider things from his point of view—"

"Sir?"

"—until you climb into his skin and walk around in it."

Harper Lee, *To Kill a Mockingbird*

No one, of course, can ever climb into another's skin, or see this construct we call the self, but we can infer that self in a number of ways. Two of these ways are: (1) "self-report," that which can be inferred from an individual's statements about himself; and (2) "observations," that which can be inferred from the individual's behavior. Before we turn to these methods, however, it is wise to remind ourselves that the self is multidimensional and tremendously complex and that there are two major cautions that we need to be aware of in assessing it: our *limitations* and our *biases*.

Excerpt from *To Kill a Mockingbird* by Harper Lee, Copyright © 1960, is reprinted by permission of J. B. Lippincott Company and William Heinemann Ltd.

Limitations. Ideally, when you desire to assess the self, you need training and supervised experience in measurement, clinical psychology, and personality theory. Even without this preparation, however, it is possible to understand the concept of the self and to be aware of the means of measuring it. Regardless of your training, you should seek out counselors, school psychologists, and other qualified helpers to assist you in your assessments. It would also be helpful to seek out and read some of the References at the end of this book and give you a clearer understanding of the complexity of measuring the self.

Above all, keep in mind your own limitations. This means being aware of the extent of your training and of the possible cost of errors in judgment, being able to tolerate ambiguity, not being too hasty with answers but instead trying to base your inferences on sufficient evidence, and that remembering that the self is many times more difficult to assess than is some tangible object.

Biases. It is helpful to keep in mind that a self must be studied through the perceptions of someone. Even when you try to describe your *own* self, it can only be a rough approximation. As we shall see later, one's observation of oneself is open to distortion, either involuntarily or deliberately. Therefore, in making inferences about the self, it is vital to recognize your own biases and try to take them into account as much as possible. Your task is to gain a clearer understanding of the student's self, not to try to give him yours. To put it another way, you should have a fair understanding of yourself before you attempt to evaluate the self of others.

Evaluating the Self Through Self-Reports

Through the years there has been controversy over the validity and reliability of self-report inventories. One is dealing with validity when he asks the question: *Is the instrument measuring what it claims to measure?* If so, it is a "valid" instrument. One is dealing with reliability when he asks: *How consistent are the findings through various administrations?* If the findings are consistent through repeated administrations, the instrument is considered "reliable."

Rogers (1951) has taken the position that self-reports are valuable sources of information about the individual. And Allport (1955, 1961) has written that the individual has the right to be believed when he reports his feelings about himself. Both these authorities believe that if we want to know more about a person, we should ask him directly. Sarbin and Rosenberg (1955) concluded from their research that their self-report instrument was useful in getting at meaningful self-attributes quickly and with a minimum of effort. Perhaps this general viewpoint can best be summarized by a statement of Strong and Feder: "Every evaluative statement that a person makes concerning himself can be considered a sample of his self concept, from which inferences may then be made about the various properties of that self concept" (1961, p. 170). Numerous other studies have been based on the assumption that evaluative statements made by the individual about himself are valid and reliable data.

The major critics of self-reporting believe that while the self concept is what an individual believes about himself, the self-report is only what he is willing and able to disclose to someone else. Combs, Courson, and Soper (1963) argue that these are rarely, if ever, identical. They refer to Combs and Soper (1957), who reported that the degree to which the self-report can be relied upon as an accurate indication of the self concept depends upon such factors as: (1) the clarity of the subject's awareness; (2) his command of adequate symbols for expression; (3) social expectancy; (4) the cooperation of the subject; and (5) his freedom from threat.

Three additional variables which might influence self-reports are the *familiarity of the item, response set,* and *social desirability.* Purinton (1965) reported that changes in self-reports wth repeated usage could be related to the student's familiarity with the items and would not necessarily reflect a change in his self concept. Shulman (1968) found that there are yea-sayers and nay-sayers who respond in a particular pattern irrespective of the inventory questions. Heilbrun (1965) has maintained that the social desirability of a response has something to do with its probability of endorsement on a self-report test.

Wylie (1961) concluded from her comprehensive review of research on self concept:

> We would like to assume that a subject's self-report responses are determined by his phenomenal field. However, we know that it would be naive to take this for granted, since it is obvious that such responses may also be influenced by the: (a) subject's intent to select what he wishes to reveal to the examiner, (b) subject's intent to say that he has attitudes or perceptions which he doesn't have, (c) subject's response habits, particularly those involving introspection and the use of language, and (d) host of situational and methodological factors which may not only induce variations of (a), (b), and (c) but may exert other more superficial influences on the responses obtained (1961, p. 24).

Clearly, there are a host of contaminating variables in self-reports. For the teacher, this means that conclusions about self concept based solely on self-reports must be taken with a great deal of salt. However, in spite of their weaknesses and limitations, self-reports do reveal characteristics of the self and are important to teachers. Used sensitively in conjunction with other evidence, self-reports give rich insights into how the child sees himself and his world. A few of the better known self-report inventories are listed below. For a more complete description of these and other self-report inventories, the reader is referred to Purkey (1968).

- *The Self-esteem Inventory.* The SEI was developed by Stanley Coopersmith of the University of California. It was especially constructed for the research reported in *The Antecedents of Self-esteem* (Coopersmith 1967). All the statements in the scale have been worded for use with children 8 to 10.
- *The Bledsoe Self Concept Scale.* The BSCS, which was designed by Joseph Bledsoe of the University of Georgia, has been used with success from the third through the eighth grades, (Bledsoe 1967). It consists of a checklist of 30 trait-descriptive adjectives.
- *The Self-appraisal Scale.* Another recent self-report inventory is the SAS, developed by Helen Davidson and Judith Greenberg of the City College of the City University of New York for their research on scholastic achievers from a deprived background (Davidson and Greenberg 1967.) It consists of 24 items, each of which has been tested for its intelligibility to fifth-grade children.
- *The How-I-See-Myself-Scale.* This popular instrument was developed by Ira Gordon of the University of Florida from 1958 to 1967. It was devised from the categories developed by Jersild (1952), out of the compositions of children. The scale consists of a 40 (elementary form) or 42-item (secondary form) five-point scale. Additional information may be found in Gordon (1966, 1968) and Yeatts (1967).
- *Q-Sort.* Q-sort is not so much an instrument as it is a method. It requires the subject to sort a number of self-reference statements (usually 70 to 150 items) into a series of piles or classes along a continuum of appropriateness of self-description, from those "most like" him to those "least like" him. The number of items sorted into each pile is specified in such a way that the resulting frequency distributions approximates that of a normal distribution. For an extensive reference on this method, see Cummins (1963).
- *Semantic Differential.* The semantic differential technique of measuring the "meaning systems" of individuals was developed by Charles Osgood of the University of Illinois. The method is described in detail in Osgood, Suci, and Tannenbaum (1957). Basically, it involves sets of polar adjectives such as Happy–sad, Hard–soft, and Slow–fast, with five to seven spaces between each set. The concept to be measured is placed at the top of the scale and the subject is to place a check somewhere along the continuum to indicate his attitude. It is a popular and flexible

method of measuring the dimensions of one's system of meaning about himself and the world in which he lives.

There are other commercially produced self-report inventories which are designated to be used by individuals with special training in psychometrics. Two of the more popular are the *Tennessee Self Concept Scale* (Fitts 1964) published by Counselor Recordings and Tests, Box 6184, Acklen Station, Nashville, Tennessee, 37212, and the *California Psychological Inventory* (Gough 1956) published by Consulting Psychologists Press, Inc., 577 College Ave., Palo Alto, California.

Whether the self-report inventory you use is commercially prepared or locally produced, it is a good idea to remember four rules in giving self-report scales:

1. When working with younger students, items should be read to the students while the children read silently.
2. Stress the fact that there are no *right* or *wrong* answers. The student is to express those ideas he holds true about himself.
3. All self-report inventories should be administered under conditions which are as unthreatening as possible.
4. Maintain the confidentiality of the results.

Evaluating the Self Through Observations

Traditionally, observers of human behavior have been encouraged to be as passive, uninvolved, and detached as possible, in order to facilitate their learning and avoid disrupting the person being observed. The goal was to strive for objective perception of the individual and his behavior and to separate the observer's self from that which is being observed (Carbonara 1961). In fact, the more like a camera, the more depersonalized and detached the observer became, the better.

A more recent approach to observation is that of Combs (1965a) who believes that observations are unnecessarily frustrating because "of a mistaken belief that observations must be made objectively" (1965a, p. 64). He believes that sensitivity is a matter of commitment, and that the observer should be looking for *reasons* for behavior rather than at behavior itself. He explains (p. 66):

> I have given up asking my students to make coldly factual, detailed observation reports. I now ask them to do what I do myself when I watch a child behaving or a teacher teaching—to get the "feel" of what's going on, to see if they can get inside the skin of the person being observed, to understand how things look from his point of view. I ask them, "What do you think he is trying to do?" "How do you suppose he feels?" "How would you have to feel to behave like that?" "How does he see the other kids?" "What does he feel about the subject?" and so on.

It seems that Combs' approach encourages the teacher's exploration, involvement, and sensitivity to the individual.

For our purposes, we can utilize both approaches. We can be as objective as possible when making observations, and then we can be free to form our more subjective inferences.

Making observations. We can never view ourselves or anyone else with complete objectivity, for the meanings we assign things, people, and events are products of our past experience and the processes of how we view ourselves, as we have seen. Yet teachers need to minimize bias as much as possible. A good way to do this is to understand the process of observation.

In observing a person we usually begin with his appearance. We can become aware of the clothes he wears and the way he wears them. We can consider his height and weight, his posture, his grooming, and his general cleanliness. We can take note of any physical problems and his apparent state of health. Next we can take into account his behavior—his speech, his movements, his facial expressions, his manner, his habits and his reactions. We can be particularly alert to fleeting clues which tell us how he relates to his peer group and to adults, taking into account the things he seeks out and the things he avoids, the way he reacts to success and to failure, to approval and disapproval, and the ways he spends his spare time. From all these observations we gather the raw material which we may use to draw inferences. Always, we should keep in mind that *his perceptions* of his appearance and behavior are more important to our understanding of him than his appearance and behavior in themselves. Sometimes a student with a seriously negative self concept will look fine.

Often it is possible for us to structure our observations by having the student respond to stimuli like those presented in structured interviews or simple quasi-projective techniques. In the structured interview, questions are carefully organized and may be open-ended. They usually deal with the student's hopes, fears, likes, dislikes, family, and school life, and are posed in an atmosphere of acceptance and permissiveness. Sacks (1966) gives a number of tips on the techniques involved in using such structured interviews.

Simple quasi-projective techniques, which we can think of as the process of drawing inferences from the student's productions, involve having the student evaluate himself by writing an autobiography, complete interest records, participate in play situations, or make up stories or complete sentences. The younger child's drawings can be used as indications of his self (Harris 1963). Dinkmeyer (1965) provides some useful tips on the inferential aspect of child study.

Before you draw inferences about a student, it will be helpful to ask yourself: "How do I feel about this person?" "What things might distort my perceptions of how this student sees himself and others?" Try to include a number of observations on different days, to avoid misunderstandings based on a person's "off-day." Finally, avoid jumping to conclusions. If a student spends some time alone, it may stem merely from his enjoyment of solitary activities. For a more detailed treatment of methods of observation, Gordon's book (1966) provides a comprehensive treatment.

Drawing inferences. Inference is a valuable scientific tool whose reliability between and within observers has been demonstrated (Courson, 1965). Once appearance and behavior have been carefully observed, we are prepared to draw some inferences. On the basis of what we've seen, we should ask ourselves: "What are some of the beliefs he holds about himself?" "Does he see himself as a student, a leader, an athlete, a popular fellow, a son, or whatever, and in what order?" "Are his beliefs about himself generally positive or negative?" "Which beliefs are more central?" "Which are more value-laden?" "Which beliefs are most likely to resist change?" "What problems does the student have, and what is his most pressing problem *right now?*" It is in the answers we give to questions like these that we find what the individual student is like, how he feels about himself and the world, and why he behaves as he does.

One particular caution should be noted in drawing inferences, and that is the importance of being *conservative* about the use of case histories, cumulative folders, anecdotal reports, information picked up in the teachers' lounge, or any other secondary or indirect information. They involve the perceptions of a third party. While they are sometimes useful, they are also an important source of bias and misunderstanding.

In this final chapter we have seen the importance of what the teacher believes about himself and about his students, and how attitudes toward students are more important than techniques and materials. We've considered some of the things the teacher does: the attitudes he conveys, the atmosphere he creates, and the sensitivity he develops through self-report inventories and observations.

References

Allport, G. W. *Becoming*. New Haven, Conn.: Yale University Press, 1955.

Berger, E. M. "The Relation Between Expressed Acceptance of Self and Expressed Acceptance of Others." *J. Abn. and Soc. Psychol,* 47 (1953): 778–782.

Birney, R. C.; Burdick, H.; and Teevan, R. C. *Fear of Failure*. Princeton, N.J.: D. Van Nostrand, 1969.

Bledsoe, J. "Self-Concept of Children and Their Intelligence, Achievement, Interests, and Anxiety." *Child. Educ.,* 43 (1967): 436–438.

Brookover, W. B. et al. *Self-Concept of Ability and School Achievement. II: Improving Academic Achievement Through Students' Self-Concept Enhancement.* U.S. Office of Education, Cooperative Research Project No. 1636. East Lansing: Office of Research and Publications, Michigan State University, 1965.

———; Erickson, E. L.; and Joiner, L. M. *Self-Concept of Ability and School Achievement. III: Relationship of Self-Concept to Achievement in High School.* U.S. Office of Education, Cooperative Research Project No. 2831. East Lansing: Office of Research and Publications, Michigan State University, 1967.

Carbonara, N. T. *Techniques for Observing Normal Child Behavior.* Pittsburgh: University of Pittsburgh Press, 1961.

Carlton, L., and Moore, R. H. "The Effects of Self-Directive Dramatization on Reading Achievement and Self Concept of Culturally Disadvantaged Children." *Reading Teacher,* 1966, 20, 125–130.

———. *Reading, Self-Directive Dramatization and Self Concept.* Columbus, Ohio: Charles E. Merrill, 1968.

Christensen, C. M. "Relationships Between Pupil Achievement, Pupil Affect-Need, Teacher Warmth, and Teacher Permissiveness." *J. Educ. Psychol.,* 51 (1960): 169–174.

Clarke, W. E. "The Relationship Between College Academic Performance and Expectancies." Doctoral dissertation, Michigan State University, 1960.

Cogan, M. "The Behavior of Teachers and the Productive Behavior of Their Pupils." *J. Exptl. Educ.,* 27 (1958) : 89–124.

———. *The Professional Education of Teachers: A Perceptual View of Teacher Preparation."* Boston: Allyn & Bacon, 1965. (a)

———; Courson, C. C.; and Soper, D. W. "The Measurement of Self-Concept and Self-Report." *Educ. and Psychol. Measmt.,* 23 (1963a) : 493–500.

Combs, A. W., and Soper, D. W. "The Self, Its Derivate Terms, and Research." *J. Individual Psychol.,* 13 (1957) : 135–145.

———. "The Perceptual Organization of Effective Counselors." *J. Counsl. Psychol.,* 10 (1936b) : 222–226.

Combs, A. W., and Snygg, D. *Individual Behavior.* 2nd ed. New York: Harper & Row, 1959.

Combs, A. W. et al. *Florida Studies in the Helping Professions.* University of Florida Social Science Monograph No. 37, 1969.

Coopersmith, S. *The Antecedents of Self-Esteem.* San Francisco: W. H. Freeman, 1967.

Costello, C. G. "Ego Involvement, Success and Failure: A Review of the Literature." In H. J. Eysenck, ed., *Experiments in Motivation.* New York: Macmillan, 1964, pp. 161–208.

Courson, C. C. "The Use of Inference as a Research Tool." *Educ. and Psychol. Measmt.,* 25 (1965): 1029–1038.

Crovetto, A. M.; Fischer, L. L.; and Boudreaux, J. L. *The Pre-School Child and his Self-Image.* Division of Instruction and Division of Pupil Personnel, New Orleans Public Schools, 1967.

Cummins, R. E. "Some Applications of "Q" Methodology to Teaching and Educational Research." *J. Educ. Res.,* 57 (1963) : 94–98.

Davidson, H. H., and Greenberg, J. W. *School Achievers from a Deprived Background.* U.S.O.E. Project No. 2805, Contract No. OE–5–10–132. New York: The City College of the City University of New York, 1967.

Davidson, H. H., and Lang, G. "Children's Perceptions of their Teachers' Feelings Toward Them Related to Self-Perception, School Achievement, and Behavior." *J. Exptl. Educ.*, 29 (1960) : 107–118.

Dinkmeyer, D. C. *Child Development: The Emerging Self.* Englewood Cliffs, N.J.: Prentice-Hall, 1965.

Fey, W. F. "Acceptance of Self and Others, and Its Relation to Therapy Readiness." *J. Clin. Psychol.*, 10 (1954) : 266–269.

Fitts, W. *Tennessee Self-Concept Scale.* Nashville: Counselor Recordings and Tests, 1964.

Frankel, E. "Effects of a Program of Advanced Summer Study on the Self-Perceptions of Academically Talented High School Students. *Exceptional Children,* 30 (1964) : 245–249.

Gill, M. P. "Pattern of Achievement as Related to the Perceived Self." Paper read at the annual meeting of the American Educational Research Association Convention, Los Angeles, February 1969.

Gordon, I. J. *Studying the Child in the School.* New York: Wiley, 1966.

———. *A Text Manual for the How-I-See-Myself-Scale.* Florida Educational Research and Development Council. Gainesville: University of Florida, 1968.

Gough, J. C. *California Psychological Inventory.* Palo Alto, Calif.: Consulting Psychologist Press, 1956.

Harris, D. B. *Children's Drawings as Measures of Intellectual Maturity.* New York: Harcourt, Brace, 1963.

Heilbrum, A. B., Jr. "The social desirability variable: Implications for test reliability and validity." *Educ. and Psychol. Measmt.*, 25 (1965) : 745–756.

Jersild, A. T. *In Search of Self.* New York: Bureau of Publications, Teachers College, Columbia University, 1952.

———. *Child Psychology.* Englewood Cliffs, N.J.: Prentice-Hall, 1960.

———. "Voice of the Self." *NEA J.*, 54 (1965) : 23–25.

Jourard, S. M. *The Transparent Self: Self-Disclosure and Well-Being.* Princeton, N.J.: D. Van Nostrand, 1964.

Kowitz, G. T. "Test Anxiety and Self-Concept." *Childhd. Educ.*, 44 (1967) : 162–165.

Ludwig, D. J., and Maehr, M. L. "Changes in Self-Concept and Stated Behavioral Preferences." *Child Developmt.*, 38 (1967) : 453–467.

Luft, J. "On Nonverbal Interaction." *J. Psychol.*, 63 (1966) : 261–268.

Moustakas, C. *The Authentic Teacher: Sensitivity and Awareness in the Classroom.* Cambridge, Mass.: Howard A. Doyle Publishing Company, 1966.

Omwake, K. T. "The Relation Between Acceptance of Self and Acceptance of Others Shown by Three Personality Inventories." *J. Consult. Psychol.*, 18 (1954) : 443, 446.

Osgood, C. E.; Suci, G. J.; and Tannenbaum, P. H. *The Measurement of Meaning.* Urbana: University of Illinois Press, 1957.

Purinton, D. E. "The Effect of Item Familiarity on Self-Concept Sorts." *Dissertation Abstr.*, 26 (1965): 2325.

Purkey, W. W. "The Search for Self: Evaluating Student Self Concepts." *Ibid.* 4 (2), 1968.

Reed, H. B. Implications for Science Education of a Teacher Competence Research. *Science Educ.*, 46, (1962): 473–486.

Rogers, C. R. *Client-Centered Therapy.* Boston: Houghton-Mifflin, 1951.

———. The Therapeutic Relationship: Recent Theory and Research. Reprinted in G. Babladelis and S. Adams, eds., *The Shaping of Personality.* Englewood Cliffs, N.J.: Prentice-Hall, 1965, 1967.

Rosenthal, R., and Jacobson, L. 1968a. "Teacher Expectations for the Disadvantaged." *Scientific Amer.,* 218 (1968a) : 19–23.

———. *Pygmalion in the Classroom: Teacher Expectations and Pupils' Intellectual Development.* New York: Holt, Rinehart, 1968. (b)

Sacks, B. M. *The Student, the Interview, and the Curriculum.* Boston: Houghton-Mifflin, 1966.

Sarason, I. G. The Effects of Anxiety and Threat on the Solution of a Difficult Task. *J. Abn. and Soc. Psychol.,* 62 (1961) : 165–168.

Sarbin, T. R., and Rosenberg, B. G. "Contributions to Role-Taking Theory: IV. Method for Obtaining a Quantitative Estimate of Self." *J. Soc. Psychol.,* 42 (1955) : 71–81.

Shulman, L. S. "Multiple Measurement of Self-concept." Paper presented at the meeting of the American Educational Research Association, Chicago, February 1968.

Spaulding, R. L. "Achievement, Creativity, and Self Concept Correlates of Teacher-Pupil Transactions in Elementary Schools." U.S. Office of Education, Cooperative Research No. 1352. Urbana: University of Illinois, 1963.

———. Achievement, Creativity, and Self Concept Correlates of Teacher-Pupil Transactions in Elementary Schools. In C. B. Stendler, ed., *Readings in Child Behavior and Development,* 2nd ed. New York: Harcourt, Brace, 1964, pp. 313–318.

Staines, J. W. "The Self-Picture as a Factor in the Classroom." *British J. Educatl. Psychol.,* 28 (1958) : 97–111.

Strong, D., and Feder, D. "Measurement of the Self Concept: A Critique of the Literature." *J. Counslg. Psychol.,* 8 (1961) : 223–229.

Trent, R. D. "The Relationship Between Expressed Self-Acceptance and Expressed Attitudes Toward Negro and White in Negro Children." *J. Genet. Psychol.,* 91 (1957) : 25–31.

Walsh, A. M. *Self-Concepts of Bright Boys with Learning Difficulties.* New York: Bureau of Publications, Teachers College, Columbia University, 1956.

Wylie, R. C. *The Self-Concept: A Critical Survey of Pertinent Research Literature.* Lincoln: University of Nebraska Press, 1961.

Yeatts, P. P. "Developmental Changes in the Self-Concept of Children Grades 3–12." *Florida Educatl. Res. and Developmt. Council Res. Bull.,* no. 2. Gainesville: University of Florida, 1967.

Neurotic Interaction Between Counselor and Counselee

GEORGE LAWTON

Marriage counseling is increasingly viewed as a form of short-term psychotherapy (1, 2, 3, 4). Only on rare occasions, however, is it analytically oriented and on even rarer occasions is the analytic approach Freudian in character.

Marriage counseling may deal with the unmarried, the married, and the in-between. It differs from ordinary short-term psychotherapy in that the chief and often the only presenting symptom of the candidate for therapy is some phase of his relationship with the opposite sex or one representative of it. The unmarried candidate is likely to make it the opposite sex in general, and the married candidate one representative in particular.

It has been the writer's experience that the problem of an unmarried adult who has a difficulty with the opposite sex which makes him seek professional help nearly always needs long-term psychotherapy. Since the writer is probably better known as a psychoanalyst than as a marriage counselor, his sampling of both married and unmarried clients is probably somewhat skewed. Within the confines of this nevertheless broad and lengthy experience with this group of unmarried adults we are now discussing, the writer has found a considerable number with strong unconscious homosexual trends, another fairly large group with psychotic patterns in their thinking, and some borderline psychotics. Most of the remainder are severely disturbed neurotics.

The *couple* who applies for pre-marital guidance generally presents relatively simple problems in comparison with the group just mentioned. These couples more nearly fit the stereotype of premarital counseling as

From *Journal of Counseling Psychology,* 1958, 5, 28–33. Copyright 1958 by the American Psychological Association. Reprinted by permission.

a form of educational guidance regarding mate suitability, preparation for a sexual life, how to draw up a budget, etc.

As for the problems of the married, here we enter upon one of the most difficult and challenging areas in all of psychotherapy. Those with marital problems are generally the most disturbed patients the writer has, and the most difficult to treat. Those with a marital syndrome constitute for the writer's practice the same order of magnitude as schizophrenics, those with psychosomatic problems, homosexuals, alcoholics, and severely disturbed children.

A man or woman whose marriage is in serious trouble is a person in a state of crisis, an emergency perhaps as great as any he can face. He is obsessed with the problem, which he generally defines as due to something his partner is doing, or not doing, of a very drastic kind. He or she wants to talk only about his obsession, namely, how his partner, for some reason, is destroying his every chance for happiness. This is stating the problem in extreme form, but the reality is most often not too far behind. A great number of the cases seen by at least *this* marriage counselor are examples of a (possibly transient) psychosis which may be called *marital paranoia*.

The relationship with individuals of the opposite sex is one of the most important experiences in the life of a patient, but it is equally important to the therapist, who is also a patient only temporarily on the other side of the desk and presumably a little further advanced in understanding and therefore in a position to be helpful to one less advanced.

Since for the writer marriage counseling in a form of psychotherapy, in the discussion that follows, the practitioner will be referred to as a therapist and the person with a problem, a patient. Since the observations made apply to various kinds of psychotherapy, most references from this point onward will not specify "marriage counseling" as such. And, while we speak of neurotic interaction in this symposium, it should be realized that the interaction can also be psychotic on one or both sides, depending on the makeup of the therapist and patient and the type of problem in this area which one or both have still failed to solve.

INTERFERING MOTIVATIONS: COUNTER-IDENTIFICATIONS AND COUNTER-TRANSFERENCES

Neurotic interaction in this paper will be considered under the head of counter-transference and counter-identification phenomena. The therapist acts in a complementary manner to a neurotic or psychotic need of the patient; or the patient's appearance, personality, or problem stirs up in the therapist an old or current problem which has either not been perceived or not been solved. In such a case, the original signal for psychotic or neurotic interaction may unconsciously be sent out by the therapist, and the patient unconsciously responds with the type of behavior which the therapist indicates he (the therapist) needs.

A study of the variety of unconscious motivations which may intrude into the dynamics of the therapeutic relationship is important because they: (a) increase the strain and tension of the therapist's work, (b) complicate the therapeutic relationship unduly, and (c) jeopardize the success of therapy.

Therapist Insecurities Variously Expressed

There are many ways the therapist may unconsciously act on his own insecurities in his interactions with the patient. Out of his fear that he will lose control of the relationship, the therapist may, first of all, *tend to dominate the patient.* He may, for example, determinedly proceed to get the patient to break up a courtship, a marriage, or an extra-marital affair in order to prove his (the therapist's) power. I must put an end to this and fast! the therapist resolves.

A second way a therapist's insecurities may appear is in his competition with other significant authority figures in the life of the patient. He may offer advice in opposition to the minister, physician, spouse, sibling, parent, or friend and see to it that this opposing advice is carried out by the patient in ways of doubtful relevance to the therapy. In extreme cases, this may be a real drive toward omnipotence in the life of the patient: "I, your therapist, am Jehovah. Do unquestioningly what I say and have no other gods before me."

Other therapists evidence their insecurities in a third way: by showering the patient with excessive love and attention. The therapist probably felt himself unloved and neglected by a parent and therefore redresses the old hurt by reliving the roles of parent and child. He now acts both roles at once by making the patient the child he once was and by also becoming his own parent. He is over-parentalizing the patient in return for the patient's grateful affection. Here we find the therapist who goes to extreme lengths to prevent a marriage failure: "This marriage *must* succeed." Glover speaks of "the eagerness of some therapists to give suck."

A fourth form of insecurity expression by a therapist is to function as the child of the patient. He identifies the patient with his own parent. He misses the patient when he is away and welcomes him back with a sigh of pleasure and relief. Parental security is re-established for the child.

Fifthly, the therapist's insecurities may take the channel of the Pygmalion complex. The need to manipulate and to resolve one's own problems in other people's lives leads to the need to make the patient like the therapist.

The therapist, in a sixth fashion, may find his insecurities take the form of resentment of the patient's demands. He may become vindictive toward the patient for his hostility, his negative transference. The resentment may openly emerge in the form of anger toward the patient for his failure to improve or more covertly as despair. Some therapists unconsciously use silence as counter-resistance, counter-attack. They use "controlled apathy" as a punitive measure.

Seventhly, some therapists fear the patient's hostility and try to appease the patient. Such therapists have a need for friendliness, are afraid of their patient's aggression, feel vulnerable to attack and criticism. Whenever a therapist hides behind his beard—that is, uses some ritualistic practice or professional mumbo-jumbo—he should ask himself whether what he is doing is prompted by a desire to cure the patient, or by insecurity.

An eighth form of insecurity expression on the part of the therapist is closely related to the foregoing: his inability to stand the patient's tension and anxiety. Often the patient reminds the therapist too much of his own problems—sexual, marital, illness, death, parent-child interactions. This type of insecurity is apt to result in a glittering pseudo-optimism: "Don't worry; everything will be all right." Such pseudo-optimism creates resistance and counter-resistance to therapy.

Sweet and Aggressive Therapists

Two types of counter-transference that deserve our particular attention are (a) the sweet and (b) the aggressive patterns of therapists in their interactions with patients. These patterns (as well as those to be considered later) are also reflective of insecurity feelings of therapists, but are considered under a separate heading merely for convenience.

The sweet therapist has a need to overintellectualize and over-emphasize logic and common sense. The hour is sweetly reasonable, rather than filled with emotions and thoughts that can lead only to storm and trouble, tears and the gnashing of teeth, bloodshed.

The over-emphasis on logic and common sense may represent resistance on the therapist's part to the possibility of the patient's voicing transference feelings which the therapist may find distressing. It may also represent the therapist's resistance to the possibility that he may take the lid off the Pandora box of his counter-transference feelings.

Here belongs the tendency of some therapists to round off each hour with a complete explanation, a summary of important points covered. Is this educational zealousness? Or compulsion? What does the therapist hope to ward off by this ritual of giving a summary at the end of the hour? Persons may become therapists because they seek an intellectual system for their personal problems, but patients don't get cured so cleanly and so sweetly.

Distinguished sharply from the therapist who handles his counter-transference problems in this sweet fashion is the aggressive type of therapist. Some therapists have contempt for their patients. The patient is always wrong; he is an opponent to be outwitted. The therapist says to himself as he faces the patient: "You are going to like what I do or else . . ." The writer knew a therapist who stood up, faced his patients, and thundered angrily and sarcastically at them.

More often, however, aggressions of therapists take somewhat more subtle forms. As expressed earlier, silence may be used punitively. Contempt may slip into the tone of voice, the gesture, the facial expression. Humor is used to "draw blood."

Seduction: A Two-Way Street

Insufficiently analyzed therapists may have difficulty resisting temptations both to seduce and be seduced by their patients. Attempts at the seduction of the therapist by the patient are a form of resistance to therapy, though both patients and therapists may regard it as a means of therapy and proof of it.

Patient seduction may take both verbal and non-verbal forms. Examples of non-verbal seduction devices are glances, gifts, smiles, and payment of bill in advance or over-payments. Verbal wooing devices consist of the outpouring of love and sexual thoughts and feelings and sometimes outright pleas and arguments in favor of sexual response by the therapist. It is here worth noting that the seduction of the therapist may be homosexual as well as heterosexual and that homosexual counter-transference can be a greater source of counter-resistance than heterosexual.

Immature and disturbed therapists may be tempted in the direction of an actively seductive role themselves, for the submissive, child-like patient offers "easy pickings." Some of the verbal wooing devices of a therapist follow: calling the patient by his first name too soon and without ascertaining patient's wishes; using affectionate or meaningful intonation or words; engaging in long, cosy telephone conversations; talking, explaining, interpreting excessively; asking for deep material too soon or too obviously. Non-verbal seduction of the patient by the therapist may take such means as the following: visiting the patient's home at the request of the patient whenever the latter undergoes an emotional emergency of a transference kind; giving affectionate or meaningful glances; putting an affectionate hand on the patient's shoulder or giving a parental pat; allowing the patient to telephone regularly after hours to see the therapist at ordinarily non-office hour times; charging the patient a fee which the patient feels is lower than called for in a particular situation and letting the patient know this is done because the therapist likes him; and regularly over-running usual and conventional time limits for sessions.

Therapist Projections

Some therapists see in their work an opportunity to project their personal attitudes. All marital problems are due to the same causes, some marriage counselors believe, and all difficulties are to be solved in the same way. This is the Procrustean school of marriage counseling. Here are some examples:

(a) *The therapist himself is a convert to defeat and self-pity.* He believes privately that the world is a vale of tears and that human beings generally don't or can't get what they want. *He* has not achieved what he hoped for in life, so why should this patient? Let him adjust himself to a world where truth, justice, and love do *not* prevail.

(b) *Then, on the other hand, we find the therapist who believes that life is grand and glorious.* To this therapist, people who have problems do so most unnecessarily: a smile, a cheerful up and at 'em attitude, a hearty, reassuring clap on the back will solve all difficulties. This type of marriage counselor believes that the unhappy, cantankerous husband will change over night if his wife will only make apple pie.

(c) *Some marriage counselors believe that the answer to a sick marriage is inescapably divorce, and others believe that reconciliation is always possible.* Both are likely to be *projecting their own personal marital attitudes.* The one kind of therapist says to himself: when marriage reaches this point, or when a person has this kind of spouse, divorce *must* be the answer. The other type of therapist is just as incapable of taking an objective view of a particular marriage and will insist on reconciliation in marriages which are obviously distorting the personalities of the participants.

(d) *Some therapists believe that technically satisfactory sexual intercourse is the cure for all emotional problems.* Since most patients, with or without opportunities for satisfactory sexual intercourse, share this point of view, patient and therapist are more in agreement on this attitude than many another. This doctrine starts with the idea that satisfactory sexual intercourse is always good and leads on to the notion that more of it is even better, for you can never have too much of a good thing. Some therapists keep pushing their patients into heterosexual intercourse whether the patient wants it or not, is ready for it or not, is benefited by it or not, or whether it is nis problem or not.

(e) *There are therapists at the other end of the sex-projection con-*

tinuum, however, who over-spiritualize the man-woman relationship. They are the ones who recommend cold showers and a run around the block for teen-agers with strong sexual urges. Having their own private feud with the sexual impulse, they are glad in a marriage counseling situation to play down the importance of satisfactory sexual experiences and to play up the sublimations.

Summary

We have considered various types of neurotic interactions between counselor and counselee which interfere with therapeutic effectiveness. These were dealt with under the general heading of interfering motivations (of the therapist) in the forms of counter-transferences and counter-identifications. For convenience of discussion we sub-divided these interfering motivations into various expressions of therapist insecurities, sweet and aggressive therapists, seductive processes, and therapist projections.

In the light of this discussion, it would seem evident that the psychotherapist who has undergone successful psychoanalysis, or at least psychotherapy, is less likely to get involved in neurotic interactions between himself and his patient. He is also better equipped than the unanalyzed practitioner to deal with neurotic interactions when they do arise. And it is also clearly important that the psychotherapist who is dealing with marital problems should himself have a happy marriage, for such a practitioner is apt to be better equipped to detect and deal with neurotic interactions between himself and his patients.

Our concluding point of emphasis, then, is this: *the most important instrument* in our attempt to understand and treat successfully the problems which a patient may have in relationship to a member of the opposite sex *is our knowledge of our own problems in this area and our ability either to solve or handle these problems in life in general* and in our interactions with patients in particular.

References

1. Alexander, F. "Principles and Techniques of Briefer Psychotherapeutic Procedures." *Psychiatric Treatment.* Proceedings of the Assn. for Research in Nerv. and Ment. Disease, 21, 1953, 16–20.
2. Ellis, A. "A Critical Evaluation of Marriage Counseling." *Mar. & Fam. Liv.,* 18 (1956): 65–71.
3. Harper, R. A. "Failure in Marriage Counseling." *Mar. & Fam. Liv.,* 17 (1955): 359–362.
4. Laidlaw, R. W. "The psychiatrist as marriage counselor." *Am. J. Psychiat.,* 106 (1950): 732–736.

How Did He Get There?

DAVID N. ASPY

A few days ago several of my friends and I held a reunion, and as usually happens, we began to talk about what our old acquaintances were doing. Since we all were either currently teaching or had been, most of those we discussed were also members of that profession. The conversation was *most* illuminating.

One fellow whose name came up had just returned from Harvard. "You know what he's doing?" someone contributed. "He's in charge of research for a large urban school system!" The shock that ran through the group was obvious on every face. The comments included, "He was the most trifling kid I ever knew," "He has the most 'country' sounding voice I ever heard," and "He's so dumb it hurts." We finally resolved our dissonance by concluding that Harvard was either overrated or had lowered its academic standards drastically.

Another choice morsel for gossip was tossed out when we discovered that a second "old colleague" was the president of a college! Of course we found ways to downgrade this accomplishment. Our statements were, "They must have been desperate," "I understand he has an awful case of ulcers," and "Some guys are consistently lucky."

After this kind of conversation had run its course, one of our group said, "You know, I wonder how many of our friends are surprised at what we're doing. How many people thought you'd be a college professor? How many thought you'd be a successful businessman? How many thought you'd be a prominent school official? In a way all of us are surprises to most people, even ourselves." These observations stopped our conversation by making us think about the course of our own lives.

Reprinted from *Peabody Journal of Education,* George Peabody College for Teachers, 1969, 47, 152–153, by permission of the author and publisher.

Our reunion was not unique. Time after time this type of conversation has been repeated, and it seems to stem from some basic concepts deep in most of our beings. Remember, we were all teachers, which means we were engaged in the facilitation of human growth, and yet we were surprised at the development of our former acquaintances. In a sense we were expressing a disbelief in the very process to which we ostensibly were devoting our time and effort. You see, we believed in our own growth, but not in that of others. This is one part of a facilitating life—that of self fulfillment; but a truly facilitative life extends to promoting growth in others, and this we cannot do unless we actually *believe* in it. In other words, we cannot facilitate growth in others until we are convinced that it can be done.

Another revealing aspect of our conversation was reflected by our lack of surprise at others' failures. We expected them! We even pointed out flaws in their personalities which predicted failure. Perhaps the last straw in our negative set was shown in our satisfaction at "being right" in our prediction of failure. In fact, we were more concerned with being right than with the tragedy of some of our friends' lives.

All of the foregoing may make us a little sensitive about expressed cruelty toward others, but there is a potentially constructive element of this kind of experience. At least two major lessons emerge. First, there is a strong possibility that our lack of "positive expectancy" for our former acquaintances retarded their growth. That is, each man is a part of all the people he meets, and, as research indicates, people tend to behave as others expect. Of course, these same acquaintances may have retarded our emergence. The true picture is that we probably retarded each other's growth, but happily most of us found enough constructive people to "make it." Our mutual challenge is to become that kind of facilitative person.

The second lesson is a deeper one and more painful. It is found in the fact that we seemed pleased or relieved that some of our colleagues either had not grown or had actually deteriorated. Of course, we didn't smile on obvious tragedy such as serious illness or death. In fact, we were quite sympathetic with those. The stories which brought pleasure or relief were those about people who were less successful than we. It is as if our hold on our own success was so tenuous that one way to enhance it was by comparing it to that of our colleagues. The subtlety of this fact makes it potent indeed, because it means that we probably functioned in ways which actively promoted the failure of those with whom we were in competition. You see, we were still in a kind of competition with them, because they were our reference points. It was relieving to know that we were not "coming in last" in the race for life.

These lessons are vivid ones when thinking of our relationships with our former colleagues, but they become doubly significant when we bring them into our daily lives. It is imperative that we *see* our students *and* colleagues as well as ourselves as people in the process of actualizing their individual potentials. That is, we must see the human being as a growing organism whose realization can be facilitated or retarded by others' expectations. The evidence indicates that our growth is promoted by those who believe we can grow. This same evidence indicates that when we feel threatened by another person, we actively retard his growth. Thus, when we realize that we hold these attitudes toward some students and colleagues, it is our professional responsibility either to correct these perceptions or to move away from those individuals.

It may be revealing to ask yourself how you see your old colleagues. Examining our own attitudes toward others' success could be an interesting and hopefully a productive process.

On Being Number One: Competition in Education

DAVID N. CAMPBELL

I am observing in a new open-space elementary school staffed by very young and attractive people I am supposedly to help become open classroom teachers. Positioned to the rear of one pod, I can observe two women math teachers simultaneously. One is using a game of the tic-tac-toe with addition and subtraction problems instead of Xs and Os. It is boys versus girls, third grade. A small boy comes forward for 7 + 2 and guesses at 8. The boys groan; the girls cheer; the teacher looks pained. The "motivation" is high. There is good attention and "involvement." It's a good lesson—by normal standards. It seems that the girls frequently win. The chagrined boy returns to his seat and while his efficient teacher continues through *her lesson,* which she imagines is arithmetic, the real lesson is demonstrated in front of me as the little boy punches the little girl next to him as hard as he can, saying, "I hate you, I hate you, I hate you." In the adjacent bay the "innovative" teacher is using flash cards in the same manner. Children are guessing answers, "2 . . . 4 . . . 8. . . ." One boy always wins and the others hate him.

In a physical education class the children run in a wide circle, jumping hurdles. Several, as usual, cannot coordinate their bodies. They trip and fall. Finally the instructor—in what he probably believes to be a kind gesture—allows them to sit out the rest of the exercise. The embarrassment and humiliation is so heavy that their eyes remain down, looking at the floor. Later they all run in relay teams, cheering and jeering—cheering those who are fast and jeering those who are slow, and who lose the match for the whole team.

Now I'm in the reading groups, the redbirds and bluebirds (a code

Reprinted from *Phi Delta Kappan,* 1974, 56, 143–146, by permission of the author and publisher.

every child has easily broken), and the youngsters are reading out loud. In essence they are on stage performing for the others, who laugh or giggle at every mistake and wiggle hands to correct, along with "oo-ah-oo-ah." Lifelong reading problems are being ingrained.

In music class youngsters are "auditioned" by singing in front of each other, in art by some very select few having their work displayed, and in every classroom every day that common experience described so well by Jules Henry is repeated. Henry speaks of Boris, a fifth-grader, at the board attempting to reduce a fraction to its lowest terms. He is performing for the teacher and the class, and he is being judged. He is being assigned a rank, status, and role and he will carry them with him for the rest of his life. He is having trouble reducing the fraction; the teacher suggests that he "think." She is painfully patient, but Boris is mentally paralyzed. All the while hands are waving, heaving up and down, all frantic to correct Boris. Finally, the teacher gives up with Boris and calls on Peggy, who always knows the right answers (unfortunately for her).

> Thus Boris's failure has made it possible for Peggy to succeed; his depression is the price of her exhilaration, his misery the occasion of her rejoicing. This is the standard condition of the American elementary school. . . . To a Zuni, Hopi, or Dakota Indian, Peggy's performance would seem cruel beyond belief, for competition, the wringing of success from somebody's failure, is a form of torture foreign to those noncompetitive Americans. Yet Peggy's action seems natural to us; and so it is. How else would you run our world? And since all but the brightest children (i.e., less than 5%) have the constant experience that others succeed at their expense, they cannot but develop an inherent tendency to hate—to hate the success of others, to hate others who are successful, and to be determined to prevent it. Along with this, naturally, goes the hope that others will fail. . . . Looked at from Boris's point of view (which it seldom is) the nightmare at the blackboard was, perhaps, a lesson in controlling himself so that he would not fly shrieking from the room under the enormous public pressure.[1]

But of course Boris cannot fly from the room either shrieking or quietly. He will have to "adjust," for the competition will only become greater as he continues in school. By junior high school he will be tracked and rather finally labeled, his progress now strictly controlled so that he may no longer have a chance for A grades, or college prep, or A.P. He knows by now that he cannot draw, is no good at music, terrible at math, mediocre at athletics, miserable in English, passable in science; but at least his fate is somehow acceptable, because everyone in his classes is also inferior, a total or partial failure. In fact, Boris is effectively cut off from social interaction with his betters or those below him in the

1. Jules Henry, "In Suburban Classrooms," *Radical School Reform,* Ronald and Beatrice Gross, editors (New York: Simon and Schuster, 1969), p. 83.

hierarchy. He cannot think of dating an upper-track girl. He carries his books upside down so others cannot identify his status. Again, Jules Henry:

> The function of high school, then, is not so much to communicate knowledge as to oblige children finally to accept the grading system as a measure of their inner excellence. And a function of the self-destructive process in American children is to make them willing to accept not their own but a variety of other standards, like a grading system, for measuring themselves. It is thus apparent that the way American culture is now integrated it would fall apart if it did not engender feelings of inferiority or worthlessness.[2]

This is the ethic which permeates, and dominates, our society. It is intoned as the prime motivation which has made our country "great." Fathers, especially, will confront me over this issue and proclaim: "It's a dog-eat-dog competitive world out there and I want my kid to know that." I attempt to point out that this is not a very attractive world to offer to one's children, however real it may be. The idea is essentially, "Make my kid suffer now so he gets used to it. Teach him to claw his way to the top by any means necessary. Teach him to hate those who win and himself when he loses and despise those who don't make it." But the idea is so well programmed that few are converted. After all, they see Mark Spitz standing there bedecked with a necklace of Olympic gold medals and he doesn't say, "It was a great experience. It was meeting all those other athletes so well trained and so dedicated and feeling my own body respond the way I wanted." No, instead he proclaims the teaching of all his coaches throughout his schooling and training: "All that matters is winning." Thus he reinforces millions throughout his country and effectively destroys the idea of the Olympic Games.

In that sequence of the film about the 1972 Olympics which dealt with those who lost, the point was never so clearly and devastatingly made that there, as in school, most people fail. Grown men and women break down and cry. There's a degree of despair seldom witnessed except at the death of someone close, with collapsing dreams and worlds. In both school and the games the spirit of the experience has been distorted beyond recognition. Everywhere a parade of frustrated fathers determined that their son will be a winner and make up for their own personal failure. All over the country Little League and school coaches deliver Knute Rockne halftime speeches; but the emphasis is now more exaggerated, an anxiety-ridden command to win: *All that matters is winning.*

Some day compare a street baseball game to Little League, the difference between kids enjoying themselves, the game, the laughing, jokes,

2. Jules Henry, *Culture Against Man* (New York: Random House, 1965), p. 83.

bending the rules; and the other: tense kids, shouldering the responsibility of dozens of adults, making good for dad and mom, for the team, the coach, and the community. Those adults have effectively destroyed not only childhood; to an always unknown degree they have distorted that child's entire life.

I remember an exception, a male physical education teacher at a junior high school where I taught for a number of years. He had a motto which at the time I thought was terribly trite: "A sport for every boy and every boy a sport." But in practice it meant boys who looked forward to his class and respected and admired him, would in fact do anything for him. He had a competing basketball team, but the instructions were explicit and reinforced continually: Winning is *not* the most important thing. Good sportsmanship is. No dirty play, no arguments or contesting decisions, and at the end the whole team, win or lose, must en masse congratulate the other team. The gym was open every lunchtime for games and general use and it was always filled. He was rare. I am certain he could no longer exist in our winning-is-everything schools.

The counter-argument is that competition makes for betterment, higher standards; a free market creates lower prices and better and more abundant goods and services. But of course we know better now. The free market is essentially not at all free but dependent upon favors from the government; it is subject to price fixing, charging as much as the public will bear, subsidy, and campaign contributions. As to competition creating our agricultural and industrial superiority, that is largely a myth too, as any Midwestern farmer with some of the richest soil in the world will testify. It was the temperate climate with abundant mineral wealth, millions of immigrants for cheap labor, and the very fortunate circumstances of men in leadership at the beginning who were extraordinary. We should have had to try hard to make a failure of such potential.

But even on a more personal level the competition myth does not stand up well to real scrutiny. In a series of studies measuring children 5 to 10 years of age, situations were created where rewards (toys) were possible for competing children if they cooperated in manipulating the materials. American children, in general, more often reacted against their own best interests, or, as the researchers expressed it, "The American Competitive Spirit may be alive and well, but it has produced a culture whose children are systematically irrational." [3] The researchers noted that the experiments suggested that children become increasingly competitive as they grow older, i.e., it is a learned behavior pattern. "They learn to pursue personal ends and to block opponents in conflict-of-interest situations, even when mutual assistance is required for personal goal attainment."

3. Linden L. Nelson and Spencer Kagan, "Competition: The Star-Spangled Scramble," *Psychology Today*, September, 1972, pp. 58–91.

Not only did the children in the experiments work against their own best interests but were almost sadistically rivalrous. When given a choice, American children took toys away from their peers on 78% of the trials, *even when they could not keep the toys for themselves.* Observing the success of their actions, some of the children gloated: "Ha! Ha! Now you won't get a toy." And they were quite willing to make sacrifices in order to reduce the rewards of their peers.

We have created, through competition, a system based on mistrust. In school the assumption is that no one learns without threats of grades, failure, being less than first, i.e., that these extrinsic factors are prime motivation for learning. Standardized achievement tests, grading curves, entrance examinations, and now "accountability"—all are intended to set one person against another, all have nothing whatsoever to do with education and are, in fact, antithetical to education. However, the whole frantic, irrational scramble to beat others is essential for the kind of institution our schools are, i.e., sorting, ranking, and labeling places. Winning and losing are what our schools are all about, not education.

In such a system the losers must predominate and be tormented by envy and self-loathing; some sort of defense must be constructed against the assault of continued failure. It may take the common form of "turning off," non-involvement, don't-take-a-chance, keep-your-mouth-shut, or becoming a "discipline case," having a "learning problem," being "antisocial," "adjustment," or more overt behavior, e.g., physical assaults upon people and property.

Reminder: In school teachers are critics, trained in that role. All work is to be "corrected," so that for most children, all day, every day, they are being told what is wrong with them and their work. To survive 12 or more years of that sort of assault one must develop elaborate defenses, schemes and means for survival, along with a vast reservoir of smouldering hatred, resentment, need for revenge and for evening the score. Many of our school buildings record the result of this need.

But it need not be so. I have watched hundreds of children change in a short time from mistrustful, hating, suspicious, and terribly destructive children into real children who begin to trust again, help one another, smile and laugh in school and who to not want to leave for recess, lunch, or even home. They look forward to every day. It is no miracle; it requires time, but entails nothing much more than minimizing and finally removing the sorting, ranking, and labeling role of schools. It involves stopping the failure. It means establishing a classroom where competition is not used as a motivation for learning. Kids in our society may always engage in some competition, but it is not the teacher's job to promote it, for it has nothing to do with education.

During a tour of British primary schools we had a teacher who insisted on asking the children, "Who's the smartest?" He should have known better. The children didn't know what he was talking about. They had evidently never thought about it. In several British classrooms there were retarded children. Only the teacher knew, for there was no other reason for or means of knowing, since no child was forced to perform in front of others. There were no putbacks, grades, tests, gold stars. *All* stories and drawings were displayed on the walls. Children were not placed in failure situations, forced to prove themselves, to read at "grade level" every week. They were not told they had exactly 15 minutes to finish this or that. Instead, they had time to develop at their own pace, in their own fashion, with strong support from the adults and other children.

In the American school I described earlier, the destruction of other children's work was rampant, fights were frequent, and sarcastic, devastating putdowns common among the second- and third-graders with whom I worked. It required only about three weeks for the changes to emerge. The first was an end of the destruction of others' work. Later a spirit of cooperation and help began to be common. Finally there was what I look for as the real measure of success: children talking freely to every adult and stranger who walks in, leading them by the hand to see projects and explaining their activities, no longer afraid, suspicious, or turned inward. Such changed attitudes developed because we stopped comparing one child with another and stopped labeling and rank-ordering. Mistakes, "wrong answers," and pleasing the teacher were replaced with a non-judgmental, supportive "try again" climate.

Certainly much of the opposition to open education comes from those who perceive correctly that such an educational setting will indeed produce quite different individuals, youngsters who will not expend a large portion of their energies fighting one another or beating someone. The opponents view cooperation, not competition, as a threat. After all, they say, if we are engaged in training future file clerks, waitresses, and janitors, there is a need to convince them of their inferiority, that their lesser status is their own fault, i.e., that they had a fair chance and failed. My answer is: The argument is fallacious, because the deck is stacked against certain groups and individuals from the beginning. Many people win by luck of birth or skin color. They may win because of their friends, because they break the law, because they are humble or because they are male instead of female. Or perhaps they are more beautiful, tall, slender, or nondescript. Superiority in talent or learning, as the Jencks studies show, is only one factor in success.

If we can remove the school from the noneducational role of ranking, sorting, and labeling, *which is none of its business,* then perhaps we can make our schools pleasant, interesting places where people come to learn. As our schools now function they are nothing more than bargain-basement personnel screening agencies for business and government which exploit the school for their own purposes. We are saving personnel departments large amounts of money that otherwise would have to be spent for on-the-job apprenticeship training. No doubt college admissions officers love the school in its present role. It save them so much time. They simply accept or reject on the basis of class rank and grade average. No need to deal with individuals and their whole potential.

What we must do, then, is refuse to certify, i.e., to do others' dirty work, to be exploited for their purposes. In an *educational* institution there is no need for grading, promotion, ranking, tracking, labeling. We are *not* a miniature version of the larger society or a training/screening device for business and government. We *are* there to take over once a child's home and neighborhood environment is intellectually exhausted. We can provide the means for his/her further development with microscopes, libraries, and specialists, opening ever wider possibilities. We are then essentially in the service of the child. No one argues that at some point training for a profession is not necessary, but there is still the question of whether colleges or the professions themselves should finally certify doctors and teachers. After all, a musician is not certified by his degree, he must audition for every post.

What a tremendous burden will be removed and what a change worked when we can teach without "evaluating," when people come to us not for credit but to learn, and where the sole motivation for such learning is interest. We have that demonstrated in open classrooms everywhere. It works in that people do things because they are worth doing. The relationship between teacher and student is then what it is supposed to be: trusting, direct, humane, committed. It can be seen every day in such classrooms. Yes, it does effectively remove the teacher's power and control over students—which is something we should not have and which, again, has nothing at all to do with education.

Teachers at all levels must ask why they teach, ask if they chose teaching in order to sit in judgment, be critics, rank, sort, label; or did most teachers choose to teach in order to help and share in the development of others? Imagine Socrates strolling through the market places with his class and one day exclaiming, "Well, we've been talking about justice for about nine weeks now, and I suppose we'd better have a midterm. Let me see. I have to have a grading curve. Plato, not bad (not as good as me, of course). How about an A—? Meno, keep trying; how about a B, since that makes you second in our class with a GPA of. . . ." Silly? Certainly, but we all do it, every day.

5
THE PERSON IN THE PROCESS

The focus of Part 5 is on the person that is being helped. However, since the articles in this section are about basic principles of human behavior, what is written applies equally as well to the helper. As we have seen, it makes a great deal of difference what helpers believe about the nature of persons and their capacities.

The editors of this book have been very fortunate to obtain the first article in this section. Shortly before his death, Earl Kelly prepared the manuscript, "What May We Now Believe," in which he deals with the question of what may we believe about human nature. Upon finishing the manuscript, and apparently not sure whether he would be able to see it through publication, he gave it to his dear friend Morrell Clute, telling him to do with it what he would. Dr. Clute chose to let us put it in print for the first time in this volume. We are deeply grateful.

The editors believe this article constitutes a summation of Earl Kelley's basic beliefs about human beings and life. It represents a core of beliefs, based partly on research and partly on intuition, that every person must have if he or she hopes to be a successful helper.

This final section of the Sourcebook *also presents an in-depth look at self-concept. No idea in modern humanistic psychology is more important than the perceived self. Its ramifications extend into every aspect of human interaction. C. H. Patterson's article analyzes the core of this vital concept as described by Carl Rogers and others.*

The remainder of the papers in this volume are about the potentialities of people. In all of them, the position that the human being is an open, developing system that can be invited to grow and flourish or be hindered and debilitated through the conditions and persons in the environment is taken.

Arthur Combs presents the more recent conceptualization of intelligence as a mutable, modifiable, human characteristic. Combs suggests that intelligence is a function of a rich, extensive, and available field of perceptions and is therefore open to far more modification than we have traditionally believed.

Abraham Maslow describes the kind of person we would all like to be and to help others become. He defines the basic characteristics of the self-actualized individual and explains the phenomenon he refers to as "peak experience."

This volume ends with the question, "What Can Man Become?" We feel this is appropriate because it is a positive question and should be the goal of all persons engaged in helping relationships. Art Combs suggests what humans might become and presents some ideas about the necessary conditions that must exist before such goals can be met.

What May We Now Believe?

EARL C. KELLEY

The usual way to start an article is to devote the first part to the changing social scene and our changing culture. Often there is a good deal of viewing with alarm. Our society has been viewed with alarm by expert viewers. While some of the facets we see are indeed alarming, this approach does not seem to be very effective. Our society and culture seem to take them in stride.

It appears to me that it might be more effective to start off with a series of statements concerning education and life on which we may be able to get some agreement. These could give us something to hang other ideas and techniques onto. If these statements are true as of now, what other ideas are consistent with them? What ways of operating are therefore suggested?

I propose to set forth a series of twelve statements which seem as near truth as I can get at this time. At first I tried to organize them into two categories, those which are established by research data, and those which come by going somewhat farther beyond the data. Research has no value until someone takes the data and asks what it means. In other words, research data have no value until someone argues beyond them into meaning for whatever human enterprise they apply to.

This division into these two categories turned out to be impracticable. The twelve statements are all related to research data, some more closely than others, but the line is too fine to be discriminating. I then tried to arrange them in a more or less logical order. I do not think the order matters too much.

The list of statements could be called a set of beliefs. The word "be-

Unpublished manuscript printed by permission of Morrell Clute (see introduction to Part 5).

lief," however, is a tricky one, and since I will doubtless use it in reference to the statements, I would like to clarify my use of it.

What one believes is one of the most important things about a person. Beliefs control behavior if one is free to act as he thinks he should. The trouble comes when one holds a belief without support. Some people believe that 13 is an unlucky number; others believe that seeing the new moon for the first time over the right shoulder assures a month of good fortune. The trouble with such beliefs is that there is no support in nature or research for them. When one holds beliefs too far at variance with the nature of the universe and what has been learned about it, he is apt to behave in ways which are irrational, even harmful to himself and others. The closer one's beliefs are related to what is known about man and the universe, the more likely it is that his behavior will enhance self and others.

Each person then has the task of getting his beliefs as much in line with what is known of the nature of man and his universe as he can. The teacher needs to hold beliefs about children which he can justify. I believe the following twelve statements, and could give reasons why I believe them. If I believed the number 13 was unlucky, I could not support that belief.

When we realize that what people believe, including attitudes and feelings, control their behavior, it is frightening to realize that many of their beliefs are unrelated to the nature of man and his universe. These people fall victim to irrational behavior, which affects not only them but everyone else. An example of such a belief is that all children can and must learn to read at age six. This belief, held alike by many teachers, school administrators and parents, has no support either from research or from performance. Behavior of adults who hold this belief wreaks havoc with our little children, dooming many of them to become bad school citizens, teacher baiters, home disturbers, and finally dropouts. Many of our mentally ill and delinquent come from this group. If one asks why these adults believe this, the answer often is, "We always have."

If we can accept some beliefs which are in keeping with what is known about the nature of man and his universe, our practices will improve. It is in the hope that this may occur that I submit the following statements together with brief elaboration to clarify meaning.

1. *Human beings are the most important things in the world.* Of course a human being has to have an environment. He has to have a planet to be on, and this planet ought to provide him with the food and shelter, and, hopefully, such things as beauty. These, however, facilitate humans and are not the object of the whole enterprise.

In fact, the world around us exists, has reality, only as it is perceived by somebody. This is not to deny it is there but only to point out that unless it is perceived by someone, its existence does not matter. And it *is* what the perceiver makes it to be.

Every human being, if not too damaged before or after birth, is an asset. To put it more narrowly, he produces more than he consumes. Far more important, he adds to humanness. He is able to supply humanness to the very young, who cannot develop without other people. He adds to the sum of human creativeness.

The person is more important than the textbook.

2. *Children are people.* They are therefore entitled to be treated with human dignity and respect at all times. They are not something to do something to, but to live with and grow with. They are to be treated as assets with potentiality.

This needs to be said because we often do things to children that we would not even consider doing to adults. Citizenship starts at birth, or so our constitution says. The twentieth century is sometimes referred to as the century of the child, but we have a long way to go before children are really included in the human race. I do not think that this should be the century of the child, but I do believe that we must admit children to their fair share of the human adventure. This should be the century of the human family, with all enjoying the dignity—the valuing—that goes with being human.

Are your children free from search and seizure?

3. *Each person is unique.* It would hardly seem necessary to mention this except for three points. The first is that we understand better now how it is that the psychological self is built. We have known for a long time how the physical self is so made that it is virtually impossible for two people (except identical twins) to have the same cell structure. We now understand how the perceptive stuff of growth, which builds the psychological self, is selectively taken in. Nature's effort to achieve complete uniqueness is astonishing. Nature must cherish uniqueness.

The second point is that while we have talked about individual differences (uniqueness) for generations, we do not yet believe in them. If we did we would cease trying to get everybody to learn the same things in the same way.

The third is that since each human organism is unlike any other, each has something that nobody else has. This is the individual's significance, his reason to be.

4. *When any human being is lost or diminished, everybody loses.* This is directly related to man's uniqueness. When anyone dies, something goes out of this world which was not here before, and which cannot be replaced. This is what John Donne was saying centuries ago when he said, "Ask not for whom the bell tolls—it tolls for thee." He did not have the advantage of modern research, but his idea has been corroborated in our laboratories.

We often hear that the world has become very small. This is based on the fact that I can get from here to the other side of the world in much less time than would have been necessary only a generation ago. This is a superficial time-space concept. Since people are the most important things in the world, the size of my world depends upon the number of people I have to relate to, the number of people whose unique behavior can affect me. My world is not smaller, but infinitely larger than the one I knew when I was a boy. It is a matter of seeing the individual's world as people or as things.

Physical death, previously referred to, is not the only form of death, or of being diminished. When anybody is made to think less of himself, to feel less able, it is partial death, and if it continues, the individual can become so disabled that he is dead in the sense that he has become ineffective, immobilized, unable to enhance self or others.

5. *Our children are all right when we get them.* By this I mean they are all right when they are born, not necessarily so when they come to school. There are a few defectives, damaged before they are born, and a few are damaged by the transition from the womb to the air. There are not very many of these. Many more defectives are made after birth than are born defective.

My purpose in putting this statement in at this point is to remind us, when a child behaves in a way detrimental to us and to himself, he has been made this way by the life he has been required to live in an adult-managed world over which he has no control. We (adults in general) have made him that way. His psychological self has been damaged, as truly as one's physical self may be damaged by disease or accident. If we could see the psychological self, as we can the physical, our hearts would go out to them. We are prone to pity the physical cripple and blame the psychological cripple.

When we see a child behaving in a harmful way, it will help us if we can remember that he did not get that way by himself. He was born with a potential for good, but has been prevented from growing in that direction. Every individual has to *learn* to be responsible for his own behavior, but this can only be learned in an atmosphere where cooperation and affection naturally lead to responsibility.

6. *Every human being can change and change for the better as long as he lives.* There are a very few exceptions to this. These are the ones whose early infancy and childhood have been so hostile that they have completely withdrawn and become quite inaccessible. Autistic babies and catatonic older people are examples of this. But we do not even get these in school. They are in hospitals. So I feel that the above statement is true for everyone who gets to school.

A good deal has been said over the years about the importance of the first year. Some have gone so far as to say that by the end of the third year the die is cast for life. I do not here mean to deny the importance of these years. These damaged ones will never be what they might have been. An unloved and unwanted child will doubtless carry symptoms of this deprivation throughout life. We are all handicapped, however, in one way or another, by life's vicissitudes. We take these handicaps and make what we can of life as we are.

Anyone who is still accessible can improve, and this leads to more improvement. If it were true that nothing can be done for a child after the age of five, there would be little need for teachers. The possibility of change is the teacher's great reason-to-be. If teaching were confined to the dreary business of getting people who have already been ruined to read, write and cypher, followed by drilling on the "facts," the teacher's life would indeed be bleak. But when one realizes that he or she has the opportunity to take damaged young ones and show them ways to growth and fulfillment, the task of teaching takes on new meaning.

7. *No one of any age does anything with determination and verve without being involved in it.* The task has to seem worth doing to the individual. It has to make sense to him. This is well known and accepted in the adult world but too often little considered in the school.

This is not to say that the child, or anyone else, has the right to "do just as he pleases." No responsible educator has ever advocated this. It is a canard invented by authoritarians to make democratic behavior seem ridiculous. The idea of change frightens the authoritarian, because he might have to learn new behavior.

I know of no way of involving people in tasks except through consultation. It is through this process that the learner can come to see the reasons for doing whatever lies ahead. He does not have to have his own way, but he has to see that the task is a worthy one before he can spend his energy on it in any true sense.

We teachers are so accustomed to deciding what the tasks will be before we even see the learner that most of us lack skill in consultation. We are so full of our own compulsions and purposes that even when we attempt to consult with the learner, we wait for what we had in mind to emerge before we register approval.

If we do not know how to consult unique learners; if learners must be consulted about what is to be learned in order that they may best learn, then we must learn how to consult. To do this, we must free ourselves of our own compulsions, since unique human beings a generation or two removed from us are not likely to choose what we have in mind. How much happier the lives of early elementary teachers and their children would be if, in teaching reading, the learners saw it as a worthy task or the teacher was free and willing to wait until the learner *could* see some sense or purpose in it!

8. *How a person feels is more important than what he knows.* This is true because one's feelings and attitudes control behavior while one's knowledge does not.

This is not to imply that what one knows is not important. Of course it is. Some of the worst people the world has ever known, however, were exceedingly well informed. The Nazis who slaughtered millions of people in many ingenious ways knew too much, felt too little.

We have been working altogether too hard trying to get our learners to know. We have even sought to have them know exactly what we know, in the same way. We have not realized that the knower and the known are inseparable; that knowledge is what we know after we have learned; that this learning can only occur in the light of the unique learner's experience and purpose and therefore can never be exactly the same in two different people.

We have, as a rule, paid too little attention to how our learners feel. This, however, is what makes knowledge useable. If a person comes to think too little of himself, to feel too inferior, he may come to the point where he cannot do anything, cannot function.

It comes about, therefore, that our attention needs to be directed to a different outcome. At the end of a school day, each child needs to feel better about himself than he did the day before. He needs to feel more able to meet whatever problems life may present; more courageous and more confident. The vicissitudes of life cannot be foreseen, but what we can do is to make each child more able to meet them in all of their variety.

There are those who may worry about the neglect of the "fundamentals" and of subject matter. This need not concern us. The person who feels good about himself will learn to read, for example, better and sooner than he will if he sees himself unable to do so. He will learn more about the world about him (his proper subject matter) when he can look at himself and say, "It is enough." So we gain not only in the direction of human adequacy but also in the things we have always cherished.

9. *Freedom is a requirement for humanness.* By this I do not mean freedom to do just as one pleases. Nobody has this. The instant one starts living anywhere near anyone else, he loses his freedom to do just as he pleases, because he must take this other person into account. I mean freedom within the social scene. I mean having some choices, the chance to decide whether to do this or that. It automatically involves other people.

Every human being is uniquely purposive. Purpose has no meaning in the absence of freedom to choose paths down which one's energies can best be spent. The whole history of mankind has been a struggle between those who would be free and those who would oppress. This is the struggle that goes on in many classrooms. A child who is told exactly what to do, watched and tested to see whether or not he did it, has sanctions applied when he does not or cannot do it, knows not freedom. Of course, he can reject the whole thing, as many do. This is not a real choice, but a negation. It is not a choice between two or more paths for positive action.

Freedom begets creativity. The person who is free to make choices will in some degree be creative. A person is creative when he is faced with a unique dilemma, and devises a solution not necessarily new to all the world, but new to him. Creativity is the growing edge of life; it can only occur in an atmosphere of freedom. A slave cannot create.

It would be good if we would look to our young in this tightly packed industrial society to see how fares freedom. How many choices do our "good" children really have? And if they do not have it in this "land of the free," where else will it be nourished?

10. *All forms of exclusion and segregation represent the evil use of power, and are evil.* In order to avoid long and tiresome debate about the meanings of "good" and "evil," I will define them as I use them. That which facilitates self and others is good. That which diminishes self or others is evil.

I do not limit this discussion to the obvious and ever present exclusion and segregation on the basis of skin color or creed although they are a prominent part of our social problem. This exclusion is only a part of the evil of exclusion. I wish to include the segregation of blue-birds from crows, the exclusion of accessible people from school, the disfranchisement of those whom adults frown upon from participation in the school council; the denial to some of the right to take part in student activities; the separation of children into *X, Y,* and *Z* groups to suit adult convenience. The child in the X group is robbed of part of his human birthright as surely as the one in the *Z* group. The list could be extended almost indefinitely.

If each human being is a potential asset (see 1), we are far from the point where we have too many assets. Man's and the machine's ingenuity in the production of food, clothing and shelter has not even been tested so far. What we need to learn is better development of human potential, better ways for people to spend their energies, better ways of distributing the goods of earth. These cannot be attained through humiliation of the individual by exclusion or segregation, either in school or out.

11. *All forms of rejection are evil.* I refer here not only to the obvious instances where, in later years, children are expelled or frozen out of school. I am thinking of the many subtle forms of rejection which go on in the lives of so many children of all ages. We are all aware of the low grade on the report card, which has to be taken home and often has the effect of increasing distance between parent and child. Little chil-

dren, often too young to understand what it is all about, are subjected to emotional tones of disapproval which they know only too well.

Rejection takes innumerable forms, shows up when least expected. Many teachers whom we all consider excellent, who love children, habitually operate in ways which damage some of their children. When a child is unfavorably compared with another who may be what adults call "bright;" when a child's failure to comprehend is made conspicuous; when he is called upon to compete in an area for which he is not ready and cannot come out well, it is like entering a cripple in a foot-race and then making him feel inferior because he did not win it.

Here we set in motion a whole cluster of feelings and attitudes which grow and fester. Here we sow the wind; the whirlwind is reaped later in drop-outs, mental illness, delinquency and attendant evils. Research experts tell us that most high school drop-outs can be identified by the time they are in the third grade, many even earlier. Thus the drop-out probably is an elementary school one. The future drop-out is the non-reader, the over-aged, sometimes the rebel.

I believe that we cannot afford to reject anybody. I say this not alone for humanitarian reasons, but also for practical, economic, social, reasons. The rejected are too expensive. Rejection causes feelings of hostility, which leads to aggression, to alienation from self and others, to withdrawal, to delinquency, to adult crime and prison or to the mental hospital.

How to teach without rejection is a matter which each must study because each must work out his own way. If we do not know how, we must learn how. Our present curriculum, made by adults without even knowing who the learner is or what he is like, has rejection of some of our young planned and built-in in advance. If the program is such that everybody can master it, then it is too easy, and has to be made difficult enough so that there will be human waste. This is because there is one program for all members of any particular class of learners, be they X or Z. A proper and urgent study for all teachers is how to individualize learning so that there will be something for everyone; so that everyone can hold up his head.

12. *Our task is to build better people.* This appears to be a truism, but it is in fact a switch in objectives. It has been assumed that that which lies outside the learner is what is important. This outside material, often called "knowledge," when injected, will of itself make better people. This has not worked, because too often the injection has called for too much coercion, and this has damaged the psychological self and reduced self-esteem. It is here that the individual learns hate instead of love. It has been self-defeating because whatever value the injected knowledge might have had is rendered unusable.

There is a difference. The self-esteem must come first, and what the child learns about his world will follow, but it will not be the first objective. We have all heard "Teach the child" as long ago as we can remember. It gains real meaning when our first consideration is how the child feels about himself, others, and his world, not how he can perform on tests, or how he can give evidence of possession of the items of subject matter which adults cherish.

The Self in Recent Rogerian Theory

C. H. PATTERSON

The objective of this paper is to sketch the place of the self in the current client-centered approach to personality. While the self is today becoming of central importance in all theories of personality, it constitutes the core of the Rogerian approach which has, in fact, been designated by some writers (e.g., 9, 15) as "self-theory." Perhaps this is because client-centered theory is based upon the observations of individual clients in therapy.

ROGERS' FORMULATIONS

1947

Rogers' earliest formulation was presented in 1947 (17): "The self is a basic factor in the formation of personality and in the determination of behavior." As the perception of self changes, behavior changes. The person's feeling of adequacy is basic to psychological adjustment. The absence of threat is important for the development of an adequate self-concept and is a condition for changes in the self-concept. The self-concept is, by definition, a phenomenological concept: it is the self as seen by the experiencing person.

1951

In 1951 Rogers (18) amplified and extended his discussion of the self in nineteen propositions. The point of view remained perceptual and

Reprinted from *Journal of Individual Psychology* 17, 1961, 5–11, by permission of the author and the publisher.

phenomenological: there is no reality for the individual other than that given by his perceptions. The self is the central concept of personality and behavior. While the basic drive of the organism is the maintenance and enhancement of the organism, the psychological self may take precedence over the physiological organism.

Once the self has developed, experiences are perceived and evaluated in terms of their relevance and significance to the self. Behavior is normally consistent with the self-concept, even at the expense of the organism. However, organic experiences or needs which are unsymbolized (because they are unacceptable) may at times lead to behavior inconsistent with the self-concept ("I was not myself"), or to psychological tension and maladjustment. Experiences which are inconsistent with the self-concept may be perceived as threatening, and may be rejected, denied, or distorted; the self-concept is defended.

Psychological adjustment or integration, on the other hand, exists when the self-concept is congruent with all the experiences of the organism. Under conditions of absence of threat to the self, all experiences —including the organismic—may be examined and assimilated into the self-concept, leading to changes in the self-concept. This occurs in therapy.

1959

The most recent and most detailed of Rogers' theoretical discussions, a more systematic and extended formulation of earlier expressions, appeared in mimeographed form in 1955 and in print in 1959 (19). Self-actualization becomes an important aspect of a general actualizing tendency.

The self-concept is defined as "the organized, consistent conceptual Gestalt composed of characteristics of the 'I' or 'me' and the perceptions of the relationships of the 'I' or 'me' to others and to various aspects of life, together with the value attached to these perceptions" (19, p. 200). The ideal self is introduced into the theory and is defined as "the self-concept which the individual would most like to possess, upon which he places the highest value for himself" (19, p. 200).

Several concepts having to do with regard are included. Rogers postulates a basic, though secondary or learned, need for positive regard from others—that is for warmth, liking, respect, sympathy, and acceptance—and a need for positive self-regard, which is related to or dependent upon positive regard from others.

Unconditional self-regard is a state of general positive self-regard, irrespective of conditions. Positive self-regard may be conditional, however, when the individual "values an experience positively or negatively solely because of . . . conditions of worth which he has taken over from others, not because the experience enhances or fails to enhance his organism" (19, p. 209). In this case the individual is vulnerable to threat and anxiety.

The central ideas in Rogers' theory of the self may be stated as follows:

1. The theory of the self, as part of the general personality theory, is phenomenological. The essence of phenomenology is that "man lives essentially in his own personal and subjective world" (19, p. 191).
2. The self becames differentiated as part of the actualizing tendency, from the environment, through transactions with the environment—particularly the social environment. The process by which this occurs is not detailed by Rogers, but is presumably along the lines described by the sociologists Cooley (8) and Mead (13).[1]
3. The self-concept is the organization of the perceptions of the self. It is the self-concept, rather than any "real" self, which is of significance in personality and behavior. As Combs and Snygg note, the existence of a "real" self is a philosophical question, since it cannot be observed directly (6, p. 123).
4. The self-concept becomes the most significant determinant of response to the environment. It governs the perceptions or meanings attributed to the environment.
5. Whether learned or inherent, a need for positive regard from others develops or emerges with the self-concept. While Rogers leans toward attributing this need to learning, I would include it as an element of the self-actualizing tendency.
6. A need for positive self-regard, or self-esteem, according to Rogers, likewise is learned through internalization or introjection of experiences of positive regard by others. But, alternatively, it may be an aspect of the self-actualizing tendency.
7. When positive self-regard depends on evaluations by others, discrepancies may develop between the needs of the organism and the needs of the self-concept for positive self-regard. There is thus incongruence between the self and experience, or psychological maladjustment. Maladjustment is the result of attempting to preserve the existing self-concept from the threat of experiences which are inconsistent with it, leading to selective perception and distortion or denial of experience.

1. Sociology, I think, anticipated psychology in reacting against behaviorism and recognizing the importance of the self. In the middle thirties, as an undergraduate in sociology at the University of Chicago, I was exposed to the writings of Cooley (8) and Mead (13) on the self. This was where I took on the phenomenological approach. Not until several years later were the self and phenomenology introduced, or rather reintroduced, into psychology. I say reintroduced because James (12) had recognized the importance of the self, and was a phenomenologist as well.

This highly condensed summary does not include the vicissitudes of the self through the processes of disorganization, or the processes of reorganization which take place in therapy.

While a number of persons have contributed to the theory, including Raimy (16), Snygg and Combs (21), and many others who have been associated with Rogers, there has been no other comparable exposition of the theory nor are there any adequately stated alternatives or variations of it. Rogers' terminology differs in some respects from that used by other client-centered writers, but the basic concepts are similar if not identical. For example, some theorists, including myself (14), have used the term self-esteem to refer to what Rogers designates as positive self-regard.

COMPARISON WITH OTHER FORMULATIONS

"Me" versus "I"

Several theorists (2, 4, 13, 22) have emphasized two aspects of the self, essentially distinguishing between the *self as object,* the "me," and the *self as subject,* the "I." The first is often referred to as the *self-concept,* the second as the *ego,* although, as Hall and Lindzey (9, p. 468) point out, there is no general agreement upon terms. James called the "me" the empirical self and the "I" the pure ego—the sense of personal identity or the judging thought. This personal identity, he suggested, may not exist as a fact, "but it would exist as a *feeling* all the same; the consciousness of it would be there, and the psychologist would still have to analyze that" (12, p. 333). The ego would appear to be self-consciousness. Mead's conceptions of the "I" and the "me" appear to be similar, although his discussion is difficult to follow. The "I" appears to be the awareness of the self as of the moment of action (13, pp. 173–178, 192).

These concepts, while preferable to the idea of the "I" as an executive, which lends itself to reification, are vague and difficult to pin down. At least I am not able to differentiate actually, practically, or operationally between the executive aspects of the self, and the self as an object to the self. The self of Snygg and Combs is both an object and doer. Others, including Allport (1) and Sherif and Cantril (20), also appear to adopt this view. Hilgard (10) suggests that the concept of the self as a doer is an error into which psychologists have been led by the common-sense or lay view that behavior seems to be self-determined.

In Rogers' theory the self-concept, although an important determiner of behavior, is not an executive or doer. There is no need for positing such an executive. The organism is by nature continually active, seeking its goal of actualization, and the self as part of the organism is also seeking actualization through its constant activity. The self-concept thus influences the direction of activity, rather than initiating it and directing it entirely. Thus Rogers avoids the problem of reification and the ambiguousness of the concept of the "I" or the ego as an executive. James' sense of personal identity might be considered a part of the self-concept, and the ego or "I" as the awareness of the self-concept. However, I am not sure that this solution is entirely satisfactory.

Ideal Self

In his recent formulation of the concept of the ideal self Rogers indicates that the perception of the ideal self becomes more realistic, and the self becomes more congruent with the ideal self, as an outcome of therapy. This suggests that personality disturbance is characterized by an unrealistic self-ideal, and/or incongruence between the self-concept and the self-ideal. This formulation has been the basis of some research by the client-centered school (e.g., 3). But it is not incorporated in Rogers' statement of the theory. The theory apparently does not recognize conflict between the self-concept and the self-ideal as a source of disturbance, but emphasizes the conflict between the self-concept and organismic experiences as its source. This is in contrast to some other theories in which the self-ideal is a central concept and an important factor in psychological adjustment or maladjustment, e.g., Horney (11).

The Self

The notion of the self, or the self-structure, is broader than the self-concept. It includes the self-concept and the ideal self. What else it includes, is not clear. Combs and Snygg speak of the phenomenal self, defined as the "organization of all the ways an individual has of seeing himself" (6, p. 126). The self-concept includes "only those perceptions about self which seem most vital or important to the individual himself" (6, p. 127). How these are to be differentiated is not indicated. Rogers considers the self-concept to be in the person's awareness, whereas the self may include aspects not in awareness.

PROBLEMS OF OPERATIONAL DEFINITION

Rogers made an effort to keep his constructs and concepts so that they can be operationally defined. The phenomenological approach, it seems to me, fosters this effort. One is not concerned about the "real" self, the "real" environment, etc., but with the perceptions of particular individuals. The self-concept and the self-ideal are perceptions which can be studied and objectified by instruments such as the Q-sort, or by tests of the 'Who am I" variety. The latter, though ideally suited for use with client-centered theory, have not, however, to my knowledge, been used in connection with this theory.

Rogers points out the problem of operationally defining the organismic experiences which, it is assumed, conflict with the self-concept. The aspects of the self other than the self-concept and the self-ideal, are also not operationally defined. Maybe we do not need these concepts. I see no need for unconscious elements of the self, for example. Aspects of the self which are not in awareness but which can be brought into awareness, can be tapped by instructions such as "Sort these statements in terms of your concept of yourself as a father." The self, insofar as it is behaviorally effective, may consist only of the various self-perceptions—thus resolving the problem posed above about the area of the self apart from the self-concept and the self-ideal. The organismic experiences, on the other hand, as an essential aspect of the theory, must be brought within the realm of measurement. The approach of Chodorkoff (5), using Q-sorts of self-referent items by clinicians as an "objective description" of the total experience of the individual, though operational, may be questioned as to its validity.

There is also the problem, pointed out by Combs and Soper (7), that although the self-concept may be operationally defined as the individual's statements about himself, these statements do not necessarily correspond to his perception of himself. His statements may be inaccurate for a number of reasons, including inability or unwillingness to give an accurate report. Yet there is no other approach to determining the self-concept, since by definition it is the perception of the self by the individual, and no one else can report upon it or describe it.

In general, what is needed is a more formal theoretical statement which would lead to testable hypotheses for research, not only with clients in therapy, but in many other situations, with many other kinds of subjects.

Summary

The aspects of Rogers' theory which relate to his central formulation of the self-concept have been summarized. A comparison with the thinking of others regarding the self attempted to clarify some differences and showed other differences in need of resolution. Some problems of operational definition were briefly discussed.

References

1. Allport, G. W. "The Ego in Contemporary Psychology." *Psychol. Rev.,* 50 (1943): 451–468. Also in *Personality and Social Encounter: Selected Essays.* Boston: Beacon Press, 1960, pp. 71–93.
2. Bertocci, P. A. "The Psychological Self, the Ego and Personality." *Psychol. Rev.,* 52 (1945): 91–99.
3. Butler, J. M., & Haigh, G. V. "Changes in the Relation Between Self-Concepts and Ideal Concepts Consequent upon Client-Centered Counseling." In C. R. Rogers and R. F. Dymond, eds., *Psychotherapy and Personality Change.* Chicago: University of Chicago Press, 1954, pp. 55–76.
4. Chein, I. "The awareness of the self and the structure of the ego." *Psychol. Rev.,* 51 (1944): 504–514.
5. Chodorkoff, B. "Self-Perception, Perceptual Defense, and Adjustment." *J. Abnorm. Soc. Psychol.,* 49 (1954): 508–512.
6. Combs, A. W., and Snygg, D. *Individual Behavior,* rev. ed. New York: Harper, 1959.
7. Combs, A. W., and Soper, D. W. "The Self, Its Derivative Terms, and Research." *J. Indiv. Psychol.* 13 (1957): 134–145. Also in A. E. Kuenzli, ed., *The Phenomenological Problem.* New York: Harper, 1959, pp. 31–48.
8. Cooley, C. H. *Human Nature and the Social Order.* New York: Scribner's, 1902.
9. Hall, C. S., and Lindzey, G. *Theories of Personality.* New York: Wiley, 1957.
10. Hilgard, E. R. "Human Motives and the Concept of the Self." *Amer. Psychologist* 4 (1949): 374–382. Also in H. Brand, ed., *The Study of Personality.* New York: Wiley, 1954, pp. 347–361.
11. Horney, K. *Neurosis and Human Growth.* New York: W. W. Norton, 1950.
12. James, W. *The Principles of Psychology.* vol. 1. New York: Holt, 1890.
13. Mead, G. H. *Mind, Self and Society.* Chicago: University of Chicago Press, 1934.
14. Patterson, C. H. *Counseling and Psychotherapy: Theory and Practice.* New York: Harper, 1959.
15. Pepinsky, H. B., and Pepinsky, P. N. *Counseling: Theory and Practice.* New York: Ronald Press, 1954.
16. Raimy, V. C. "Self-Reference in Counseling Interviews." *J. Consult. Psychol.,* 12 (1948): 153–163. Also in A. E. Kuenzli, ed., *The Phenomenological Problem.* New York: Harper, 1959, pp. 76–95.
17. Rogers, C. R. "Some Observations on the Organization of Personality." *Amer. Psychologist* 2 (1947): 358–368. Also in A. E. Kuenzli, ed., *The Phenomenological Problem.* New York: Harper, 1959, pp. 49–75.
18. Rogers, C. R. *Client-Centered Therapy.* Boston: Houghton-Mifflin, 1951.
19. Rogers, C. R. "A Theory of Therapy, Personality, and Interpersonal Relationships, as Developed in the Client-Centered Framework." In S. Koch, ed., *Psychology: A Study of a Science.* vol. 3. New York: McGraw-Hill, 1959, pp. 184–256.
20. Sherif, M., and Cantril, H. *The Psychology of Ego-Involvements.* New York: Wiley, 1947.
21. Snygg, D., and Combs, A. W. *Individual Behavior.* New York: Harper, 1949.
22. Symonds, P. M. *The Ego and the Self.* New York: Appleton-Century-Crofts, 1951.

Intelligence from a Perceptual Point of View

ARTHUR W. COMBS

There is a growing trend in psychology toward viewing behavior as a function of perception. More and more we have come to understand that the individual's behavior is not so much a function of the physical stimulus as it is a function of his perceptions of the events to which he is exposed. It is the meaning of events to the individual rather than the externally observed nature of events which seems crucial in behavior. As a result, psychologists in increasing numbers are turning their attention to the problems of human perception and are attempting to observe behavior, not from an external point of view, but from the point of view of the individual who is behaving. This paper is an attempt to relate this method of observation to the problem of intelligence. The question we wish to explore in this paper is: "What is the nature of intelligence viewed from a perceptual or phenomenological frame of reference?"

INTELLIGENCE AS A PROBLEM OF PERCEPTION

By the term *intelligence* we ordinarily refer to the effectiveness of the individual's behavior. In a personal frame of reference the individual's behavior is described in terms of the perceptions that he can make his own unique perceptive field. This perceptive field has been called by Snygg and Combs *The Phenomenal Field* and has been defined by them as "the universe of experience open to the individual at the moment of his behavior." In other words, the behavior of the individual will be

Reprinted from *Journal of Abnormal and Social Psychology* 47, 1952, 662–673. Copyright 1952 by the American Psychological Association. Reprinted by permission.

dependent upon the perceptions that the individual makes in his phenomenal field at the moment of action. The effectiveness of his behavior will necessarily be a function of the adequacy of those perceptions.

If an entity in the perceptive field is vague and ill defined, the behavior of the individual will be correspondingly vague and lacking in precision. Until the child has clearly differentiated that 2 plus 2 equals 4, this function is comparatively meaningless and his behavior in arithmetic is correspondingly inaccurate and ineffective. Thus, the precision and effectiveness of the individual's behavior will be dependent upon the scope and clarity of his personal field of awareness. Intelligence, then, from a perceptual point of view becomes a function of the factors which limit the scope and clarity of an individual's phenomenal field.

The perceptions that could be made of any given situation, such as looking at a stone wall, for example, are, theoretically, practically infinite in number and quality. As a matter of fact, however, we are strictly limited in our perceptions of a stone wall to those which we, as human beings, can make. The perceptions possible to us are only those that people can make. We cannot, for instance, perceive the wall as it would appear to a man from Mars, or from the interior of an atom, or as it would appear to a centipede. What is more, we cannot even perceive it as it would appear to all people. Different people will perceive different aspects of the wall differently, even at the same instant. I can only perceive the wall, and hence behave toward it, in terms of the perceptions that I, as an individual, can make regarding it. I may, for instance, perceive it as a fine, sturdy fence enclosing my property, while a stone mason friend might perceive it as having been poorly designed, or as having been built with too little cement in the mortar mixture. The perceptions open to my mason friend are the result of his unique experience. I, not having such experience, am incapable of those perceptions at this moment.

POTENTIAL AND FUNCTIONAL PERCEPTIONS

Before proceeding further with our discussion of the limiting factors in perception, it is necessary for us to pause for a moment to distinguish between potential and functional perceptions. By potential perceptions I mean those perceptions that exist in the individual's unique field of awareness and that, given the right circumstances at any particular moment, *could* occur. The fact that a perception is potentially possible to any individual, by no means, however, means that it will occur at the moment of action. Even those perceptions that I can make potentially may not be active for me at any given moment. Potentially, I might be able, for instance, to perceive the wall that we have just been using as an example as a barrier to be gotten over, as an eyesore to be beautified, as composed of 687 bricks costing me $80.27, or as providing pleasant shade on a hot day. These are all potential perceptions I am capable of making about the wall. They will affect my behavior, however, only when they are active or functioning in my field of perceptions. When I am beating a hasty retreat pursued by a neighbor's angry dog, perceptions about the shade, beauty, or cost of the wall, though potential, are not functional in affecting my behavior. I behave only in terms of my functioning perception of the wall as something to get over—and quickly. The fact that particular perceptions may exist potentially in the phenomenal field of an individual is by no means a guarantee that they may exist functionally at the moment of action.

While the potential intelligence of the individual is of interest in judging his capacities, it is practically always a matter impossible to measure with any degree of accuracy. We can only sample those parts of a phenomenal field that *we* happen to feel are important. Obviously the measurement of a person's potential perceptions in these terms is open to extremely grave sampling error and improves in accuracy only as the individuals tested have common experience in the materials chosen for testing. It seems probable that an intelligence test cannot accurately measure the potential differentiations that he individual can make in his phenomenal field. Rather, what we usually measure are the subject's functional perceptions. That is, we measure what differentiations he can make when confronted with the necessity to do so for one reason or another. We may define these functional perceptions as: those perceptions in the field experienced by the individual at the moment of behaving.

From a perceptual viewpoint, if intelligence is the capacity for effective behavior, *the intelligence of an individual will be dependent upon the richness and variety of perceptions possible to him at a given moment.* To understand and effectively to foster intelligent behavior, it will be necessary for us to be concerned with the limiting factors upon the perceptions of an individual. We need to know not only what the individual *could* perceive, but what he *would* perceive at a given moment of behaving.

PHYSIOLOGIC LIMITATIONS UPON PERCEPTION

Certainly the physical limitations upon the organism affect the differentiations possible in the phenomenal field. Some forms of prenatal anomalies, like mongolism, microcephalia, and similar disorders, indubitably reduce the level of operation at which the individual can function and seriously impair the ability of the organism to make adequate perceptions. Similarly, there seems good reason to believe that some types of mechanical or disease injury to the central nervous system may result in impaired functioning, such as occurs in cerebral palsy, birth injuries, prefrontal lobotomy, the aftermath of such diseases as encephalitis or, even, in common childhood diseases accompanied by prolonged high fever. Various forms of endocrinopathies, particularly cretinism, also appear to have limiting effects upon differentiational capacity for some individuals. Such physical or biological limitations upon the organism have been widely studied but account for only a small proportion of those persons operating at impaired intelligence levels.

Other less dramatic forms of physical handicaps may also have important effects upon the perceptions possible to the individual, however. This is particularly true of individuals suffering impairment of various sense modalities which may inhibit the clarity or even the existence of some perceptions. We need to remind ourselves, however, that such persons may have as rich and varied a perceptive field within their own limitations as we have within ours. Testing persons living in one frame of reference with tests based on those of another can easily lead us astray, a fact well known to the makers of some tests for the handicapped. The limitations imposed upon perception by such physical handicaps as the loss or impairment of locomotion or the use of arms or hands are also important in limiting certain kinds of perceptions. These people experience different, but not necessarily fewer or poorer, perceptions of events than socalled "normals."

Perhaps less well recognized in their effects upon perception are such factors as malnutrition, focal infections, and chronic fatigue, which may reduce both the need for and the ability to make adequate perceptions. It is well known in industrial psychology, for example, that fatigued workers are more likely to have accidents, perhaps because of failure to make the right differentiations at the right time. It is conceivable that persons suffering from chronic fatigue over long periods similarly fail to make differentiations useful to them on later occasions.

Certainly such physical factors as these have important effects upon the ability of the individual to make adequate differentiations in his perceptive field. The more dramatic of these have often been recognized and studied. Others, such as the effects of malnutrition, fatigue, and the like, have been less adequately explored. In spite of the lack of research in respect to some of the physical limitations upon intelligence, far more work has been done in this area, however, than in some of those to be discussed below.

ENVIRONMENT AND OPPORTUNITY AS A LIMITATION UPON PERCEPTION

The differentiations in the phenomenal field that an individual can make will, of course, be affected by the opportunities for perception to which he has been exposed. To appear in the perceptive field an event must have been, in some manner, experienced by the person who perceives it. Environmental effects upon perception appear to be of two types, actual or concrete and symbolic or vicarious.

Exposure to Actual Environmental Events

In the first place the perceptions possible to any individual will be limited, in part, by the actual environmental factors to which he has been exposed. Eskimos ordinarily do not comprehend bananas, nor African Bushmen, snow, since neither has had the opportunity to experience these events in their respective environments. It is not necessary to go so far afield for illustration, however. In our own country our experience with the testing of children in various parts of the nation has shown that perceptions are highly limited by the environmental conditions surrounding the individual. Mountain children, for example, often give bizarre responses on intelligence tests. Sherman and Henry found intelligence test results on such children arranged themselves in order of the opportunities provided by their environment.

There are differences also between the perceptions of rural and urban children, children from the North and children from the South, mountain and valley, seaboard and plains. Nor are such differences confined only to children. Adults, too, are limited in their perceptions by environmental factors. During the war I worked for a time in an induction station receiving men from the mountains of Kentucky, West Virginia, and southern Ohio. An intelligence test in use at this station was composed of a series of five pictures with instructions to the subject to cross out that one of each series of five objects that did not belong with the others. One set of five pictures showed four stringed instruments, a guitar, harp, violin, bass fiddle, and a trumpet. Large numbers of these back country men crossed out the harp because they had never seen one or because "all the others are things in our band." We cannot assume that these men were less able to make differentiations or had perceptive fields less rich than their examiner on the basis of these tests. We can only suggest that their perceptions are different from those who made the test. Presumably, had they made the test and administered it to the psychologist, the psychologist would have appeared rather dull!

Exposure to Symbolic or Vicarious Events

Differentiations may occur in the perceptive field upon a symbolic basis as well as from exposure to an actual event. That is, perceptions may occur in the individual's field through indirect exposure to experience as in reading, conversation, movies, and other means of communication. Although I cannot directly perceive that it is dangerous to expose myself to rays from an atomic pile, for example, I can differentiate this notion through what others whom I respect have told me. Ideas and concepts are largely differentiations of this sort, and it is probable that many of our perceptions are acquired through a symbolic rather than an actual exposure. Certainly most of our formal schooling falls in this category which may explain, in part, why so little of it is effective in our behavior.

It will be recognized at once that exposure to events in no sense completely determines the perceptions that the individual will make. Exposure to events is only one of the factors involved in determining whether or not an event will be differentiated. Even with equivalent exposure, the perceptions we make are not alike. Perception is not an all or none proposition but a selective process. The same person in the same situation at different times may perceive quite different aspects of the situation and behave accordingly. The provisions of opportunity to perceive is by no means a guarantee that a particular perception will occur, a phenomenon of which teachers are only too aware. The personal field of the individual is always organized and meaningful and, even with exposure to events, only those aspects that have meaning for the individual in his own unique economy will be differentiated with permanence.

The individual in a particular culture perceives those aspects of his environment that, from his point of view, he needs to perceive to maintain and enhance his self in the world in which he lives. This does not mean he makes fewer perceptions than an individual in another culture; he makes only *different* perceptions. Thus, intelligence tests made in one culture and applied in another do not measure the ability to differentiate, nor do they measure the richness of the individual's field. Perhaps what they really measure is no more than the difference between cultures. American-made intelligence tests applied to other cultures generally show the following arrangement of nationality groups in decreasing order: British Isles, Germany, France, Italy, the Balkans, Asiatic countries. It will be noted that these nationality groups are also roughly arranged in order to the degree of commonality with our own culture.

TIME AS A LIMITATION UPON PERCEPTION

Differentiation requires time. The richness of perception, therefore, will be in part a function of how long the individual has been in touch with experiences. While it is true that a perception is possible only when confronted by an experience, it is also true that this exposure must be long enough to make differentiation possible. This principle is familiar to anyone who has looked at a painting for a period of time. The perceptions which can be made are almost limitless if one looks long enough.

In thinking of the effect of time upon differentiation, it is necessary for us to keep in mind that we are speaking of the duration of the individual's experience with an event and not of the observer's experience. Thus, while it may appear to an outside observer that an individual is confronted by an experience, from the individual's own point of view, he may have no contact with it whatever. A child may sit in school all day, apparently exposed to the curriculum, but may actually be experiencing and perceiving quite different aspects of the situation. Perception is an internal, individual phenomenon and may be quite different from that of another person, even in the same situation.

Most perceptions that the individual makes are functions of previous differentiations he has made in his phenomenal field. For example, before one can perceive the mechanics of multiplication, he must have perceived addition. In the same way, before he can perceive the function of a sand dome on top of the locomotive, he must differentiate the fact that locomotive wheels sometimes slip. Clearly this process of differentiation takes time. It seems axiomatic that to make differentiations an individual must have lived long enough to do so, a fact that we recognize in the construction of intelligence tests calibrated for various age levels, and which teachers recognize in the concept of readiness.

Differentiations in the phenomenal field seem to be occurring continuously as the organism seeks to satisfy its needs in the myriad situations of life. In this sense, intelligence never ceases to develop but is continuously increasing so long as the individual remains alive and operating. That intelligence seems to level off at age sixteen or later is probably a mere artifact of our method of observation. So long as the individual remains in school we have at least a modicum of comparable experience which can be tested in different persons. After the school years, when individuals are free to go their separate ways, this modicum of comparable experience rapidly disappears. The older one gets, the more diverse is his experience. Intelligence tests based upon comparability of experience may thus fail to evaluate properly the effectiveness of adults.

THE INDIVIDUAL'S GOALS AND VALUES AS A LIMITING FACTOR UPON PERCEPTION

Up to this point in our discussion we have been dealing with factors affecting perception that are widely discussed in the literature and for the most part as well understood. In the remainder of this paper let us turn our attention to several factors less well explored as they appear in a phenomenological setting. The first of these has to do with the effects of the individual's own goals and values as a limiting factor on perception.

From a phenomenological view the individual is forever engaged in a ceaseless attempt to achieve satisfaction of his need through the goals and values he has differentiated as leading to that end. These goals and values may be explicit or implicit, simple or complex, but they are always unique to the personality itself. The goals of an individual will vary in another respect as well. The individual's goals and values may be either positive or negative. That is, in the course of his experience, the person may differentiate some things as matters to be sought, while other things may be differentiated as matters to be avoided. What is more, although there is a considerable degree of stability in the major goals and values of a particular individual, there may be great fluctuations on how some goals are perceived from time to time, depending upon the total organization of the perceptual field at any moment.

The goals and values an individual seeks have a most important effect upon the perceptions he can make. Once goals have been established by the individual they continue to affect his every experience. Thus, the person who has differentiated good music as a goal to be sought perceives music more frequently. His entire experience with music is likely to be affected. Certainly his experience will differ markedly from the person who has formulated a goal to avoid music at all costs. In the same way the experiences of children who perceive schooling as something to be sought are vastly different from those of children who try to avoid all aspects of schooling. If the fundamental thesis of this paper is accurate, that intelligence is a function of the variety and richness of the perceptive field, then the individual's goals must have a most important effect upon intelligence. A considerable body of research has been accumulating over the past several years, demonstrating this controlling effect of goals and values on the individual's perceptive experience. Such studies as those of J. M. Levine, R. Levine, Postman, and Bruner are fascinating cases in point.

This effect of goals on perception is by no means limited to the subject whose intelligence we wish to measure. It is equally true of the intelligence test constructor. It leads to the very confusing situation wherein the test constructor with one organization of goals perceives certain experiences to be marks of intelligence for another person who may or may not have similar goals. Indeed, the likelihood is that he, almost certainly, does not have similar goals. Intelligence tests thus become highly selected samplings of perception in terms of what the testers consider important. Low scorers do not necessarily mean less rich and varied fields of perception; they may mean only fields of perception more widely divergent from those of the examiner. A young man whom the writer tested at an induction center during the war illustrates the point very well. This young man was a newsboy on the streets of a West Virginia city. Although he had failed repeatedly in grammar school and was generally regarded as "not bright," he appeared on a national radio hook-up as "The Human Adding Machine." He was a wizard at figures. He could multiply correctly such figures as 6235941 × 397 almost as fast as the problem could be written down. He astounded our induction center for half a day with his numerical feats. Yet, on the Binet Test given by the writer he achieved an IQ of less than 60! People in his home town, who bought his papers, amused themselves by giving him problems to figure constantly. When not so occupied this young man entertained himself by adding up the license numbers of cars that passed his corner. He was a specialist in numbers. Apparently as a result of some early success in this field, he had been led to practice numbers constantly, eventually to the exclusion of all else. This was one area in which a poor colored boy could succeed and he made the most of it. His number perceptions were certainly rich and varied but other things were not. Although he was capable of arithmetic feats not achieved by one in millions, he was classified as dull! I do not mean to argue that variety of perception is unimportant in effective behavior. I do mean to suggest the importance of goals in determining perception.

CULTURAL EFFECTS ON GOALS AND PERCEPTIONS

We have stated here that the richness of the individual's perceptive field is in part a function of the goals he has differentiated as important or threatening to him. But, clearly these goals are themselves the results of the individual's experience. The culture one grows up in deeply affects the goals one holds. Cultures both restrict and encourage, approve and disapprove the formulation of goals in the individual. This selective effect of the culture in large measure determines the goals sought and avoided by the individual. These goals in turn must exert important effects upon the perceptions that become part of the individual's perceptive field.

I remember the Kentucky moonshiner to whom I once administered the Wechsler-Bellevue. This man could not tell me "how many pints in a quart" although he had certainly been taught this fact in his early schooling. Knowing that my client did a considerable business in bootleg liquor, I framed the question differently and asked "Well, how do you sell your liquor?" He smiled tolerantly and replied, "Oh Boss, I just sell it by the jug full!" In his community to have done otherwise would have been to risk bankruptcy. In a culture where a jug is standard container for spirits, what do we need to know about quarts?

It is conceivable that low intelligence may be, at least in part, no more than a function of the goals an individual is striving to reach in achieving his need satisfaction. The well-known phenomenon in which intelligence tests give best results in the school years, when experience and goals have a degree of commonality, and break down badly following those years would seem to corroborate this point. Perhaps by concerning ourselves with human goals we can affect perception, and thus intelligence, much more than we believed possible. Can it be that the child of low apparent intelligence is not so much a problem of an unfortunate heredity as an unforunate constellation of goals or values? We could do a great deal about intelligence if that were true.

THE SELF-CONCEPT AS A FACTOR LIMITING PERCEPTION

We are just beginning to understand the tremendous effects of the individual's concept of self upon his perceptions and behavior. Lecky, for instance, reports the effect of a change in self-concept in improving the ability of children to spell. Other researchers have reported similar effects of the self-concept upon the perceptions which the individual may make. Clinical experience would tend to bear out such observations. Any clinician is familiar with numerous instances in which a child's conception of his abilities severely limited his achievement, even though his real abilities may have been superior to his perception of them. One needs but to go shopping with one's spouse to discover again how one's conception of himself as a male or female affects the things he sees and the things he hears.

Perception is a selective process, and the conception one holds of himself is a vital factor in determining the richness and the variety of perception selected. It makes a great deal of difference, for example, how one perceives the president of our country if one conceives of himself as a Democrat, a Republican, or a Communist. One needs but to observe a group of children to become aware that little boys perceive things quite differently from little girls. Professors do not perceive like truck drivers, although when I have had to ride with professor automobile-drivers, I have often wished they did. Thousands of people in our society avoid perceptions having to do with mathematical functions by their firm concept of themselves as people who "cannot do mathematics." The self-concepts we hold have a very vital effect in selecting the perceptions which become part of our perceptive fields. If the effectiveness of behavior is dependent on our perceptive fields, it follows that the self-concepts we hold must affect the "intelligence" of our behavior.

There is another factor in the effect of the self-concept upon perception that makes it even more important as a selector of experience. That factor is the circular effect of a given concept of self. Let us take, as an example, the child who has developed a concept of himself as "unable to read." Such a child is likely to avoid reading, and thus the very experience which might change his concept of self is bypassed. Worse still, the child who believes himself unable to read, confronted with the necessity for reading, is more likely than not to do badly. The external evaluation of his teachers and fellow pupils, as well as his own observations of his performance, all provide proof to the child of how right he was in the first place! The possession of a particular concept of self tends to produce behavior that corroborates the self-concept with which the behavior originated.

Every clinician has had experience with children of ability who conceive of themselves as unable, unliked, unwanted, or unacceptable and perceive and behave in accordance with their perceptions. And this effect is not limited to children alone. It seems to me one of the great tragedies of our society that millions of people in our society perceiving themselves as able to produce only *X* amount, behave in these terms. Society, in turn, evaluates them in terms of this behavior and so lends proof to what is already conceived by the individual. Compared to this waste of human potential in our society, our losses in automobile accidents seem like a mere drop in the bucket. It is even conceivable in these terms that we create losses in intelligence. If, in our schools, we teach a child that he is unable and if he believes us and behaves in these terms, we need not be surprised when we test his intelligence to discover that he produces at the level at which we taught him!

It is conceivable that psychology has unwittingly contributed to this situation by the widespread publication of a static conception of intelligence and human capacities. The concept of severe limits upon the capacities of the organism simply corroborates the self-concept of the man in the street and decreases the likelihood of change in his concept of self. Even more important must be the effect upon our educational system. Teachers who believe in an unchanging character of child capacities provide the attitudes and experiences that produce and maintain a child's conception of self and his abilities. It is notorious that children's grades vary very little from year to year through the course of schooling. This continuous and little-changing evaluation must have important effects on the self-concept of the child. If the school system in which the child lives is thoroughly imbued with the notion that a child's capacities are comparatively fixed, it is even conceivable that the system may in large measure produce a child's intelligence level by the circular effect we have mentioned above.

THREAT AS A FACTOR IN PERCEPTION

The last of the factors I should like to discuss as a possible factor in intelligence is the effect of threat upon the perceptive field. If our fundamental assumption that intelligence is a function of the richness and breadth of the phenomenal field is correct, the effect of threat on this field becomes a most important consideration. Although these effects have been so widely understood by the layman that they have been made a part of his everyday speech, it is interesting that until very recently the phenomenon has been given little attention by psychologists. The perception by the individual of threat to himself seems to have at least two major effects upon the perceptive field.

Restriction of the Perceptive Field Under Threat

The first of these effects is the restrictive effect that the perception of threat to self seems to have on the individual's perception. When he feels himself threatened, there appears to be a narrowing of the perceptive field to the object of threat. This has often been described in the psychology of vision as "tunnel vision." The phenomenon is extremely common, and almost everyone has experienced it at some moment of crisis in his lifetime. One hears it described in such comments as "All I could see was the truck coming at us," or, "I was so scared I couldn't think of a thing." There seems reason to believe that this effect is not limited to traumatic experiences alone, but exists in lesser degree in response to milder threats as well. Combs and Taylor, for example, have demonstrated the effect under extremely mild forms of threat.

Such limiting effects on perception must certainly have a bearing upon perceptions available to the individual in his phenomenal field. Subjects who have participated in food deprivation experiments report uniformly that when threatened by hunger, food becomes an obsession. Recently, at the dinner table, I asked my young daughter what she had learned at school that day. "Oh nothing," said she with much feeling, "but was our teacher mad! Wow!" It would appear from her remarks that, feeling threatened by an angry teacher, it was difficult for her to perceive much else. Her perceptions of the day were apparently entirely concerned with the nature of anger. No doubt these are valuable perceptions to possess, but I know of no intelligence test which measures them.

I recall, too, the behavior of two little girls whose mother was taken to a mental hospital at the beginning of the summer. The matter was kept a deep secret from these two children for fear they "would not understand." The children spent most of the summer with the writer's daughter in an incessant game of "hospital." From morning to night this game went on outside our living-room window. Apparently, this preoccupation was the direct outcome of the threat they felt in the loss of their mother, for with the mother's return the game ceased as suddenly as it had begun. To the best of my knowledge it has not occurred since. Under threat there seem to be severe limits imposed upon the breadth and character of perception.

Defense of the Perceptive Field Under Threat

There is a second effect of threat upon the individual's perceptions. This effect has to do with the defense reactions reduced in the individual on perceiving himself to be threatened. The perception of threat not only narrows the field and reduces the possibility of wide perceptions, but causes the individual to protect and cling to the perceptions he already holds. Thus, the possibility of perceptual changes is reduced, and the opportunities for new perceptions or learning are decreased. Under threat, behavior becomes rigid. The fluidity and adaptation which we generally associate with intelligent behavior is vastly decreased. A number of interesting experiments in the past few years have demonstrated this phenomenon. Cowen, for example, illustrated this effect in problem solving.

Our own experiment previously mentioned also demonstrated this effect with even very mild forms of threat. This rigidity or resistance of perception to change under threat is well known to the layman and is well illustrated in some of the sayings of our culture. Such aphorisms as "Nobody ever wins an argument" or "You can lead a horse to water but you cannot make him drink" seem to be illustrations of a vague understanding of the phenomenon in the public mind. It is surprising that this principle has been so long overlooked.

I think it will be generally agreed that intelligent behavior is quite the antithesis of rigidity. In the terms we have used in this article, intelligent behavior is a function of the variety and richness of perception in the phenomenal field. Whatever produces narrowness and rigidity of perception becomes an important factor in limiting intelligence. If this reasoning is accurate, or even partly so, one is led to wonder about the effects of long-continued threat upon the development of intelligence. What of the child who has suffered serious threats to himself for long periods of his life, as in the case of the delinquent, for example? Or what of the child who has been seriously deprived of affection and warmth from those who surround him over a period of years? Is it possible that we have created low intelligence in such children? Axline has reported a number of cases in which intelligence scores improved considerably under therapy. We have observed similar changes in our own clinical practice.

It may be argued that, although threat seems to reduce perception, some people under threat apparently produce more effectively. I think, however, it is necessary for us to distinguish between "threat" and "challenge." In threat, the individual perceives himself in jeopardy and feels, in addition, a degree of inadequacy to deal effectively with the threat perceived. In challenge, the individual perceives himself threatened but feels at the same time a degree of adequacy to deal with the threat. It would appear that whether an event is perceived as threatening or challenging is a function of the individual's feeling of competence to deal with it. If this analysis is correct, it would explain why a situation that appears threatening to a person, from the viewpoint of an outside observer, might one time produce rigidity and another highly effective behavior. This description of events seems characteristic of the history of civilization as well as of individuals, if Toynbee's explanation can be given credence. He points out that the most productive (more intelligent?) societies are those in which the society faces some crisis within its capacities to cope with the situation (challenge), while societies without crisis or in which the crisis is overwhelming produce very little or collapse entirely.

SOME IMPLICATIONS OF THIS CONCEPTION OF INTELLIGENT BEHAVIOR

If the conception of intelligence we have been discussing in this paper should prove accurate, it seems to me to raise serious questions about some of our common assumptions with respect to intelligence and, at the same time, opens some exciting new possibilities for the treatment or education of persons we have often assumed to be beyond help. It implies that our conception of the limiting factors of intelligence may have been too narrow. It would suggest perhaps that our very point of view with respect to intelligence may have resulted in our own tunnel vision, such that we have not been able to perceive other factors given little attention to this point. Perhaps we have been too impressed with the limitations upon growth and development which we observe in physical maturation. We may, for instance, have jumped too quickly to the assumption that intelligent behavior was limited as severely as physical growth and that we have explored to exhaustion other factors that may limit intelligence.

I am not suggesting that physiologic limits do not exist in respect to intelligence. I am suggesting that we may have conceded too early that we had approached those limits. There is no doubt that we can demonstrate in some cases, such as mongolism, cretinism, and the like, that physical factors severely limit intelligence. But these cases are comparatively few compared to the so-called "familial" cases of low intelligence that we often assume are hereditary in origin. What evidence do we really possess that would lead us to the position that an individual of "normal" physical condition and vigor may be limited in his capacity for effective behavior by some physical condition? We assume there must be such factors operating because we cannot explain his handicap otherwise. That biological science has not yet been able to demonstrate such physical bases has not deterred us in this. On the contrary, we have simply deplored the lack of sufficient advance in that discipline to demonstrate our conclusion! I should like to suggest that this may not be their failure but ours. Until it can be definitely established that limitations exist as biological functions, our task as psychologists is to assume that they may just as well be social or psychological in character and to work just as hard exploring the matter in our discipline as we expect the biologist to work in his.

Let us, for example, explore to the very fullest the possibility that in those cases where we cannot demonstrate biologic impairment, the limitations upon intelligence may be psychological. If it turns out not to be true, we shall find out in time. I do not believe we can afford to limit the places where we look by the preperceptions we have about the matter. Our responsibility here is too great. Education, to name but the most obvious of our social institutions, has in large measure predicated its goals and methods on a concept of humanity with certain static limitations on intelligence. If these limitations are not static, it is up to us as psychologists to find out. The task of the scientist is to question, not to be content with answers. We cannot afford to accept an undemonstrated point of view that prevents us from asking questions.

SOME IMPLICATIONS FOR INTELLIGENCE TESTING

If the concepts of intelligence we have been discussing prove accurate, another area of psychological thought toward which we must cast a quizzical eye is the area of intelligence testing. This is particularly important at a time when our culture has come to accept these instruments as trustingly as the family doctor's prescription. If our approach to intelligent behavior as a function of the variety and richness of the perceptual field is a valid consideration, we need to ask regarding these tests at least the following questions:

1. Is our sampling of the perceptive field truly adequate? If I lived for years in a prison cell, I presume I should become expert in perceptions about that cell. Unfortunately, they would be of little value outside the prison walls, but can it truthfully be said that my perceptions are less rich or varied, or only that they are less rich and varied about things I have not had opportunity to experience? Is the delinquent, with rich and varied perceptions on how to elude the police, less intelligent or has he simply not perceived things society wishes he had?

2. Since perceptions are always closely affected by need, by whose need shall we sample perceptions—yours, mine, society's, the subject's own? I suspect that in terms of his own needs and perceptions the subject might be deemed quite brilliant, though he might or might not appear so from the point of view of society. For the most part our tests are based on the assumption that academic, upper middle-class, intellectual perceptions are important. But are they? Can we assume that the expert machinist, who can perceive things "out of this world" for most of the rest of us about a piece of stock on his lathe, is less intelligent than a diplomat who perceives many things about foreign affairs? Can we be so sure of our values as to call one bright and the other dull? Can we blame the machinist for his lack of perception about foreign affairs without asking the diplomat to be equally skilled in the machinist's field of perceptions?

3. Finally, if perceptions are affected by the factors we have discussed in this paper, is it fair to sample intelligence irrespective of the control of such factors? Shall we, for example, examine the child who has lacked opportunity to perceive, has possessed a concept of self or been so threatened over a long period of time so as to have been unable to perceive what we wish to sample without consideration of those factors? Shall we overlook such factors and be satisfied that the perceptions important to us are not there, or shall we seek for ways to make it possible for the child to have them? Shall we assume that our failure to discover a particular perception present in the field is, *ipso facto,* evidence of lack of capacity; or seek to discover why it is not? On the positive side of the picture, if the concepts we have here been discussing are sound, there is reason to believe that intelligence may be far less immutable than we have thought. It may be that we can do far more than we have dreamed we could. Perhaps we may even be able to create intelligence!

IMPLICATIONS FOR CONSTRUCTIVE ACTION

Who can say, for example, what results we might be able to achieve by a systematic effort to remove or decrease the effectiveness of the limitations on perception discussed in this paper? It is fascinating to speculate on the possibilities one might try in constructing a situation for a child, or adult, consciously designed to minimize the limitations imposed on perception by physical condition, environment, goals, the individuals' self-concept, and the effects of perceived personal threat.

If the position we have taken is accurate, it would suggest that there is much we can do (*a*) to free individuals from the restraints upon perception and (*b*) to provide the opportunities for perception to occur.

1. First and most obviously, we should be able to discover and make available to far more people the means to achieve better physical condition. We have already done a good deal in this area but much needs yet to be done. Who can say, for instance, what completely adequate medical care for all our people might mean a generation hence?

2. If this discussion has merit, there lies the possibility of providing experiences for people that will make adequate perceptions possible. We have tried to do this in our schools, but have not always accomplished it. We have succeeded very well in gathering information and in making it available to students. We have not succeeded too well in making such information meaningful. Can it be that the decreases in school success with advance through the school years is more a function of lack of meaning for students than lack of intelligence? Is it enough to assume that experience provided by us to the student is truly provided when he is free to experience it? Has the child in school, who is so worried about his relationship with his peers that he cannot perceive what his book is saying, truly been provided opportunity to perceive?

In our training of children of "low intelligence," we often provide sit uations wherein they are carefully taught to perform repeatedly a simple act. Is it possible that in so doing we may be further narrowing their fields of perception and building self-concepts that produce even narrower perceptive fields?

What kinds of environments could we construct that might more effectively result in increased perception? Such experiments as Lippitt and White have carried on with democratic and autocratic environments suggest some possibilities, but we need to know much more. Perhaps we could learn to build such environments from observing with greater care and understanding the methods of good teachers.

3. Who can say what possible effects might occur from a systematic release of the individual's perceptions by the satisfaction of his most press-

ing needs or goals? We college professors insist we can produce more, which is another way of saying perceive more, when we have the leisure time to do so, when we are freed from the necessity of spending our time satisfying our needs for sheer existence. Can this be less true of others? It is possible that the child with needs of love, affection, status, prestige, or a girl friend might also be freed to perceive more widely and richly, if we could but find ways of helping him satisfy his needs. Ordinarily, we pay a good deal of attention to the physical needs of a child, understanding that with these needs unfulfilled, he makes a poor student. Is there any good reason to suppose his psychological needs are less pressing or less important in freeing him to perceive widely and accurately? We spend much time and energy trying to find ways of "motivating" people or blaming them for not being motivated to do what we need them to do. We assume that if permitted to seek their own needs, people will not satisfy ours. Perhaps we should get further by helping them satisfy their needs; they might then be free to satisfy ours.

4. Most of our educational methods are directed at the provision of perceptions for the student. He is lectured, required, shown, exhorted, and coerced to perceive what someone thinks he should. It seems possible that with equal energy devoted to the matter of creating needs, goals, and values in students, rich and varied perceptions might be more efficiently produced.

What effects might we be able to produce by providing experiences that build adequate concepts of self in children and adults? What differences in the richness and variety of perception might result from a generation of people with "I can" rather than "I can't" conceptions of themselves? What possibilities of increased perceptions and hence increased intelligence might accrue to such a program? Clinical experience has demonstrated frequently how a changed perception of self as a more adequate personality can free children for improved school performance, for example.

What would happen if we were consciously and carefully to set about the task of providing experiences that would lead people to conceptions of themselves as adequate, worthy, self-respecting people? If freedom to perceive is a function of adequate perceptions of self, it should not surprise us that the child who perceives himself as unwanted, unacceptable, unable, or unliked behaves in rigid fashion. It should be possible, too, to reverse this process and produce more adequate perceptions by systematic efforts at producing more adequate definitions of self. The possibilities seem tremendous but we have scarcely scratched the surface of this problem.

Finally, if threat to the individual has as important effects as seem indicated in this discussion, the removal of threat would seem a most important factor to consider in the release of the individual to perceive more adequately. The work of Rogers and his students in client-centered therapy has already illustrated to some degree what possibilities freeing the individual to perceive more adequately may accomplish through the provision of a permissive nonthreatening relationship between counselor and client. We have already mentioned the effects Axline has reported following a permissive, nonthreatening form of play therapy.

Such effects do not seem limited to the therapeutic situation, however. A number of workers have applied this principle of permissiveness to the classroom situation with equally gratifying results. Experiments in student-centered teaching at Syracuse have led many of us to believe in the tremendous educational possibilities in the removal of threat.

This paper has asked many questions. Indeed, it has asked far more questions than it has presumed to answer. That, it seems to me, is the function of theory. The picture of intelligence presented here as it seems from a phenomenological viewpoint may be accurate or false or, more likely, partly true and partly false. Only time and the industry of many observers can check its adequacy or inadequacy. It seems to me to pose problems that are both exciting and challenging. If it proves as stimulating to the reader as it has to the author, I shall rest content that a theory has achieved its purpose.

The Creative Attitude

ABRAHAM H. MASLOW

My feeling is that the concept of creativeness and the concept of the healthy, self-actualizing, fully human person seem to be coming closer and closer together, and may perhaps turn out to be the same thing.

Another conclusion I seem to be impelled toward, even though I am not quite sure of my facts, is that creative art education, or better said, Education-Through-Art, may be especially important not so much for turning out artists or art products, as for turning out better people. If we have clearly in mind the educational goals for human beings that I will be hinting at, if we hope for our children that they will become full human beings, and that they will move towards actualizing the potentialities that they have, then, as nearly as I can make out, the only kind of education in existence today that has any faint inkling of such goals is art education. So I am thinking of education through art not because it turns out pictures but because I think it may be possible that, clearly understood, it may become the paradigm for all other education. That is, instead of being regarded as the frill, the expendable kind of thing which it now is, if we take it seriously enough and work at it hard enough and if it turns out to be what some of us suspect it can be, then we may one day teach arithmetic and reading and writing on this paradigm. So far as I am concerned, I am talking about all education. That is why I am interested in education through art—simply because it seems to be good education in potential.

Another reason for my interest in art education, creativeness, psychological health, etc., is that I have a very strong feeling of a change of pace in history. It seems to me that we are at a point in history unlike anything that has ever been before. Life moves far more rapidly now

Reprinted from *The Structurist* 31, 1963, pp. 4–10, by permission of the author and the publisher.

than it ever did before. Think, for instance, of the huge acceleration in the rate of growth of facts, of knowledge, of techniques, of inventions, of advances in technology. It seems very obvious to me that this requires a change in our attitude toward the human being, and toward his relationships to the world. To put it bluntly, we need a different kind of human being. I feel I must take far more seriously today than I did twenty years ago, the Heraclitus, the Whitehead, the Bergson kind of emphasis on the world as a flux, a movement, a process, not a static thing. If this is so and it is obviously much more so than it was in 1900 or even in 1930—if this is so, then we need a different kind of human being to be able to live in a world which changes perpetually, which doesn't stand still. I may go so far as to say for the educational enterprise: what's the use of teaching facts? Facts become obsolete so darned fast! What's the use of teaching techniques? The techniques become obsolete so fast! Even the engineering schools are torn by this realization. M.I.T. for instance, no longer teaches engineering *only* as the acquisition of a series of skills, because practically all the skills that the professors of engineering learned when they were in school have now become obsolete. It's no use today learning to make buggy whips. What some professors have done at M.I.T., I understand, is to give up the teaching of the tried and true methods of the past, in favor of trying to create a new kind of human being who is comfortable with change, who enjoys change, who is able to improvise, who is able to face with confidence, strength and courage a situation of which he has absolutely no forewarning.

Even today as I read the morning newspaper before coming here, *everything* seems to be changing; international law is changing, politics are changing; the whole international scene is changing. People talk with each other in the United Nations from across different centuries. One man speaks in terms of the international law of the nineteenth century. Another one answers him in terms of something else entirely, from a different platform in a different world. Things have changed that fast.

To come back to my title, what I'm talking about is the job of trying to make ourselves over into people who don't need to staticize the world, who don't need to freeze it and to make it stable, who don't need to do what their daddies did, who are able confidently to face tomorrow not knowing what's going to come, not knowing what will happen, with confidence enough in ourselves that we will be able to improvise in that situation which has never existed before. This means a new type of human being. Heraclitian you might call him. The society which can turn out such people will survive; the societies that *cannot* turn out such people will die.

You'll notice that I stress a great deal improvising and inspiration, rather than approaching creativeness from the vantage point of the finished work of art, of the great creative work. As a matter of fact, I won't even approach it today from the point of view of completed products at all. Why is this? Because we're pretty clearly aware now from our psychological analysis of the process of creativeness and of creative individuals, that we must make the distinction between primary creativeness and a secondary creativeness. The primary creativeness or the inspirational phase of creativeness must be separated from the working out and the development of the inspiration. This is because the latter phase stresses not only creativeness, but also relies very much on just plain hard work, on the discipline of the artist who may spend half a lifetime learning his tools, his skills, and his materials, until he becomes finally ready for a full expression of what he sees. I am very certain that many, many people have waked up in the middle of the night with a flash of inspiration about some novel they would like to write, or a play or a poem or whatever and that most of these inspirations never came to anything. Inspirations are a dime a dozen. The difference between the inspiration and the final product, for example, Tolstoy's "War and Peace," is an awful lot of hard work, an awful lot of discipline, an awful lot of training, an awful lot of finger exercises and practices and rehearsals and throwing away first drafts and so on. Now the virtues which go with the secondary kind of creativeness, the creativeness which results in the actual products, in the great paintings, the great novels, in the bridges, the new inventions and so on, rest as heavily upon other virtues–stubbornness and patience and hard work and so on, as they do upon the creativeness of the personality. Therefore, in order to keep the field of operation clean, you might say, it seems necessary to me to focus upon improvising, on this first flash and, for the moment, not to worry about what becomes of it, recognizing that many of them do get lost. Partly for this reason, among the best subjects to study for this inspirational phase of creativeness are young children whose inventiveness and creativeness very frequently cannot be defined in terms of product. When a little boy discovers the decimal system for himself this can be a high moment of inspiration, and a high creative moment, and should not be waved aside because of some a priori definition which says creativeness ought to be socially useful or it ought to be novel, or nobody should have thought of it before, etc.

For this same reason I have decided for myself not to take scientific creativeness as a paradigm, but rather to use other examples. Much of the research that's going on now deals with the creative scientists, with people who have proven themselves to be creative, Nobel prize winners, great inventors, and so on. The trouble is, if you know a lot of scientists, that you soon learn that something is wrong with this criterion because scientists as a group are not nearly as creative generally as you would expect. This includes people who have discovered, who have created actually, who have published things which were advances in human knowledge. Actually, this is not too difficult to understand. This finding tells us something about the nature of science rather than about the nature of creativeness. If I wanted to be mischievous about it, I could go so far as to define science as a technique whereby non-creative people can create. This is by no means making fun of scientists. It's a wonderful thing it seems to me, for limited human beings, that they can be pressed into the service of great things even though they themselves are not great people. Science is a technique, social and institutionalized, whereby even unintelligent people can be useful in the advance of knowledge. That is as extreme and dramatic as I can make it. Since any particular scientist rests so much in the arms of history, stands on so many shoulders of so many predecessors, he is so much a part of a huge basketball team, of a big collection of people, that his own shortcomings may not appear. He becomes worthy of reference, worthy of great respect through his participation in a great and respect-worthy enterprise. Therefore, when he discovers something, I have learned to understand this as a product of a social institution, of a collaboration. If he didn't discover it, somebody else would have pretty soon. Therefore, it seems to me that selecting our scientists, even though they have created, is not the best way to study the theory of creativeness.

I will make one last point before I get to my paper proper. I believe also that we cannot study creativeness in an ultimate sense until we realize that practically all the definitions that we have been using of creativeness, and most of the examples of creativeness that we use are essentially male or masculine definitions and male or masculine products. We've left out of consideration almost entirely the creativeness of women by the simple semantic technique of defining only male products as creative and overlooking entirely the creativeness of women. I have learned recently (through my studies of peak experiences) to look to women and to feminine creativeness as a good field of operation for research, because it gets less involved in products, less involved in achievement, more involved with the process itself, with the going-on process rather than with the climax in obvious triumph and success.

This is the background of the particular problem I'd like to talk about today.

II

The puzzle that I'm now trying to unravel is suggested by the observation that the creative person, in the inspirational phase of the creative furore, loses his past and his future and lives only in the moment. He is all there, totally immersed, fascinated and absorbed in the present, in the current situation, in the here-now, with the matter-in-hand. Or to use a perfect phrase from *The Spinster* by Sylvia Ashton-Warner, the teacher absorbed with a new method of teaching reading to her children says "I am utterly lost in the present."

This ability to become "lost in the present" seems to be a sine qua non for creativeness of any kind. But also certain *prerequisites* of creativeness—in whatever realm—somehow have something to do with this ability to become timeless, selfless, outside of space, of society, of history.

It has begun to appear strongly that this phenomenon is a diluted, more secular, more frequent version of the mystical experience that has been described so often as to have become what Huxley called *The Perennial Philosophy*. In various cultures and in various eras, it takes on somewhat different coloration—and yet its essence is always recognizable—it is the same.

It is always described as a loss of self or of ego, or sometimes as a transcendence of self. There is a fusion with the reality being observed (with the matter-in-hand, I shall say more neutrally), a oneness where there was a twoness, an integration of some sort of the self with the nonself. There is universally reported a seeing of formerly hidden truth, a revelation in the strict sense, a stripping away of veils, and finally, almost always, the whole experience is experienced as bliss, ecstasy, rapture, exaltation.

Little wonder that this shaking experience has so often been considered to be superhuman, supernatural, so much greater and grander than anything conceivable as human that it could only be attributed to trans-human sources. And such "revelations" often serve as basis, sometimes the *sole* basis, for the various "revealed" religions.

And yet even this most remarkable of all experiences has now been brought into the realm of human experience and cognition. My researches on what I call peak experiences (3,4), and Marghanita Laski's on what she calls ecstasies (1), done quite independently of each other, show that these experiences are quite naturalistic, quite easily investigated and, what is to the point right now, that they have much to teach us about creativeness as well as other aspects of the full functioning of human beings when they are most fully realizing themselves, most mature and evolved, most healthy, when, in a word, they are most fully human.

One main characteristic of the peak-experience is just this total fascination with the matter-in-hand, this getting lost in the present, this detachment from time and place. And it seems to me now that much of what we have learned from the study of these peak-experiences can be transferred quite directly to the enriched understanding of the here-now experience of the creative attitude.

It is not necessary for us to confine ourselves to these uncommon and rather extreme experiences, even though it now seems clear that practically all people can report moments of rapture if they dig around long enough in their memories, and if the interview situation is just right. We can also refer to the simplest version of the peak-experience, namely fascination, concentration or absorption in *anything* which is interesting enough to hold this attention completely. And I mean not only great symphonies or tragedies; the job can be done by a gripping movie or detective story, or simply becoming absorbed with one's work. There are certain advantages in starting from such universal and familiar experiences which we all have, so that we can get a direct feeling or intuition or empathy, that is, a direct experiential knowledge of a modest, moderate version of the fancier "high" experiences. For one thing we can avoid the flossy, high-flying, extremely metaphorical vocabulary that is so common in this realm.

Well then, what are some of the things that happen in these moments?

GIVING UP THE PAST

The best way to view a present problem is to give it all you've got, to study *it* and its nature, to perceive *within* it the intrinsic interrelationships, to discover (rather than to invent) the answer to the problem within the problem itself. This is also the best way to look at a painting or to listen to a patient in therapy.

The other way is merely a matter of shuffling over past experiences, past habits, past knowledge to find out in what respects this current situation is similar to some situation in the past, i.e., to classify it, and then to use *now* the solution that once worked for the similar problem in the past. This can be likened to the work of a filing clerk. I have called it "rubricizing" (2). And it works well enough to the extent that the present *is* like the past.

But obviously it *doesn't* work in so far as the matter-in-hand is different from the past. The file clerk approach fails then. This person confronting an unknown painting hurriedly runs back through his knowledge of art history to remember how he is supposed to react. Meanwhile of course he is hardly looking at the painting. All he needs is the name or the style or the content to enable him to do his quick calculations. He then enjoys it if he is supposed to, and doesn't if he is *not* supposed to.

In such a person, the past is an inert, undigested foreign body which the person carries about like keys in his pocket. It is not yet the person himself.

More accurately said: The past is active and alive only in so far as it has re-created the person, and has been digested into the present person. It is not or should not be something *other* than the person, something alien to it. It has now become Person, (and has lost its own identity as something different and other) just as past steaks that I have eaten are now me, *not* steaks. The digested past (assimilated by intussusception) is different from the undigested past. It is Lewin's "ahistorical past."

GIVING UP THE FUTURE

Often we use the present not for its own sake but in order to prepare for the future. Think how often in a conversation we put on a listening face as the other person talks, secretly however preparing what we are going to say, rehearsing, planning a counter-attack perhaps. Think how different your attitude would be right now if you knew you were to comment on my remarks in five minutes. Think how hard it would be then to be a good, total listener.

If we are totally listening or totally looking, we have thereby given up this kind of "preparing for the future." We don't treat the present as merely a means to some future end (thereby devaluating the present). And obviously, this kind of forgetting the future is a prerequisite to total involvement with the present. Just as obviously, a good way to "forget" the future is not to be apprehensive about it.

Of course, this is only one sense of the concept "future." The future which is within us, part of our present selves, is another story altogether (3, pp. 14–15).

INNOCENCE

This amounts to a kind of "innocence" of perceiving and behaving. Something of the sort has often been attributed to highly creative people. They are variously described as being naked in the situation, guileless, without *a priori* expectations, without "shoulds" or "oughts," without fashions, fads, dogmas, habits or other pictures-in-the-head of what is proper, normal, "right," as being ready to receive whatever happens to be the case without surprise, shock, indignation or denial.

Children are more able to be receptive in this undemanding way. So are wise old people. And it appears now that we *all* may be more innocent in this style when we become "here-now."

NARROWING OF CONSCIOUSNESS

We have now become much less conscious of everything other than the matter-in-hand (less distractible). *Very* important here is our lessened awareness of other people, of their ties to us and ours to them, of obligations, duties, fears, hopes, etc. We become much more free of other people, which in turn, means that we become much more ourselves, our Real Selves (Horney), our authentic selves, our real identity.

This is so because *the* greatest cause of our alienation from our real selves is our neurotic involvements with other people, the historical hangovers from childhood, the irrational transferences, in which past and present are confused, and in which the adult acts like a child. (By the way, it's all right for the *child* to act like a child. His dependencies on other people can be very real. *But,* after all, he *is* supposed to outgrow them. To be afraid of what daddy will say or do is certainly out-of-place if daddy has been dead for twenty years.)

In a word, we become more free of the influence of other people in such moments. So, in so far as these influences have affected our behavior, they no longer do so.

This means dropping masks, dropping our efforts to influence, to impress, to please, to be lovable, to win applause. It could be said so: if we have no audience to play to, we cease to be actors. With no need to act we can devote ourselves, self-forgetfully, to the problem.

LOSS OF EGO: SELF-FORGETFULNESS, LOSS OF SELF-CONSCIOUSNESS

When you are totally absorbed in non-self, you tend to become less conscious of yourself, less self-aware. You are less apt to be observing yourself like a spectator or a critic. To use the language of psychodynamics, you become less dissociated than usual into a self-observing ego and an experiencing ego; i.e., you come much closer to being *all* experiencing ego. (You tend to lose the shyness and bashfulness of the adolescent, the painful awareness of being looked at, etc.) This in turn means more unifying, more oneness and integration of the person.

It also means less criticizing and editing, less evaluating, less selecting and rejecting, less judging and weighing, less splitting and analyzing of the experience.

This kind of self-forgetfulness is one of the paths to finding one's true identity, one's real self, one's authentic nature, one's deepest nature. It is almost always felt as pleasant and desirable. We needn't go so far as the Buddhists and Eastern thinkers do in talking about the "accursed ego"; and yet there *is* something in what they say.

INHIBITING FORCE OF CONSCIOUSNESS (OF SELF)

In some senses consciousness (especially of self) is inhibiting in some ways and at some times. It is sometimes the locus of doubts, conflicts, fears, etc. It is sometimes harmful to full-functioning creativeness. It is sometimes an inhibitor of spontaneity and of expressiveness (*But* the observing ego is necessary for therapy).

(And yet it is also true that some kind of self-awareness, self-observation, self-criticism; i.e., the self-observing ego *is* necessary for "secondary creativeness." To use psychotherapy as an example, the task of self-improvement is partly a consequence of criticizing the experiences that one has allowed to come into consciousness. Schizophrenic people experience many insights and yet don't make therapeutic use of them because they are too much "totally experiencing" and not enough "self-observing-and-criticizing." In creative work, likewise, the labor of disciplined construction succeeds upon the phase of "inspiration.")

FEARS DISAPPEAR

This means that our fears and anxieties also tend to disappear. So also our depressions, conflicts, ambivalence, our worries, our problems, even our physical pains. Even—for the moment—our psychoses and our neuroses (that is, if they are not so extreme as to prevent us from becoming deeply interested and immersed in the matter-in-hand).

For the time being, we are courageous and confident, unafraid, unanxious, unneurotic, not sick.

LESSENING OF DEFENSES AND INHIBITIONS

Our inhibitions also tend to disappear. So also our guardedness, our (Freudian) defenses, and controls (brakes) on our impulses as well as the defenses against danger and threat.

STRENGTH AND COURAGE

The creative attitude requires both courage and strength and most studies of creative people have reported one or another version of courage: popularity becomes a minor consideration, stubbornness, independence, self-sufficiency, a kind of arrogance, strength of character, ego-strength, etc. Fear and weakness cast out creativeness or at least make it less likely.

It seems to me that this aspect of creativeness becomes somewhat more understandable when it is seen as a part of the syndrome of here-now self-forgetfulness and other-forgetfulness. Such a state intrinsically implies less fear, less inhibition, less need for defense and self-protection, less guardedness, less need for artificiality, less fear of ridicule, of humiliation and of failure. All these characteristics are *part of* self-forgetfulness and audience-forgetfulness, Absorption casts out fear.

Or we can say in a more positive way, that becoming more courageous makes it easier to let oneself be attracted by mystery, by the unfamiliar, by the novel, by the ambiguous and contradictory, by the unusual and unexpected, etc., instead of becoming suspicious, fearful, guarded, or having to throw into action our anxiety-allaying mechanisms and defenses.

ACCEPTANCE: THE POSITIVE ATTITUDE

In moments of here-now immersion and self-forgetfulness we are apt to become more "positive" and less negative in still another way, namely, in giving up criticism (editing, picking and choosing, correcting, skepticism, improving, doubting, rejecting, judging, evaluating). This is like saying that we accept. We don't reject or disapprove or selectively pick and choose.

No blocks against the matter-in-hand means that we let it flow in upon us. We let it wreak its will upon us. We let it have its way. We let it be itself. Perhaps we can even approve of its being itself.

This makes it easier to be Taoistic in the sense of humility, non-interference, receptivity.

TRUST VS. TRYING, CONTROLLING, STRIVING

All of the foregoing happenings imply a kind of trust in the self and a trust in the world which permits the temporary giving up of straining and striving, of volition and control, of conscious coping and effort. To permit oneself to be determined by the intrinsic nature of the matter-in-hand here-now necessarily implies relaxation, waiting, receiving. The common effort to master, to dominate, and to control are antithetical to a true coming-to-terms with or a true perceiving of the materials, (or the problem, or the person, etc.). Especially is this true with respect to the future. We *must* trust our ability to improvise when confronted with novelty in the future. Phrased in this way, we can see more clearly that trust involves self-confidence, courage, lack of fear of the world. It is also clear that this kind of trust in ourselves-facing-the-unknown-future is a condition of being able to turn totally, nakedly, and wholeheartedly to the present.

(Some clinical examples may help. Giving birth, urination, defecation, sleeping, floating in the water, sexual surrender are all instances in which straining, trying, controlling, have to be given up in favor of relaxed, trusting, confident letting things happen.)

TAOISTIC RECEPTIVITY

Both Taoism and receptivity mean many things, all of them important, but also subtle and difficult to convey except in figures of speech. All of the subtle and delicate Taoistic attributes of the creative attitude which follow have been described again and again by the many writers on creativeness, now in one way, now in another. However, everyone agrees that in the primary or inspirational phase of creativeness, some degree of receptivity or non-interference or "let-be" is descriptively characteristic and also theoretically and dynamically necessary. Our question now is how does this receptivity or "letting things happen" relate to the syndrome of here-now immersion and self-forgetfulness?

For one thing, using the artist's respect for his materials as a paradigm, we may speak of this respectful attention to the matter-in-hand as a kind of courtesy or deference (without intrusion of the controlling will) which is akin to "taking it seriously." This amounts to treating it as an end, something *per se,* with its own right to be, rather than as a means to some end other than itself; i.e., as a tool for some extrinsic purpose. This respectful treatment of its being implies that it is respectworthy.

This courtesy or respectfulness can apply equally to the problem, to the materials, to the situation, or to the person. It is what one writer (Follett) has called deference (yielding, surrender) to the authority of the facts, to the law of the situation. I can go over from a bare *permitting* "it" to be itself, to a loving, caring, approving, joyful, *eagerness* that it be itself, as with one's child or sweetheart or tree or poem or pet animal.

Some such attitude is *a priori* necessary for perceiving or understanding the full concrete richness of the matter-in-hand, in *its* own nature and in *its* own style, without our help, without our imposing ourselves upon it, in about the same way that we must hush and be still if we wish to hear the whisper from the other.

This cognition of the Being of the other (B-cognition) has been fully described in (2, 3, 5).

INTEGRATION OF THE B–COGNIZER (VS. DISSOCIATION)

Creating tends to be the act of a whole man (ordinarily); he is then *most* integrated, unified, all of a piece, one-pointed, totally organized in the service of the fascinating matter-in-hand. Creativeness is therefore systemic; i.e., a whole—or Gestalt—quality of the whole person; it is not added-to the organism like a coat of paint, or like an invasion of bacteria. It is the opposite of dissociation. Here-now-allness is less dissociated (split) and more one.

PERMISSION TO DIP INTO PRIMARY PROCESS

Part of the process of integration of the person is the recovery of aspects of the unconscious and preconscious, particularly of the primary process (or poetic, metaphoric, mystic, primitive, archaic, childlike).

Our conscious intellect is too exclusively analytic, rational, numerical, atomistic, conceptual and so it misses a great deal of reality, especially within our selves.

ESTHETIC PERCEIVING RATHER THAN ABSTRACTING

Abstracting is more active and interfering (less Taoistic); more selecting-rejecting than the esthetic (Northrop) attitude of savoring, enjoying, appreciating, caring, in a non-interfering, non-intruding, non-controlling way.

The end-product of abstracting is the mathematical equation, the chemical formula, the map, the diagram, the blueprint, the cartoon, the concept, the abstracting sketch, the model, the theoretical system, all of which move further and further from raw reality ("the map is *not* the territory"). The end-product of esthetic perceiving, of non-abstracting is the total inventory of the percept, in which everything in it is apt to be equally savored, and in which evaluations of more important and less important tend to be given up. Here greater richness of the percept is sought for rather than greater simplifying and skeletonizing.

For many confused scientists and philosophers, the equation, the concept, or the blueprint have become more real than the phenomenological reality itself. Fortunately now that we can understand the interplay and mutual enrichment of the concrete and the abstract, it is no longer necessary to devalue one or the other. For the moment we intellectuals in the West who have heavily and exclusively overvalued abstractness in our picture of reality, even to the point of synonymizing them, had better redress the balance by stressing concrete, esthetic, phenomenological, non-abstracting, perceiving of *all* the aspects and details of phenomena, of the full richness of reality, including the useless portions of it.

FULLEST SPONTANEITY

If we are fully concentrated on the matter-in-hand, fascinated with it for its own sake, having no other goals or purposes in mind, then it is easier to be fully spontaneous, fully functioning, letting our capacities flow forth easily from within, of themselves, without effort, without conscious volition or control, in an instinct-like automatic, thoughtless way; i.e., the fullest least obstructed, most organized action.

The one main determinant of their organization and adaptation to the matter in hand, is then most apt to be the intrinsic nature of the matter in hand. Our capacities then adapt to the situation most perfectly, quickly, effortlessly, and change flexibly as the situation changes; e.g., a painter continuously adapts himself to the demands of his developing painting; as a wrestler adapts himself to his opponent; as a pair of fine dancers mutually adapt to each other; as water flows into cracks and contours.

FULLEST EXPRESSIVENESS (OF UNIQUENESS)

Full spontaneity is a guarantee of honest expression of the nature and the style of the freely, functioning organism, and of its uniqueness. Both words, spontaneity and expressiveness, imply honesty, naturalness, truthfulness, lack of guile, non-imitativeness, etc., because they also imply a non-instrumental nature of the behavior, a lack of willful "trying," a lack of effortful striving or straining, a lack of interference with the flow of the impulses and the free "radioactive" expression of the deep person.

The only determinants now are the intrinsic nature of the matter-in-hand, the intrinsic nature of the person and the intrinsic necessities of their fluctuating adaption to each other to form a fusion, a unit; e.g., a fine basketball team, or a string quartet. Nothing outside this fusion situation is relevant. The situation is not a means to any extrinsic end; it is an end in itself.

FUSION OF THE PERSON WITH THE WORLD

We wind up with the fusion between the person and his world which has so often been reported as an observable fact in creativeness, and which we may now reasonably consider to be a *sine qua non.* I think that this spider web of inter-relationships that I have been teasing apart and discussing can help us to understand this fusion better as a natural event, rather than as something mysterious, arcane, esoteric. I think it can even be researched if we understand it to be an isomorphism, a molding of each to each other, a better and better fitting together or complementarity, a melting into one.

It has helped me to understand what Hokusai meant when he said "If you want to draw a bird, you must become a bird."

References

1. Laski, M. *Ecstasy*. London: Cresset Press, 1961.
2. Maslow, A. H. *Motivation and Personality*. New York: Harper, 1954.
3. Maslow, A. H. *Toward a Psychology of Being*. New York: Van Nostrand, 1962.
4. Maslow, A. H. "Lessons from the Peak-Experiences." *Journal of Humanistic Psychology*, 2 (1962): 9–18.
5. Maslow, A. H. "Notes on a Psychology of Being." *Journal of Humanistic Psychology*, 1962.
6. Maslow, A. H. "Emotional Blocks to Creativity." *Journal of Individual Psychology*, 14 (1958): 51–56.
7. May, R., ed., *Existential Psychology*. New York: Random House, 1961.

What Can Man Become?

ARTHUR W. COMBS

In his inaugural address President Kennedy said to us, "Ask not what your country can do for you. Ask, rather, what you can do for your country?"

This eloquent plea was immediately met with an answering cry from millions of Americans. "Tell us what we can do," we cried. We long for a goal to live for and die for. We long for goals that will define for us where we should stand, what we should work for, what we can commit our lives and fortunes to. These are not idle questions. They are deeply serious ones, for upon our answers to these questions will rest the outcome of the great ideological struggle in which we are now engaged. In such a struggle it is the beliefs, convictions, values we hold that will determine whether we win or lose. We simply cannot sit down at the same table to bargain with adversaries who have already decided before they begin, that they are willing to die for their beliefs unless we have an equally firm commitment. A man without conviction, engaged in discussion with one whose convictions are practically a religion, is a sitting duck to be changed. This is one of the things we learned from our research on the "brain-washed" soldiers who returned from Korea.

Well, what is our commitment? What do we stand for? Freedom, we have said, is our goal. For our forefathers this was easy to define. It was freedom from the tyranny of the British kings, freedom from religious persecution, freedom from want, freedom for the slaves. Even in our own times when we have been attacked we have risen magnificently to defend ourselves against outside aggressors. But what shall be our goals in times of peace and plenty or when outside forces do not press upon

Reprinted from *California Journal for Instructional Improvement* 4, 1961, 15–23, by permission of the author and the publisher.

us? Goals for the have-nots are self-evident. Goals for those whose basic needs are satisfied are more difficult to define and less pressing to pursue.

REDEFINING FREEDOM IN TERMS OF BECOMING

We all recognize that meaning and character come from striving. We are most alive when happily engaged in the pursuit of a goal. Freedom, we have said, is our goal—but freedom for what? What does freedom mean in a nation of incredible wealth? It is apparent we need a redefinition of freedom translatable into action, not in a time of crisis alone, but applicable as well in times of peace and security.

We have stated our fundamental belief in democracy in these terms: "When men are free, they can find their own best ways." But what is a free man? A man with a full belly? A man without problems? A man with no pressures? Free to do as he pleases? When such things are achieved, a man is still no more than a vegetable. It is not enough to be free to *be*. We need freedom to *become*.

But what can man become? What is the ultimate in human freedom? What does it mean for a man to achieve the fullest possible fulfillment of his potentialities? This is a question which a number of psychologists, sociologists, educators, and humanitarians have been asking for a generation. What does it mean to be a fully functioning person, operating at the highest peak of his potentialities? What does it mean to be self-actualizing, self-realizing, a truly adequate person in the fullest possible sense of the word?

It would be hard to overestimate the importance of this search. For whatever we decide is a fully functioning, self-actualizing human being must, automatically, become the goal for all of us engaged in the helping relationships. These are the kinds of people we are trying to produce. It is to produce such people that our public schools exist, and the descriptions of these people provide us with the criteria in terms of which we can measure our success or failure.

As a result of the thinking and study of scholars and researchers, little by little, the picture begins to unfold. We begin to get some inkling of what the fully functioning person is like. This is no average man they are describing. Who, after all, wants to be average? This is a Free man with a capital F. This is a goal for us to shoot for, a picture of what can be and might be. Here is a concept of a free man that lifts our sights to what, perhaps, one day man may become.

What is more, a study of the characteristics emerging from the studies provides us with a blueprint for education practice. I believe the work of these people in defining the nature of self-actualization is certainly among the most exciting steps forward in our generation. For me, it has provided new meaning in life. It provides new goals and direction for me, not just in times of crisis, but in the quiet hours between, and in my professional work as well.

I cannot discuss all of the characteristics of these fully functioning, self-actualizing people which have now been described. In the time we have here together, let me describe only two or three of these characteristics and go on to discuss what these characteristics seem to me to mean for education. Each of the characteristics of these people could be spelled out in many aspects of curriculum in terms of what we need to do to produce that kind of characteristic. In fact, this is what the 1962 ASCD Yearbook attempts to do and I recommend it to your attention when it appears.

SELF-ACTUALIZING PEOPLE SEE THEMSELVES IN POSITIVE WAYS

Highly free people, the studies seem to show, see themselves as liked, wanted, acceptable, able, dignified, and worthy. Feeling this way about themselves, moreover, they are likely to have a deep feeling of personal security which makes it much easier to confront the emergencies of life with far less fear and trembling than the rest of us. They feel about themselves that they are people of dignity and worth and they *behave* as though they were. Indeed, it is in this factor of how the individual sees himself that we are likely to find the most outstanding differences between well-adjusted and poorly adjusted people. It is not the people who feel about themselves that they are liked and wanted and acceptable and able and so on who fill our jails and mental hospitals. Rather, it is those who feel themselves deeply inadequate, unliked, unwanted, unacceptable, unable, and the like.

This characteristic of fully functioning personalities, it seems to me, has at least four distinctly important implications for us in education.

In the first place, it seems to me, it means *we must regard the individual's self as a recognized part of the curriculum.* People learn who they are and what they are from the ways in which they are treated by those who surround them in the process of their growing up. What we do in class, therefore, affects the individual's ways of seeing himself whether we are aware of our impact or not. We *teach* children who they are and what they are by the kinds of experiences we provide. Many school deficiencies we now know are the results of a child's *belief* that he cannot read, write, or do math. A child may be taught that he cannot read from the impatience and frustration among those who sought to teach him.

We cannot rule the self out of the classroom, even if we wanted to. A child does not park himself at the door. The self is the dearest thing he owns, and he cannot be induced to part with it for any reason. Even a poor, ragged, and unhappy self must be dragged along wherever he goes. It is, after all, the only one he owns. The self, we now know, determines even what we see and what we hear. Right now in this audience as you listen to me speak, you are judging, determining, deciding about what I am saying, and you will carry away from here only that which, for one reason or another, has basically affected your very personal self.

For some time now it has been a part of our education in philosophy that we need to be concerned about the learner as well as the subject. Consequently, we have emphasized the importance of the child in the process and have developed a so-called, child-centered school. Indeed, we have sometimes carried this so far that the general public has sometimes become concerned lest we get so involved in understanding the child that we forget to teach him something!

Sometimes this has been expressed in the question, "Are you educating for intellect or educating for adjustment?" Such a dichotomy is, of course, ridiculous. Surely, we are not seeking to produce either smart psychotics, on the one hand, nor well-adjusted dopes, on the other! The fact of the matter is, we simply cannot separate what an individual learns from the nature of the individual himself. Indeed, we do not have to. This is nicely demonstrated in a recent experiment by Staines in New Zealand.

As you know, at the end of the fourth year under the British system children take an examination which determines the direction of their educational program from that point on. Staines studied two groups of fourth-grade children preparing for these examinations. One group was taught by a teacher who paid no attention to the self-concepts of the children. The other class was taught by a teacher who was simply aware of and thinking about the self-concept of the children, although he did nothing specifically planned to make changes in these matters. At the end of the year the two groups of children did about equally well on the academic aspects of the examination they took.

The adjustment level of the children in the two grades, however, was quite different. Adjustment levels in the classes taught by the teacher who was interested in the youngsters' self-concepts rose, while the adjustment level of the youngsters taught by the teacher who had ignored this factor actually decreased. Being concerned about the child's self-concept does not mean in any sense of the word that it is necessary for us to teach him any less.

Learning, itself, is a highly personal matter. Whether or not any given piece of information will be really learned by a youngster, we now know, is dependent upon whether or not he has discovered the personal meaning of that bit of information for him. It is the personal feeling I have about information, the personal commitment I have with respect to it that determines whether or not I behave differently as a result of having that information. Learning is not the cold, antiseptic examination of facts we once considered it. This is perhaps nowhere better illustrated than in the matter of dietetics. Dietitians have at their fingertips vast stores of information about what people *ought* to eat. Even you and I who are far less well informed know a good deal about what we ought to eat—but don't eat that! We go right on eating what we *want* to eat and *like* to eat, in spite of our information about the matter, until one day we cannot get into our favorite dress or a son says, "Gee, Mom, you're getting fat" or when, perhaps, like me, you visit your doctor for your annual check-up and, poking his finger in your stomach, he says, "Blubber! Sheer blubber!" Then, suddenly the information you have had all along takes on a new meaning and may even, just possibly, begin to affect your behavior.

Learning only happens to people. To ignore the presence of the person in the process simply runs the risk of failing to accomplish anything of very much importance. We cannot afford to ignore this important aspect of our problem. To do so runs the risk of making ourselves ineffective. The self is a part of the learning process and to ignore it is about as silly as saying, "I know my car needs a carburetor to run, but I think I'll run mine without one!"

Since the self is what matters to each of us, if we cast this out of school, we run the serious danger of teaching children that school is only about things that don't matter. If we are totally preoccupied with teaching subject matter, we may miss entirely the child to whom we are trying to teach it. We are all familiar with the examination time "boners." These represent the way the things we taught were seen by those whom we tried to teach.

Secondly, it seems to me, *the need for people who see themselves positively means that whatever diminishes the child's self has no place in education.* Humiliation, degradation, and failure are destructive to the self. It is commonly assumed in some places that shame and guilt are good for people, but this is rarely true, for the people who feel these things the most are the people who need them least.

Whatever makes the self smaller and meaner is not just bad for mental health. It undermines confidence and produces fear and withdrawal. It cuts down freedom of movement, the possibilities of intelligent behavior. What diminishes the self is stupefying and stultifying. Such people are a drag on the rest of us. Even worse are those who see themselves in negative terms as unliked, unwanted, unacceptable, unable, undignified, unworthy, and so on. These are the dangerous people of our society.

A positive self calls for success experience for everyone. People learn they *can* by succeeding, not by failing. There is a general feeling abroad in some places that failure is good for people, but nothing could be further from the truth. Self-actualizing people see themselves in positive ways, and you do not get this from having failures. If we teach a child he is a failure, we have no one to blame but ourselves if he comes to believe us and after that behaves so.

I do not believe it is an accident that for most children, after the third grade, there is very little variation in their grades for the rest of the time they are in school. It is as though, by the time a child reaches the third grade, he has discovered what his quota is, and after that he lives up to it. One learns he is *able* only from his successes. Even the "self-made man" who beats his chest and says, "What a fine fellow I am! I came up the hard way. Kids ought to have it hard," got this way precisely because he did *not* fail. He is a walking example of the man who did not fail.

But failure and success are feelings. They have to do with how the person to whom something happens sees the situation, not how it seems to those who look on from the outside. Success or failure does not happen unless the individual thinks it so. If a child believes he has failed, it doesn't make much difference whether other people think so or not. The important thing is what *he* believes, not what someone else does.

The provision of success for all students obviously calls for widespread curricula changes. Some sixty years ago we decided to educate everyone in this country, but we are still a long ways from discovering how to carry that out. We are still spending vast amounts of money, time, and energy trying to find ways to treat everyone alike. This, despite the fact that the most outstanding thing we know about human beings is that they are almost infinitely different. We are still providing many children with experiences of failure and self-reduction, not because we want to but because we seek to force them into a common mold which they do not fit.

We must provide for individual differences. We have talked now for a generation or more about individual differences, but we have made only a little progress in this direction. We see little in our elementary schoils, practically none in our secondary schools, and in our colleges we are not even sure it is a good idea in the first place. Despite all our talk about individual differences we still continue to insist upon group goals and standards, to organize our schools around age groups with thirty students to a class. Many teachers are fearful and insecure when they leave the familiar territory of the textbook or traditional methods and the familiar lock-step of lecture, recitation, and grades. Even our beautiful new buildings are often no more than a dull series of similar boxes, light and airy and cheerful to be sure, but still designed for fixed-size groups.

What would it mean, I ask myself, if we were to organize in such a fashion as to *really* give each child an experience of success? We have talked about it, discussed it, even advocated it on occasion, but mostly we have been too timid and fearful to put it into effect.

The plain fact of the matter is we often impose failure on students by the kind of structure upon which we insist. Many a child in our large modern high school gets lost in the shuffle. What high school teacher can know all 300 students drifting through his class in the course of the day? Adolescence is lonely enough without further subjecting the child to this kind of experience.

We have decided that rich curricula require schools of large size. But people can and do get lost in large schools, and we run the risk of losing on the bananas what we made on the oranges. I recall the snow sculpture standing on the lawn of one of our dormitories at Syracuse University some years ago, a kind of cartoon in 3-D. It had a freshman student jauntily walking into the University on one side and walking out the other side was, not a student, but an IBM card fully equipped with diploma and all his holes in the right places!

Surely it must be possible to organize our schools in such a way that somebody, somewhere in a junior or senior high school, is in contact with a child for a sufficiently long time to really get to know him. Guidance counselors who see him only an hour or two each semester are no solution. There is no substitute for the classroom teacher. The guidance function cannot be turned over to specialists. One good reason for this is the fact that adolescents simply do not take their problems to strangers. Adolescence is a deeply sensitive time of life, and the persons such children seek out for help are those with whom they have a continuing contact and that usually means a teacher, not a specialist. Some of the world's best guidance is done by coaches, advisers of the HiY, and even by the detention room keeper. The responsibility for knowing and understanding a child cannot be sloughed off. It remains the primary responsibility of the classroom teacher.

We must apply our criteria for self-actualization to every educational experience. Truly free, self-actualizing, fully-functioning people, we are told, are people who see themselves as liked, wanted, acceptable, able, dignified, worthy, and so on. Seeing oneself like this, however, is something one learns as a result of his experience during the years of his growing up. People *learn* that they are liked, wanted, acceptable, able from the things that happen to them and from the important people in their lives. In these statements we find the criteria for what we need to do in order to produce freer, more fully functioning people for our society. Let us apply these criteria to every aspect of educational experience. Let us ask about this school, this program, this policy, this method, this action, plan, or curriculum—does this help our students to feel more liked, wanted, acceptable, able, dignified, worthy, important, and so on? I have tried this with my own classes at the University with fascinating results. It has led me in some cases to reject time-honored methods and procedures. In others, it corroborated things I have known and believed for a long time. But perhaps best of all, it has led me in new directions, to new techniques, new principles. It has not always been easy, for sometimes I have had to give up cherished beliefs, to tread on unfamiliar paths with fear and trembling. Sometimes, even, I have gotten into trouble. I can only conclude, however, that despite the difficulties and tribulations the experimenting has been eminently worthwhile, and certainly never dull!

It is necessary for us to learn how things seem to our pupils. To produce the kinds of people the experts tell us we need and to do the kinds of things we have been talking about here require that we learn to understand how things look from the point of view of our students. Since students behave just as we do, according to how things seem to them, it follows that it is necessary for us to learn how things seem to our pupils. This, however, is not easy for two reasons: We have been taught for so long the importance of being objective, "of getting the facts," that for many of us it is a difficult thing to give up this scientific way of looking. On the other hand, how things seem to each of us seems so right and so *so* that it is a very difficult thing to understand that it may not be. Indeed the way things seem to us seems so certain that when other people do not see them the way we do we jump to either one of two conclusions: Either they must be very stupid or they are simply being perverse. Phyllis McGinley once expressed it very nicely when she said,

I think we must give up the fiction
That we can argue any view
For what in me is pure conviction
Is simply prejudice in you! *

We need to develop a sensitivity to how things seem to the people with whom we are working. For a long time we have advocated in teacher-training institutions the idea that teachers need to understand the child. What has often happened, however, is that we have confused understanding *about* a child with understanding the child *himself*. Even when I know a great deal about human growth and development I may fail to understand a given child. When I have made a careful study of him, when I have interviewed his parents, searched his school records, looked over his health and physical records, tested and examined him fore and aft, I still may not understand him. I do not really understand him until I have learned to see how he sees himself and how he sees the world in which he lives. All this information about him will be of limited value until I have come to understand the way he sees things in his private world of meaning and feeling. There is a world of difference between understanding a *person* and understanding *about* him.

The kind of understanding we are talking about here is not a *knowledge about,* but a *sensitivity* to people. It is a kind of empathy, the ability to put oneself in another's shoes, to feel and see as he does. All of us have this ability to some extent, but good teachers have a lot of it.

In some research we have been carrying on at the University of Florida we find that we cannot tell the difference between good teachers and poor teachers on the basis of the methods they use. One of the differences that does seem to exist, however, between good and poor ones has to do with this question of sensitivity. Good teachers seem to be much more sensitive to how things seem to the people with whom they are working. In fact, this sensitivity seems so important that apparently intelligent people who have it can do pretty well at teaching without any instruction in methods whatever. With such sensitivity they find their own methods. On the other hand, equally intelligent people with much instruction in methods may do very badly because they are unable to assess the effect of their methods upon the people they are trying to teach.

SELF-ACTUALIZING PEOPLE ARE OPEN TO THEIR EXPERIENCE

Let us turn now to a second characteristic of these highly self-actualizing, fully functioning personalities. All such people seem to be characterized by a highly degree of openness to their experience. That is to say, they are people who are able to look at themselves and the world about them openly and without fear. They are able to see themselves accurately and realistically. Psychologists have sometimes called this the capacity for "acceptance" by which they seem to mean the ability to confront evidence.

Highly self-actualizing people seem to have such a degree of trust in themselves that they are able to look at any and all data without the necessity for defending themselves or distorting events in ways they would like them to be. They are able to accept the facts about the world and about themselves, and because they are able to do this, they are people with a high degree of autonomy. They are free wheelers able to move off in new directions, and this of course is what is meant by creativity. Believing and trusting in themselves, they are able to move out in new directions. What is more, because they are more open to data they are much more likely to have right answers than other people and consequently are much more likely to behave intelligently and efficiently than are the rest of us.

Self-actualizers enjoy exploring; then enjoy discovering. They are not thrown by their experience or defensive against it. They are able to accept what is and to deal with it effectively. Please note that acceptance in the sense we are using it here means the willingness to confront data. It does not mean that acceptance and resignation are synonymous. Because an individual is willing to say, "Yes, it is true I am a stinker," does not mean that he is necessarily resigned to that fact!

This capacity for acceptance, trust in oneself, and openness to experience points to at least three important principles for us in educational practice.

The kind of openness to experience we have been talking about calls for rich opportunities for individuals to explore and test themselves. Such openness comes from opportunities to permit oneself to get involved in events. Like learning to swim, one needs sufficient help to be sure that he does not drown. On the other hand, one can *never* learn to swim if he never goes near the water. Such openness to experience comes about as a consequence of being sufficiently secure where one is that he is able to branch out into new events with courage and determination. This is the road to creativity, so needed in this generation.

One cannot be creative, however, without opportunities to get into difficulties. Indeed, it has been said that the characteristic of genius is the enjoyment of getting into difficulties for the sheer pleasure of getting out of them. Creativity calls for breaking with tradition, going out in the blue, trying one's wings, breaking out of the established ruts. Creativity is bound to be accompanied with a high amount of disorder. A creative class will not be a quiet one, and a rigidly ordered class will not be a creative one. An overemphasis upon order, procedure, custom, tradition, the "right" may actually destroy the kind of openness we are talking about.

This is a strange profession we are in. It is a profession built upon right answers. We pay off on right answers and discourage wrong ones at every level of the teaching profession. Now it is certainly a good thing to be right, but if we are so preoccupied with "being right" that we have no room for people to make mistakes, we may rob them of their most important learning experience. People learn from their mistakes. Some of the most important learnings that most of us have ever had probably came about as a consequence of our mistakes, much more than those instances where we were right.

The fear of making mistakes is almost a disease of our profession. However, an overemphasis on the importance of being right and insistence upon perfection may boomerang to discourage people from trying at all. We need a great deal more freedom to look, to try, to experiment, to explore, to talk about, to discuss. We need to open up our curricula to things we do not grade for. This was beautifully stated by a little boy in the fifth grade who wrote to his teacher after they had

had a discussion about love in his classroom: "I was very surprised when we talked in our class about love yesterday. I learned a lot of things and I found out about how lots of others feel. But I was surely surprised because I never knew you could talk about things in school that you didn't get grades for."

The kind of openness called for by the experts requires of us that we help young people to cut loose from dependency far earlier than they do. One of the criticisms we hear most often these days about our public schools is that we are producing a generation of irresponsibles. Like many of the criticisms leveled against us, I do not believe it is by any means as serious as that. I do believe, however, there is a germ of truth to be given some real consideration. The continued extension of childhood, characteristic of every phase of our modern life, tends to keep young people dependent far longer than they need be. Most of this dependency comes about as a consequence of our fear that young people may make mistakes if we set them free. The kind of openness characteristic of self-actualization, however, does not come about as a consequence of increased dependency. Quite the contrary, it comes about as a consequence of responsibility.

There are some who feel the setting up of a separate society by our adolescents is a consequence of this fear. The word "teenager" is practically a cuss word in our society. We simply do not like teenagers. They are permitted no real worthwhile place. We have built a world where there is little or no opportunity for them to have any feeling that they belong or are part of the larger society in which they live. They have little or no voice in what happens to them. They long for a feeling of importance and meaning, something to commit themselves to.

But the usual adult approach to these young people is to build them a new playground or Teen-Town where they are told to "go and play" some more. The plain fact of the matter is they are often an embarrassment to us. Consequently, we treat them as outsiders. It should not surprise us then if they build their own society. Look around you, and you will see that this is precisely what they have done—with their own language, their own customs, traditions, codes of values, even their own music, ways of dress, and symbols of status and prestige. They have done this because we have made no real place for them in our society.

This kind of separation of young people from their culture has the potentiality for great danger. They are people who do not feel they belong, do not feel under any necessity to pay their dues or look out for the members. Membership in a society is not felt by those who are cast out from it. Feelings of belonging and responsibility come about only as a consequence of feeling a part of and being given responsibility for other people.

Responsibility and independence, we need to remind ourselves, are not learned from having these things withheld. Take the case of the teacher who believes her class, for example. The teacher leaves her class telling the group, "I am going down to the office for a few minutes. I want you to be good kids until I get back." She goes to the office and returns to find the room in bedlam. Seeing this, she enters the room and says to her youngsters, "I will never leave you alone again!" If she means this, she has thereby robbed these youngsters of their only opportunity to learn how to behave when the teacher is not there. You cannot learn how to behave when the teacher is not there if the teacher never leaves you!

We do the same thing in the high school with student government. We are so afraid the youngsters might make a wrong decision that we do not let them make any. Whenever they make a decision, we veto that, and it doesn't take long before they get the idea that student government is only a game. Having come to this conclusion, they then tend to treat it like a game, and this infuriates us. We then cry out in despair, "See there, they do not even treat their government as anything but a game!" Perhaps, if they treat it like a game, we have no one to blame but ourselves for teaching them that that is what it is. In order to try one's wings there must be freedom of movement and opportunity to look and explore. If the fears of adults prevent this exploration, we have no one but ourselves to blame.

Let us not be misled by the cries of the young people themselves in this connection. I have often had teachers say to me, "But I want to give them responsibility and they don't want to take it!" This, of course, is often true, but should not discourage us from giving youngsters responsibility. It is only another indication that they are fearful of it because they had so little successful experience with it. The youngster who has not had much responsibility is quite likely to be frightened by having a large dose given to him before he is ready to assimilate it.

The rules of readiness that apply to everything else we know in education apply to learning about responsibility as well. Opportunities have to be paced to capacities. Readiness and capacity, however, are achieved from experience. You cannot expect a child to read if you never let him try, and you cannot expect him to be responsible without some successful experience with it. This is beautifully illustrated in the two old sayings: "If you want something done, get a busy man to do it" and "The rich get richer and the poor get poorer."

WHEN MEN ARE FREE, THEY FIND THEIR OWN WAYS

It is a basic principle of democracy that "when men are free, they can find their own best ways." Modern psychology tells us that in each of us there is a deep and never-ending drive to become the very most we can. Despite the assurances of the psychologists about man's basic nature and the beliefs we ourselves so glibly state about the nature of democracy, nevertheless, most of us still approach children with serious doubts and misgivings. We don't *really* believe they can find their own best ways if we provide the proper conditions.

Recently I have been reading A. S. Neill's fascinating book, *Summerhill.* This is a description of a school in England run by a headmaster who believes in giving children freedom, even to the extent of deciding for themselves whether they will go to class at all. (They do!) The lengths he has gone to in giving personal responsibility are fascinating, even shocking, to many people. Certainly he goes far beyond what I have been willing to do in my teaching. The fascinating thing is this: He has been doing this for forty years *and it works!* Here is a living demonstration that individual freedom can work, that we do not need to be afraid as we have been, that maybe, if we can really have the courage to try, it will work out all right.

In recent years I have been trying to place more responsibility and trust in my students. One thing I have done is to use a method of grading that places most of the responsibility for planning, study, and evaluation on the student. This has been much criticized by my colleagues, but the results it gets in more and better work, in individual commitment, in increased freedom for the student, in more reading and thought and effort are well worth the price. Besides, as one of my students expressed it, "Well, Dr. Combs, sure, some students take advantage of your method of grading, but then the old method took advantage of the student!"

The production of openness and responsibility in students requires courage and trust on the part of teachers. If we ourselves are afraid to try and let others try, if we are so fearful they may make mistakes, we may rob them of their most priceless opportunities to learn and will defeat ourselves as well. We need to remind ourselves of Roosevelt's "The only thing we have to fear is fear itself."

WHEN AN INDIVIDUAL FINDS INNER SECURITY, HE CAN BECOME OPEN TO HIS EXPERIENCE

The kind of openness characteristic of the truly adequate, full functioning personality the experts are describing for us comes about as a consequence of the individual's own feeling of security in himself. It is a product of his feeling that he is important, that he counts, that he is a part of the situation and the world in which he is moving. This feeling is created by the kind of atmosphere in which he lives and works. It is encouraged by atmospheres we are able to create in the classroom and the halls and laboratories that help young people to develop a feeling of trust in themselves.

What causes a person to feel outside undermines and destroys his feelings of trust. Differences must be respected and encouraged, not merely tolerated. As Earl Kelley has told us, the goal of education must be the increasing uniqueness of people, not increasing likeness. It is the flowering of individuality we seek, not the production of automatons. This means differences of all kinds must be encouraged, appreciated, valued. Segregation is not only socially undesirable; it is demoralizing and diminishing as well. We need to remind ourselves there is segregation on a thousand other bases than segregation of white and Negro that can equally as well get in our way. There is segregation, too, on the basis of age, social status, athletic prowess, dress, language, and religion, to name but a few.

The kind of openness we seek in the free personality requires a trust in self, and this means, to me, we need to change the situations we sometimes find in our teaching where the impression is given the student that all the answers worth having lie "out there." I believe it is necessary for us to recognize that the only important answers are those which the individual has within himself, for these are the only ones that will ever show up in his behavior. Consequently, the classroom must be a place where children explore "what I believe, what I think, what seems to me to be so" as well as what other people think and believe and hold to be true.

Since most human behavior is the product of beliefs, values, and convictions, it is these values that must make up a larger and larger part of our educational experience. We have been in the grip of a concept of teaching that worships objectivity for a long time now. Objectivity is of value to be sure, but objectivity requires looking at events with cold and dispassionate regard. People simply do not behave objectively. They behave in terms of their feelings, attitudes, and convictions even about the most scientific matters. I can be objective about your child; I cannot be objective about my own! The things that affect my behavior most importantly and most closely are those things in the realm of values and beliefs. An education system which does not permit me to explore these or which regards these vital aspects of life as unimportant or inadmissible to the classroom runs the risk of making itself an esthetic exercise valuable to only a few, having little to do with life, and making little impact upon the generations it hopes to affect.

* "Note to My Neighbor" by Phyllis McGinley is from *Times Three* by Phyllis McGinley. Copyright 1951 by Phyllis McGinley. Originally appeared in *The New Yorker*. Reprinted by permission of The Viking Press and Martin Secker & Warburg Limited, London.